Education and Development Reconsidered

Ford Foundation
Rockefeller Foundation
edited by
F. Champion Ward

The Praeger Special Studies program—utilizing the most modern and efficient book production techniques and a selective worldwide distribution network—makes available to the academic, government, and business communities significant, timely research in U.S. and international economic, social, and political development.

Education and Development Reconsidered
The Bellagio Conference Papers

PRAEGER SPECIAL STUDIES IN INTERNATIONAL ECONOMICS AND DEVELOPMENT

Praeger Publishers   New York   Washington   London

Library of Congress Cataloging in Publication Data

Main entry under title:

Education and development reconsidered.

(Praeger special studies in international economics and development)
    1. Underdeveloped areas—Education—Congresses.
I. Ward, Frederick Champion, 1910-   ed.
LC2605.E295   370'.9172'4   74-19335
ISBN 0-275-09700-5

PRAEGER PUBLISHERS
111 Fourth Avenue, New York, N.Y. 10003, U.S.A.
5, Cromwell Place, London SW7 2JL, England

Published in the United States of America in 1974
by Praeger Publishers, Inc.

Printed in the United States of America

A few years ago the heads of a number of assistance agencies agreed on their need to improve their understanding of the role of education in the general advance of "third world" nations. Having profited in previous years from informal discussions of common concerns in agriculture and population, they believed that similar discussions of education would prove useful.

As in the cases of agriculture and population, the Ford and Rockefeller Foundations were asked to prepare the agenda for these meetings. This task was undertaken by Kenneth W. Thompson and Michael P. Todaro, of the Rockefeller Foundation, and the editor of this volume, F. Champion Ward, of the Ford Foundation, with the help of foundation colleagues and members of the staffs of the participating agencies. The first meeting of heads of agencies was held at the Rockefeller Foundation's Villa Serbelloni in Bellagio, Italy, in May 1972, the second in November 1973. In addition, there has been considerable activity at staff level, in preparation for the Bellagio meetings and in pursuit of projects of common concern emerging from them. A third meeting of heads of agencies will be held in 1975.

The group now includes the following:

Canadian International Development Agency
Ford Foundation
French Ministry of Foreign Affairs
Inter-American Development Bank
International Bank for Reconstruction and Development
International Development Research Centre
Ministry of Overseas Development, United Kingdom
Organization for Economic Cooperation and Development
Overseas Economic Co-operation Fund, Japan
Rockefeller Foundation
Swedish International Development Authority
United Nations Children's Fund
United Nations Development Programme
United Nations Educational, Scientific and Cultural
   Organisation
United States Agency for International Development

From the first, it was considered essential that educators from the developing countries contribute papers and topics for the agenda and attend the Bellagio meetings. Their contributions, both as authors and participants, have been of central importance. We are particularly grateful to them, in view of the time and pains their participation has entailed.

The present volume contains papers selected or, in most cases, written for the Bellagio meetings on topics that, for reasons set out in the Introduction, appeared to be most worthy of attention at the present time. It is issued in response to wide interest shown in the Bellagio meetings within the academic and international communities. This interest has helped to convince us that the topics so far taken up, although far from exhaustive of current concerns, are important enough for educators in the developing countries and elsewhere as to justify this publication.

We would add that the papers are an attempt to open questions, not to exhaust or foreclose them. As the title of this book indicates, this is a time for reconsideration of the relations between educational and general development, and the present volume is best viewed as an attempt to enlarge the conversation about those relations which was begun at Bellagio in 1972.

McGeorge Bundy   John H. Knowles
President   President
The Ford Foundation   The Rockefeller Foundation

ACKNOWLEDGMENTS

The editor of this volume is particularly grateful to two associates: Mr. Francis Method, for his many-sided and invaluable help in preparing for the meetings at Bellagio; and Mrs. Kathryn Powell, for her editorial assistance, including the preparation of an index for the present volume.

"Education and Development," by Joseph Ki-Zerbo, was presented at a conference of CODIAM (Comité pour l'Organisation et le Développement des Investissements Intellectuels en Afrique et à Madagascar), Paris, 1970, and appeared in Tam-Tam, June 1970. It is included here with the kind permission of the author.

"Employment in the 1970's: A New Perspective," by Mahbub ul Haq, was presented at the World Conference of the Society for International Development in Ottawa, May 1971 and appeared in the International Development Review, December 1971. It is included here with the kind permission of the author and of the editor of the International Development Review, Mr. Andrew E. Rice.

"Technology, Development and Culture: A Memorandum for Discussion," by Soedjatmoko, was originally prepared for an April 1972 meeting of the Institute for Religion and Social Change on "Technology, Development and Values" in Santa Barbara, California, and is included here with the kind permission of the author and of the Director of the Institute, Dr. P. J. Philip.

"Vector Planning for the Development of Education," by William J. Platt, was excerpted from a paper, "The Faure Report: A Turning Point in Educational Planning," which was presented at Technical Symposium No. 15, Science and Man in the Americas, AAAS and CONACYT, Mexico City, June 29, 1973, and is included here with the kind permission of the author.

The papers in this volume by Michel Debeauvais and Joseph Ki-Zerbo originally appeared in French. Mr. Debeauvais's paper was translated by Mrs. Kathryn Powell, and Mr. Ki-Zerbo's paper was translated by Mrs. Jennifer Ward.

CONTENTS

LIST OF TABLES AND FIGURE

LIST OF PARTICIPANTS
IN THE VARIOUS BELLAGIO AND
BELLAGIO-RELATED MEETINGS, 1972-74

Developing Country Specialists

Abebe Ambatchew
Aklilu Habte
Fernando Henrique Cardoso
Wadi' Haddad
Abdul Razzak Kaddoura
Joseph Ki-Zerbo
Setijadi
Soedjatmoko
Gabriel Velázquez P.

Heads of Agencies Assisting Education

McGeorge Bundy, The Ford Foundation
Paul Gérin-Lajoie, Canadian International Development Agency
John A. Hannah, U.S. Agency for International Development
J. George Harrar, The Rockefeller Foundation
W. David Hopper, International Development Research Centre
John H. Knowles, The Rockefeller Foundation
Henry R. Labouisse, UNICEF
Pierre Laurent, Ministère des Affaires Etrangères (France)
Robert S. McNamara, International Bank for Reconstruction and
  Development
René Maheu, UNESCO
Edwin M. Martin, Organisation for Economic Co-operation and
  Development
W. A. C. Mathieson, Overseas Development Ministry (U.K.)
Saburo Okita, Overseas Economic Co-operation Fund (Japan)
Rudolph A. Peterson, United Nations Development Programme

Members of Agency Staffs and Specialists

James W. Armsey, The Ford Foundation
Ducan Ballantine, International Bank for Reconstruction and Develop-
  ment
James Berna, United Nations Development Programme
Joel Bernstein, U.S. Agency for International Development

Pierrette Bonnaud, Secrétariat d'Etat aux Affaires Etrangères (France)
Newton Bowles, UNICEF
James Chandler, U.S. Agency for International Development
Philip H. Coombs, International Council for Educational Development
Ralph K, Davidson, The Rockefeller Foundation
Michel Debeauvais, Organisation for Economic Co-operation and
    Development
L.-O. Edström, Swedish International Development Authority
Edgar O. Edwards, The Ford Foundation
Anders Forsse, Swedish International Development Authority
Melvin J. Fox, The Ford Foundation
Harold Freeman, U.S. Agency for International Development
Reuben Frodin, The Ford Foundation
Jacques Grunewald, Ministère des Affaires Etrangères (France)
P. O. Hanson, UNICEF
Stéphane Hessel, Ministère des Affaires Etrangères (France)
John F. Hilliard, U.S. Agency for International Development
Harold Howe II, The Ford Foundation
Torsten Husén, University of Stockholm
A. R. MacKinnon, Canadian International Development Agency
Francis J. Method, The Ford Foundation
Robert Myers, The Ford Foundation
H. M. Phillips, Independent Consultant
William Platt, UNESCO
Guelfo Pozzi, United Nations Development Programme
Daniel Rogers, U.S. Agency for International Development
Robert Schmeding, U.S. Agency for International Development
John Simmons, International Bank for Reconstruction and Development
Donald Simpson, International Development Research Centre
Tarlok Singh, UNICEF
Curt Ström, Swedish International Development Authority
Kenneth W. Thompson, The Rockefeller Foundation
J. E. C. Thornton, Overseas Development Ministry (U.K.)
Michael P. Todaro, The Rockefeller Foundation
Myron Vent, U.S. Agency for International Development
F. Champion Ward, The Ford Foundation
Francis G. Wells, Organisation for Economic Co-operation and
    Development
Kate Wild, International Development Research Centre
John Woolston, International Development Research Centre
Ruth K. Zagorin, International Development Research Centre

LIST OF CONTRIBUTORS

Aklilu Habte is the former President of Haile Sellassie I University
in Addis Ababa, Ethiopia.

C. Arnold Anderson is the former Director of the Comparative
Education Center at the University of Chicago.

Mark Blaug is Professor of the Economics of Education at the Institute of Education, University of London.

Michel Debeauvais is Professor of Economics, University of Vincennes.

Edgar O. Edwards is a member of the staff of the Ford Foundation,
now serving as Economic Advisor to the Ministry of Finance and
Economic Planning, Government of Kenya.

Mahbub ul Haq is Director of the Policy Planning and Program Review
Department of the International Bank for Reconstruction and
Development, Washington, D.C.

Torsten Husén is Director of the Institute for the Study of International
Problems in Education at the University of Stockholm.

Richard Jolly is Director of the Institute of Development Studies
at the University of Sussex, England.

Joseph Ki-Zerbo is a historian and former Minister of Education
in Upper Volta.

Francis J. Method is Project Assistant in the International Division
of the Ford Foundation

Ralph Miller is Associate Professor in the Department of Educational
Foundations at the University of Calgary, Alberta, Canada.

H. M. Phillips is an independent consultant based in Paris, France.

William J. Platt is Director of the Department of Planning and
Financing of Education of UNESCO, Paris.

T. W. Schultz is Professor of Economics at the University of Chicago.

John A. Smyth is a Project Specialist in the Educational Planning
Division of UNESCO, Paris.

Soedjatmoko is Adviser to the National Development Planning Agency in Jakarta, Indonesia.

Kenneth W. Thompson is Director of the Higher Education for Development Program, the International Council for Educational Development, New York.

Michael P. Todaro is a member of the Rockefeller Foundation staff, now serving as Research Fellow, Institute of Development Studies, Nairobi, Kenya.

Gabriel Velázquez P. is Rockefeller Foundation Advisor in Health Sciences to the University of Bahia, Brazil.

F. Champion Ward is Program Advisor in Education to the International Division of the Ford Foundation.

THE AGE OF INNOCENCE

As the drive for development began in the "less developed countries," education was perceived by the many as a social and economic advantage long confined to a favored few. Although the demand for education was strong, and the spread of education was thought to be one index of social advance, most national leaders had as yet no specific conception of the relation between education and "development." Moreover, the demand for education was itself far from homogeneous. The masses clamored for village schools, while more advantaged groups demanded (and secured) places for their children in secondary and higher education. As a result, both allocations within education and allocations to education proved to be difficult to decide upon in any rational and consistent way.

In so far as the growth of education was deliberately planned and related to economic development, the principle most often invoked was that of staffing the economy with "high-level manpower" (which led to investment in professional training facilities at the university level) and with skilled workers at lower levels (which led to the support of secondary and vocational schools). In elementary education, and in such areas as the arts faculties of universities, wild growths occurred more or less in spite of planners and finance officers. These sectors received fewer resources and much less attention from able educators than the secondary and university-level "manpower" sectors.

Western and international agencies attempting to assist education in those first years also had limited, and not fully relevant, experience on which to draw. Such plausible Western models as the Danish folk school and the American land grant college had outgrown their origins in their own societies and were familiar to most Western educators only in their evolved forms and current settings. Also, in the West it had been broadly true that centralized educational systems had not grown, and growing systems were not centralized. Therefore, combining central planning of education with its deliberate and rapid expansion was an undertaking as unfamiliar to Western "experts" as to nationals of the developing countries. There was also uncertainty concerning the relation of educational expansion to political stability. At first, social unrest was predicted if young people were denied education; later, unrest seemed equally probable if young people were given education but not jobs.

There was ambivalence, too, concerning the educational systems that already existed in the developing countries as the intense drive

xv

for development began. Advisers and consultants from nations not previously acquainted with the third world tended to ignore these extant systems or to oppose them as imperial or feudal legacies now to be swept away in favor of something more relevant to developmental needs. On their part, national elites, while often agreeing in principle with these criticisms, found it difficult, in practice, to tear their own nests; and the masses, offered education for the first time, would accept no substitutes for places in the same inherited system that had given so many social and economic advantages to the national elites. It is therefore not surprising, however deplorable, that the systems of education now to be found in the developing countries still resemble those that preceded them. They have expanded more than they have changed.

In short, the capacity of Westerners to do less harm than good as foreign advisers or donors and lenders of capital was underdeveloped, as was the capacity of recipients to make selective and systematic use of external assistance.

THE PRESENT SITUATION OF EDUCATION IN
THE DEVELOPING COUNTRIES*

Given the circumstances just cited, the sheer growth of education in the 1950s and 1960s must be viewed as an unprecedented and even heroic achievement. In gross terms, elementary education has doubled, and secondary and higher education have virtually quadrupled since 1950. Public investment in education has grown (in inconstant dollars) from approximately $1.5 billion in 1950 to approximately $12 billion in 1969. The educational system has become one of the principal employers of educated labor in many countries. Moreover, even though the relation of education to economic growth has remained unclear and even though finance officers tended for many years to see education as a social service having only a secondary claim on resources, educational expenditures have, in fact, expanded more than twice as fast as gross national products.

During this period of growth, both the planning of educational development by the developing countries and the process of technical

---

*For the purposes of this account, the "developing countries" include all African and Latin American countries and all Asian countries except Japan, the People's Republic of China, North Korea, and North Vietnam. These omissions, based (except for Japan) on UNESCO membership as of 1968, do some violence to the realities in both "developed" and "developing" continents.

assistance improved. Many of the more obvious blunders and simplified assumptions came to be avoided or at least questioned. Large numbers of educational institutions were established or enlarged, and numerous scientific and professional cadres were trained. Greater rigor in the formulation, execution, and assessment of educational programs was achieved. A chastened eclecticism and a greater respect for local initiative began to replace the confident importation of models by consultants and donors. In some instances (for example, Tanzania) the development of education was related explicitly to a specific conception of a new social order to be achieved within the constraints of a limited economy.

Yet, strenuous and impressive as this effort has been, education is now beset by major problems whose solution will require further exertions at least as great although not of the same kind as those put forth in the 1950s and 1960s. A number of factors make the future seem ominous for the further rapid growth of education.

First, there are the sheer numbers of pupils (about 300 million) who do not attend either a primary or a secondary school, even after the efforts of 20 years. In 1967-68, the following percentages of children did not attend primary school: Latin America, approximately 25 percent; Asia, 55 percent; Africa, 60 percent. The following percentages of children did not attend a postprimary school: Latin America, 65 percent; Asia, 72 percent; Africa, 85 percent.

Between 1960 and 1968, although elementary and secondary school enrollment in the developing countries increased by one-third (from about 300 million to about 400 million students), the increases in percentages of age group enrolled were far less impressive: 10 percent in Latin America (from 45 to 55 percent); 9 percent in Asia (from 36 to 45 percent); 4 percent in Africa (from 24 to 28 percent).

Other discouraging factors must be weighed. One of them is the increasing youthfulness of the population in the developing regions, whose median age is now approximately 16. It is estimated that by 1985 there will be half again as many school-age children in the developing countries (excluding China) as there were in 1965.

To the "pupil explosion" just cited must be added a slowdown in the worldwide rate of increase of expenditures on education that began in the mid-1960s (from an annual average increase of 12.1 percent between 1960 and 1965, to 10.5 percent for 1967-68). Nor can even this continuing increase be simply equated with an equal increase in numbers of pupils taught. From 1961 to 1968 the percentages of annual increase in public expenditure on education at all levels were 10 percent for Africa, 12 percent for Latin America, and 14 percent for Asia, but the corresponding rates of increase in enrollment were only 6.2 percent for Africa and Latin America and 5.6 percent for Asia.

Further doubts arise when enrollment is distinguished from educational achievement. In fact, of the pupils enrolled in elementary education in the developing countries, some 50 percent failed to complete the fourth grade. Moreover, a high proportion of these dropouts occurred in the first or second school year, making it unlikely that there is any enduring educational achievement to show for their brief attendance. This phenomenon may be called the internal inefficiency of the present systems.

Also becoming evident is a serious form of external inefficiency, in that a growing and in some cases very large proportion of school leavers and graduates are no longer assured of appropriate employment, or even of any employment at all.

In the face of the demographic and financial strains and evidence of inefficiency just cited, it is not surprising that recent reviews and planning documents by both external agencies and developing countries emphasize the improvement or alteration of education more than its further expansion. This improvement is sought along two lines, each of which has its advocates among the authors of this volume: (1) what might be called "local repairs" to the existing system, and (2) the exploration of heterodox alternatives to present educational practice.

Intersecting with these substantive matters is the procedural theme of the manner in which external assistance to education ought to evolve during the 1970s. In the current appreciations and plans of most agencies there is the explicit recognition that the design, execution, and evaluation of new educational efforts should lie with the developing countries themselves and that external assistance must be so conducted as to encourage rather than delay that result.

AREAS OF CURRENT UNCERTAINTY

The chapters that follow deal with areas of conceptual uncertainty and practical readjustment, with which both assistance agencies and developing countries appear to be most concerned at present.*

---

*Among the topics taken up in the Bellagio meetings, "nonformal" and "basic" education are not given distinct treatment in this volume, in part because of the extensive attention currently being given them in reports prepared for UNICEF and the World Bank by the International Council for Educational Development and in a forthcoming book on international aid to education by Francis J. Method and H. M. Phillips.

Education as an Economic Investment. Chapter 1 deals with education viewed as an economic investment for both states and individuals. From the beginning, some rough connection between employment and economic productivity, on the one hand, and educational achievement, on the other, has been at least surmised by both assisting agencies and developing countries. However, attempts to demonstrate the existence and nature of such a connection and to draw its implications for investment in education awaited the recent work of the economists of education.

A number of economists have contributed material for the discussion of this subject. Messrs. Todaro and Edwards, both of whom have had sustained experience in connection with economic development in East Africa, challenge some familiar assumptions underlying past investments in education in the light of growing unemployment and, on the basis of this analysis, draw implications for future investment strategies. Three economists of education, Professors Blaug, Debeauvais, and Schultz, respond to an invitation to say, in very brief compass, what guidance to "investors in education" their young discipline can now provide. Finally, Professor Jolly argues that any realistic strategy of educational planning must face the fact that the extent and effectiveness of educational "reforms" depend heavily on factors outside education proper.

Education and Social Justice. Chapter 2 addresses some of the questions of social policy and some of the operational difficulties that arise when "development" is directed toward distributive justice as well as economic growth. In the present age, education has been seen as a kind of social "equalizer" opening the door of economic opportunity to the masses. It has been widely assumed that as education expanded, its social and economic benefits would be distributed fairly. But there is now concern that, unless special and deliberate efforts are made, education may benefit most those whose parents already have advantages and who will thereby draw further away from the rest of the society to which they belong. Moreover, it is held that, in the developing countries, there has been excessive attention to higher education, at the expense particularly of primary education and therefore at the expense of the masses of the people. And even where primary education has been extended to the poor, it is pointed out that equal access to education by the "advantaged" and the "deprived" does not ensure equality of educational achievement.

The experience of developed countries suggests that time and economic development alone cannot be counted upon to correct these inequities. The student bodies of European and British universities continue to belong disproportionately to the middle and upper classes. Even where approximately half of the age group receives some form of higher education, as is the case in the United States, it remains true that a child of a fourth quartile income family in that country has about one-seventh of the chance to attend a university that a child of a first quartile income family enjoys. Similarly, in the Soviet Union there is concern that students of peasant parentage from rural areas are handicapped in attending universities with children of professional, urban parents.

For these reasons, education is now being represented by radical social critics as an advantage monopolized by a ruling class, or, if it is extended beyond that class, as a limited concession to other articulate groups or as a means of insuring a literate, skilled, and acquiescent labor force for an exploitative economy.

Donors and lenders to education have received their share of blame for these conditions. They have been charged with indifference to unjust distributions of educational opportunities and with making inequity worse through complacent acceptance of the self-serving allocations to education of developing country elites and undue stress on the production of high-level manpower by universities.

The critical theses about "development" advanced by Mahbub ul Haq and Professor Ralph Miller elaborate these concerns about the present distribution of education and other social benefits. Mr. Ki-Zerbo's paper takes up the problems faced by one developing country in trying to adapt an inherited educational system to new national aims and limited resources, and Mr. John Smyth argues that a shift from "efficiency" to "equity" criteria for investing in education entails further choices of considerable theoretical and practical difficulty.

Educational Research and Development. Chapter 3 is concerned with improvements and adjustments now called for if educational systems are to be designed and redesigned in more self-corrective and experimental ways than in the past.

Considering the age and present scale of the enterprise of education, the level of its investment in serious and sustained research and development is shockingly low. "Innovations" are undertaken from time to time, but they are frequently replicated or abandoned long before they are known to have succeeded or failed. For this reason, change in education is more cyclical than cumulative. Moreover, quite apart from change, the actual outcomes of existing systems are only grossly revealed by present measurements, and most input-output relationships remain matters of opinion only.

These deficiencies are felt acutely in international education at the present juncture, because of the strains on resources, low efficiency, and demands for "innovation" that now prevail. It seems to be widely recognized that ways must be found to enable developing countries and the world educational community to engage in research and development (R and D) on a new scale, so that investments in education by individuals, families, agencies, and nations can be made more productive.

Mr. Francis Method has provided a conspectus of what he believes to be the principal present needs in educational research and development, and Mr. William Platt has described and illustrated the kind of "vector planning" that he thinks most appropriate to an enlarged commitment to research and development. The papers of Professors Husén and Anderson, each of whom has been very widely engaged in comparative education, respond to an invitation to make practical suggestions and recommendations for improving the international performance in educational research and for relating its results to decisions about educational development, including procedural and substantive "do's" and "don'ts"; possible programs and projects; further studies that need to be made; support for and/or development of national, regional, or international resources and operating arrangements needed for an adequate, long-term attack on the problem; and any other steps they considered to be necessary.

Higher Education and Development. Chapter 4 takes up a particular question of policy that is important at the present time to both developing countries and assistance agencies. In the 1950s and 1960s very large investments were made by developing countries and by assisting agencies in the strengthening of existing universities and higher centers for research and training and in the establishment of new ones. There is now wide concern that these resources should become fully effective contributors to the progress of the nations that, together with external assistance agencies, have invested in them so heavily.

In two essays looking backward and forward in time, members of the staff of the Rockefeller Foundation provide examples and discussions of selective external support to "university development," of the assumptions on which such support has rested in the past, and of the questions that are now being raised about the developmental roles that higher education may be expected to play in the coming decades.* Two leading educators of the developing countries,

---

*With the support of 14 members of the group of donors that met at Bellagio, under the direction of Kenneth Thompson, and with the participation of a number of leading educators from the developing countries, the International Council for Educational Development is conducting a study of "Higher Education for Development," the results of which will be reported to the third meeting of heads of agencies in 1975.

Dr. Aklilu Habte and Dr. Gabriel Velázquez, give accounts of the recent development of several universities in Africa and Latin America, together with their views of the best ways for universities to contribute to national development.

Implications for External Assistance. In one way or another, all of the contributions to this volume propose or imply needed adjustments in the concepts and procedures of agencies assisting education in the developing countries, a matter of central importance in the Bellagio meetings. The first two papers in Chapter 5 deal directly with a number of these revisions and reforms of concept and practice, the one, by Mr. H. M. Phillips, being concerned with what to do, the other, by Professor C. A. Anderson, with what not to do. Finally, Soedjatmoko's "Memorandum for Discussion" is a reminder that in respect of their need for cultural "redirection and redefinition," rich and poor nations are "all in the same boat"—one more reason, and a basic one, for moving away from the unilateral transfer of models toward a shared effort to reconsider, among other things, "education," "development," and the relations between them.

Mr. Phillips believes that complex organizations require a deliberate effort over more than a few years to turn changes of policy into changes of practice. The series of meetings for which these papers were prepared bear out his view. Changes in practice and organization are occurring, some of which may have been encouraged or accelerated by the discussions at Bellagio. Jointly supported studies and projects looking toward better research and development by nationals of the developing countries, better international reporting of promising new efforts in education, and better use of university resources for national development, are under way or in prospect. There is increased realization that the effectiveness of external assistance, on whatever scale, will henceforth depend more and more on the degree of initiative and competence with which educational systems are designed and tested by educators of the developing countries themselves. Yet much clarifying of ideas and redeploying of resources remain to be done, processes that can be expected to gain from further discussion and collaboration of the kinds that these meetings of educators, specialists, and executives have so far made possible.

EDUCATION AND EMPLOYMENT IN
DEVELOPING COUNTRIES
Edgar O. Edwards and Michael P. Todaro

The idea that education in abundance beyond literacy is an unmitigated social good and an engine for development deserves challenge. That challenge is taking the form in developing countries of growing open unemployment in urban areas, reaching in the 1960s percentages such as 13.6 in Bogota, 7.9 in Venezuela, 15 in Ceylon, 9.8 in Malaya, 11.6 in the Philippines, 14.9 in Kenya, and 11.6 in Ghana.[1] Moreover, the average level of education among the unemployed appears to be rising, suggesting that the growing investment in educational systems is increasingly an investment in idle human resources. For example, in the middle and late 1960s, the highest rates and longest durations of open unemployment were found among those with a secondary level of education. The prospects, therefore, given present employment patterns, surging educational enrollments, and rapid population growth, are not encouraging. In the face of these facts, the further rapid expansion of education beyond literacy levels without constructive efforts to create meaningful employment opportunities is likely to generate political as well as educational unrest.

Obviously the numbers being educated in developing countries exceed the employment opportunities available to them when they emerge from the educational system. Yet educational ministries with the implicit endorsement of donor agencies continue to press for the expansion of educational opportunities on the tacit assumption that so long as the demand for educational places exceeds the supply, expansion is socially justified. But the signals reported above on employment suggest that the demand for education is itself excessive and a supply of education that responds exclusively to that signal may lead to a serious misallocation of development resources. It is our contention that an educational supply responsive to demand was not inappropriate in the 1950s and the early 1960s when shortages of educated manpower were general, but to continue to adjust supply to demand through the 1970s and 1980s, when opportunities for education already exceed requirements for it, is clearly bad policy. We further contend that tinkering with educational supply alone will not close the fundamental, troublesome, and growing gap between the demand for education and the supply of employment opportunities. To achieve that end, more basic policy changes will be required.

The original title of this paper was "Educational Demand and Supply in the Context of Growing Unemployment in the Less Developed Nations."

The fundamental question we address is why the demand for education in developing countries is so high and growing when job opportunities are obviously scarce and growing at a distinctly slower pace. One possibility to which we accord little weight is that education is wanted in significant quantities as an end in itself, as a consumption good. This may be an important factor in advanced countries, but given low per capita incomes, urgent needs for other consumption goods essential for a minimum standard of living, and limited numbers of families with incomes large enough to afford education as a luxury, we are not convinced of its significance in developing countries. We shall argue instead that the demand for education in the developing countries is primarily determined by the balance between (1) the prospects of earning more income through future employment in the modern sector as perceived by the student and (2) the educational costs that the student or his family must bear. An excess demand for education results then from a combination of lagging job opportunities and an overly optimistic, though privately rational, pursuit of education.

We shall also argue that employment opportunities in the modern sector are artificially restricted largely because (1) factor prices are distorted, capital being underpriced and labor being overpriced, favoring labor-saving methods of production, (2) technologies are often borrowed from advanced countries where labor is a relatively scarce resource, (3) job specifications require excessive education, partly in emulation of advanced-country standards and partly because the educational system is itself overproducing, and (4) excessive resources are devoted to education, diverting them from more productive and more labor-absorbing investment opportunities elsewhere in the economy.

On the other hand, the demand for additional education is inflated because (1) the income differential between modern- and traditional-sector employment is artificially high even when modified by the existing probability of employment, (2) perceived employment probabilities may be exaggerated because of the visible success of predecessors in the system and the temporary surfeit of employment opportunities as expatriates are replaced following independence, (3) employers give preference to the better educated even though additional education adds only marginally to productivity, and (4) the portion of the cost of education that is borne privately is usually nominal. Moreover, the demand for education may be even greater at higher levels because of the artificial stimulus created by government financial policies (in many cases made possible by the assistance of donor agencies), which reduce the proportion of total costs borne by the individual as he moves up the educational ladder. In addition to stimulating excess demand for higher education, these policies also raise serious questions of equity since they often lead to a situation in which the higher education of the rich is being subsidized out of public revenues extracted from the poor through regressive tax systems. These several factors suggest that privately perceived benefits may exceed the private costs of education even though the net social benefits are very low or even negative, and this divergence may be greater at higher than at lower educational levels.

Unlike the demand for education, which is essentially privately determined, and the supply of employment opportunities in the modern sector, which is partly privately determined, the supply of educational opportunities is almost universally a government responsibility, an important political variable, and a natural focus of government policy, often to the neglect of educational demand and employment considerations. In most developing countries today, it would appear that demand for education exceeds the supply of educational opportunities, which in turn greatly exceeds the supply of employment opportunities. The advancing educational level of the unemployed in most developing countries makes it clear that opportunities for education exceed opportunities for employment; the continuing need to ration places in educational systems suggests that the demand for education outruns enrollment capacities.

Despite these basic inequalities, little has been done in most developing countries either to temper the demand for education toward more realistic levels or to create more jobs through the elimination of factor price and other distortions. Instead, policies have focused on the supply of school places, the manipulation of which within the bounds given above has little to do with closing the gap between the demand for education and opportunities for using it productively.

In the present circumstances of most developing countries, as opposed to earlier periods when education could not meet employment needs, the supply of educational opportunities acts as a "decoy" variable, which at one extreme leaves many dissatisfied because they are locked out of the educational system and at the other spews out growing numbers of educated unemployed. When educational capacity is geared to employment opportunities, it creates an enormous and complex problem of rationing educational opportunities; when it is accommodated to educational demand, it compels the rationing of job opportunities.

In the political situation of most developing countries, it has been expedient to minimize the rationing of education and to undertake instead the rationing of jobs. Indeed, for the latter task the educational system itself can be used as a rationing device. Jobs in the modern sector can be allocated (not necessarily equitably) to those with the most advanced education, leaving others less fortunate educationally to fend for themselves on the periphery of the urban sector or in the subsistence setting of the traditional economy.

Taking these several factors into account, we feel that developing countries have overexpanded educational opportunities at levels above that necessary to ensure literacy. A continuation of this policy, therefore, must be looked upon most critically by both national governments and international donor agencies. We feel that it would be preferable to give greater weight to prospective employment opportunities in planning educational expansion. It should be recognized, however, that this can only be a partial solution since it does not come to grips with what we perceive to be the basic issue, namely, that the demand for education continues to outrun opportunities for productive employment.

To make the demand for education more realistic, governments of the developing countries should strive to bring the private calculations of the benefits and costs associated with education closer to the social benefits and costs by (1) making the beneficiary (as opposed to his family or society as a whole) bear a larger and rising proportion of his educational costs as he proceeds through the system (with appropriate subsidies for the able poor at low levels of education and through loan programs at higher levels of education) as the most effective means of rationing available places; (2) reducing income differentials between the modern and traditional sectors and within the modern sector to ensure a more realistic appraisal of the prospective benefits of education; (3) ensuring that minimum job specifications do not overvalue education; and (4) ensuring that wages are related to jobs and not to educational attainments.

To increase the supply of job opportunities, governments should (1) reduce wages relative to the price of capital as these enter into employment decisions in both the public and private sectors; (2) give more careful consideration to improving rural infrastructure and to the possible location of new modern-sector activities in areas where wages have not yet reached the distorted levels typical of established urban centers; and (3) allocate a larger share of development budgets to productive employment-creating activities as opposed to education than was the pattern in the 1960s.

We feel that reasonable efforts along these lines will leave a residual rationing problem in education of substantial magnitude. Dealing with this on the basis of merit rather than favor will be a continuing challenge for the developing countries.

The past policies of international donor agencies with respect to educational expansion were for the most part well grounded and responsive to the diverse manpower needs of developing nations. However, circumstances are changing rapidly, and donor postures must now be framed in the light of needed national policies such as

those identified above. Shortages of educated manpower are rapidly
being overcome, and a general extension into the future of present
rates of growth in educational supply will surely produce new and
hopeful school leavers greatly in excess of the new employment opportunities for which they must compete. Consequently it is now a
matter of urgency that donor agencies reexamine their educational
assistance policies. Rates of future educational expansion appropriate
to realistic appraisals of manpower needs can for the most part be
met out of national resources. Moreover, substantial outside support
even for lower levels of education where expansion continues to be
justified may simply free national educational resources for the less
economically justifiable expansion of higher levels. In short, donors
should assist the developing countries to do what is socially wise
rather than what seems to be politically expedient in the field of
education.

To the extent that developing countries can and will finance
needed educational expansion of traditional kinds out of their own
resources, donor agencies are given an opportunity to be more
selective and innovative in their own contributions to educational
development. We would give priority to the following kinds of activities:

1. Intensified and expanded applied research, particularly in
the developing countries themselves, on alternative educational and
informational delivery systems appropriate to the diverse employment needs and opportunities of these nations. Special attention
should be given to those opportunities outside of the modern sector,
the sector toward which Western-type industrial training and higher
educational systems are presently oriented.

2. Systematic and controlled pilot experimentation with educational innovations emanating from research efforts. Because of the
risks and costs associated with experimentation, it is unlikely that
developing nations will be able or willing to bear the cost of systematic experimentation.

3. Selective assistance to overcome unanticipated manpower
scarcities and bottlenecks.

The extent to which the various international aid agencies can
associate themselves with these kinds of activities will undoubtedly
vary, but we feel that they merit serious consideration.

The Private Demand for Education as a "Derived
Demand" for High-Income Modern-Sector
Employment Opportunities

In this section we will focus on an aspect of education in developing nations has been largely neglected by scholars, educational

planners, and donor agencies alike. The attention of these individuals and organizations has been devoted almost exclusively to the question of how to supply most effectively sufficient educational services to meet a set of perceived manpower needs. Implicit in this approach has been the assumption that the demand for education by individuals was some sort of given or, at any rate, the demand greatly exceeded the available supply at any point in time. The immediate need was to expand the supply in order to build up national human capital.

It is our contention that although this supply-oriented approach was useful under the circumstances of a shortage of educated manpower in the 1950s and 1960s, it is becoming increasingly less valid in the 1970s and may become totally inappropriate in the 1980s. Consequently, it is crucial that government planning and education ministries as well as international donor agencies begin to take a critical look at the factors influencing the private demand for education. The linkage between the availability of new employment opportunities and the role of the educational system in the development process is, in our opinion, most readily crystallized on the demand rather than on the supply side of the education equation.

The basic premise upon which our argument will be constructed concerns the relationship between the level and growth of modern-sector employment opportunities and the demand for education. In simple form, this premise states that to a large extent individual students and their families view education as a passport for entry into the modern, urban industrialized economy with its disproportionately high-paying employment opportunities. In this sense, the demand for education, therefore, can be seen as a "derived demand" for high-income earning employment opportunities in the modern sector. In fact, in almost all nations of Africa, Asia, and Latin America, entry into modern-sector public and private jobs is predicated upon the successful completion of the requisite years of education associated with particular jobs, often irrespective of whether or not such educational requirements are really necessary for satisfactory job performance.

Clearly, if our premise about the relationship between the demand for education and the availability of expanded employment opportunities in the modern sector is at all realistic, then the interrelationships between the "employment problem" and the "educational system" are much more intimate than one might first suspect. Central to these relationships is the individual's perception of the close linkage between his educational attainment and his employment opportunities. Individuals may correctly view the private benefits (that is, lifetime expected income-earning opportunities) of an education as greatly exceeding the private costs (that is, school fees plus "opportunity costs" of income-generating alternatives forgone while in school) so that in spite of widespread and growing unemployment among the more educated, they would continue to desire entry into and passage through the educational system. The problem arises when these "private" benefit-cost calculations diverge substantially from "social" benefit/cost calculations (that is, when what is good and rational from the individual's economic calculations is undesirable and irrational in terms of national resource allocation). Where private benefits exceed the private costs of education but the same calculation from a social viewpoint leads to a negative result, there are powerful economic and political forces pressing that society to misallocate its human and financial resources to an overexpansion of the school system, exacerbating the problem of the educated unemployed.

Eventually, of course, one could conceive of unemployment rates among the educated reaching such substantial proportions that people will start to question the utility of the heavy investment of time in an educational process that gets increasingly stretched out and for which the tangible rewards are becoming more and more uncertain. Being content with an eventual adjustment of this kind seems to us politically and economically unwise. We address instead the problem of identifying a less painful and more practical approach. Consider the following illustrative analysis.

We begin by assuming that the demand for an education sufficient to qualify an individual for entry into modern-sector employment opportunities is related to or determined by the combined influence of the following four variables:

1. The wage and/or income differential between jobs in the "modern" sector (M) and those outside the modern sector (such as family farming, rural and urban self-employment), which for simplicity we can designate as the "traditional" sector (T). Entry into modern-sector jobs is dependent initially on the level of completed education, whereas income-earning opportunities in the traditional sector do not have any fixed educational prerequisites. If we designate W_M as the modern-sector wage and W_T as the traditional-sector wage, then the greater the modern-sector-traditional-sector income differential, $M_M - W_T$ (or, for all practical purposes, we might call this the urban-rural income differential), the greater will be the demand for education. Thus, our first relationship states that the demand for education is positively related to the urban-rural or modern-traditional wage differential. Since we know from empirical studies that these differentials can be very sizable in most developing nations, one might reasonably expect the demand for education to be greater than it would be if differentials were smaller.

2. The probability of success in finding modern-sector employment (P_M). Closely related to the wage differential as a variable

affecting the demand for education on the income side is the probability that an individual who successfully completes the necessary schooling for entry into the modern-sector labor market <u>will in fact</u> get that high-paying urban job. Clearly, if urban or modern-sector unemployment rates among the educated are growing and/or if the supply of, say, secondary school graduates continually exceeds the number of new job openings for which a secondary graduate can qualify, then we need to modify the "actual" wage differential $W_M - W_T$, and instead speak about an "expected" income differential $P_M W_M - W_T$ where P_M refers to the probability or likelihood that a school graduate will be successful in securing the high-paying modern-sector job. Since the probability of success is inversely related to the unemployment rate—that is, the more people with appropriate qualifications who seek a particular job, the lower will be the probability that any one will be successful—we can argue that the demand for education through, say, the secondary level will be <u>inversely</u> related to the current unemployment rate among secondary school graduates.*

    3. The direct private costs of education (C_1). We refer here to the current out-of-pocket expenses of financing a child's education. These expenses include school fees, books, clothing, and related costs. We would expect that the demand for education would be inversely related to these direct costs—that is, the higher the school fees and associated costs, the lower would be the private demand for education, everything else being equal.

    4. The indirect or "opportunity costs" of education (C_2). An investment in a child's education involves more than just the direct, out-of-pocket costs of that education, especially when the child passes the age at which he can make a productive contribution to family income, whether in "kind" or monetarily. For example, by proceeding on to secondary school, a graduate of primary school is in effect forgoing the income he could expect to earn as a primary school graduate during the course of his years spent receiving a secondary education. These opportunity costs must also be included as a variable affecting the demand for education. One would expect the relationship between these opportunity costs and demand again to be inverse—that is, the greater the opportunity costs are, the lower will be the demand for education.

------

*In fact, since most expectations for the future tend to be based on a "static" picture of the employment situation that now prevails, we might anticipate that with a worsening employment picture, individuals will tend to overestimate their expected incomes and demand even more education than is justified in terms of "correct" private calculations.

Although there certainly are a number of other important variables, many of which are non-economic, including such factors as cultural traditions, social status, education of parents, and size of family, and which influence the demand for education, we believe that by focusing on the four variables described above, important new insights can be gained on the relationship between education and employment.

Suppose the following conditions prevail in country X:

1. The modern-traditional or urban-rural wage gap, $W_M - W_T$ is of the magnitude of, say, 100 percent for primary versus nonprimary school graduates—that is, statistics show that primary school graduates can earn starting salaries that average twice as much as a nonprimary graduate can make outside the modern sector.

2. The rate of increase of opportunities for remunerative employment for primary school graduates is slower than the rate at which new primary graduates enter the labor force—that is, the number of primary-school-leavers entering the labor market exceeds the number of jobs arising in the same period for which a primary education is the "normal" qualification. The same may be true at the secondary level and even the university level in countries such as India, Egypt, Pakistan, and, more recently, Ghana, Nigeria, and Kenya.

3. Employers, faced with an excess of applicants, tend to select by level of education since once an employer knows that there is an excess supply of more productive secondary-school-leavers, he will employ them first at the going wage, even in jobs "normally" performed by primary-school-leavers, who get the residue only.

4. Trade unions, supported by the political pressure of the educated, tend to bind the going wage to the level of educational attainment of job-holders rather than to the minimum educational qualification required for the job.

5. School fees are often very nominal or even nonexistent, and, in many cases, the state bears a larger portion of the student's costs at each successive level.

Under the above conditions, which we believe conform closely to the realities of the employment and education situation of most developing nations, one might expect the following situation to prevail. Given (1) the large and perhaps growing disparity between income-earning opportunities in the modern urban sector versus those in the traditional urban and rural sectors, (2) the requirement that entry into the modern-sector labor market necessitates a minimum but probably growing level of educational attainment, and (3) the very low private costs of education, the demand for education will be exaggerated since the anticipated private benefits are so large compared to the alternative of little or no schooling and since the direct

and indirect private costs are so low. However, as job opportunities
for the uneducated diminish, individuals must safeguard their position
by acquiring a primary education. This may suffice for a while, but
the internal dynamics of the employment demand/supply process
leads to a situation in which job prospects for those with a primary
education begin to decline. This in turn creates a demand for secondary education. But the demand for a primary education must also
increase concurrently since some who were previously content with
no education are now being "squeezed" out of the labor market. The
irony is that the more unprofitable a given level of education becomes
as a terminal point, the more demand for it increases as an intermediate stage or precondition to the next level of education! This
puts great pressure on the government in conjunction with international
donor agencies to expand educational facilities to meet the growing
demand. If they cannot respond fast enough, the people may do so
on their own, as evidenced, for example, by the Harambee school
movement in Kenya.

The upshot of all of this is the chronic tendency for developing
nations to expand their educational facilities at a rate that is extremely
difficult to justify either socially or financially in terms of optimal
human and physical capital resource allocation. Each worsening of
the employment situation calls forth an increased demand for (and
supply of) more education at all levels. Initially the uneducated swell
the ranks of the unemployed. However, over time there is an inexorable tendency for the average educational level among the unemployed to rise as the supply of school graduates continues to exceed the demand for middle- and high-level manpower. The better
educated must, after varying periods of unemployment during which
aspirations are scaled downward, take jobs requiring lesser levels
of education. The diploma and degree become requirements for employment, not the education they were intended to signify. Governments and private employers strengthen the trend by continuously
upgrading formal educational entry requirements for jobs that were
previously filled by those less educated; excess educational qualification becomes formalized and may resist downward adjustment. Moreover, to the extent that trade unions succeed in binding going wages
to the educational attainments of job holders, the going wage for each
job will tend to rise (even though worker productivity in that job
has not significantly increased) and existing distortions in wage differentials will be magnified, stimulating further the demand for education. Those who for some reason are unable to continue their education will fall by the wayside as school-leavers while the others continue to overqualify themselves through more years of education.
In the extreme case, one gets a situation like that of contemporary
India where the higher education system is in effect an "absorber of

last resort" for the great quantities of potential educated unemployed. The problem is that this is a terribly expensive form of unemployment compensation, and, short of retaining people in school until retirement, these great masses will eventually have to emerge into the cold, cruel world of tight labor markets with the result that unemployment will become more visible among those highly educated and highly vocal.

Finally, it should be pointed out that many individuals tend to resist what they see as a downgrading of their job qualifications. Consequently, even though on the demand-for-labor side, employers will attempt to substitute the more educated for the less educated for a given job, on the supply side there will be many job seekers whose expectations exceed the emerging realities of the labor market. They might prefer to remain unemployed for some time rather than to accept a job they feel is "beneath" them. It follows that as a result of these "frictional" effects and "lags" in adjustment on the supply side, unemployment will exist at all levels of education even though it is concentrated at lower levels and, in general, is inversely related to educational attainment.

The inexorable attraction of higher and higher levels of education is even more costly than this simple picture suggests. Typically in developing countries, the social cost of education increases rapidly as we climb the educational ladder while the private costs increase more slowly or indeed may decline. This widening gap between social and private costs provides an even greater stimulus to the demand for higher education than it does for lower levels so that demand is increasingly exaggerated as higher levels are considered. But educational opportunities can be accommodated to these distorted demands only at full social cost. As demands are generated progressively through the system, the social cost of accommodation grows much more rapidly than the places provided. More and more resources must be misallocated to educational expansion, and the potential for creating new jobs must diminish.

What is the purpose of going through this rather lengthy scenario of the education/employment interrelationship in developing nations? Must this story of the growing masses of educated unemployed be a necessary manifestation of the development process? We think not. We would argue that to a large degree the problem has been artificially created by inappropriate government policies fostered to a great extent by faulty advice of educational "experts" and, simply, by a questionable set of assumptions about the relationship between education and economic development upon which much of the educational philosophy has been based. Specifically, we would argue that in circumstances where modern-sector wages are set at artificially high levels in terms of the availability of human resources, where

13

time spent in the educational system serves as a prerequisite for modern-sector job market entrance, where unemployment tends to be concentrated at lower educational levels even though these levels tend to rise over time, and, finally, where the direct and to some extent the indirect costs of education are artificially low, individuals on the basis of their private benefit/cost calculations will create a sizable and growing demand for education. However, given (1) the widespread and rising unemployment problem, (2) the tendency for jobs to be filled by overqualified people in terms of length of time spent in school, (3) the heavy public subsidization of education, and (4) the significant opportunity costs of public investment in education as opposed to alternative resource uses, the social benefit-cost indicator of further expansion of the typical institutional educational system is likely to be very much less favorable than the private calculation. This phenomenon of a positive difference between private and social benefits in conjunction with a negative differential between private and social costs will typically lead to a misallocation of national resources (in this case too much education) unless the price "signals" are made to conform more closely to social realities. In other words, as long as artificial and nonmarket incentives in the form of disproportionate expected benefits and subsidized costs are established that place a premium on the number of years one spends "getting an education," the individual will decide that it is in his best private interests to pursue a lengthy educational process even though he may be aware that jobs are becoming scarcer and unemployment rates are rising.

The phenomenon of a distorted wage and price structure misallocating human resources into superfluous years of classical education (as opposed to, say, literacy training in conjunction with the provision of minimum technical or enterpreneurial skills) is analogous to the phenomenon of factor price distortions biasing production decisions toward more capital-intensive processes than are appropriate from the viewpoint of national resource endowments. In the latter case, policies that artificially cheapen capital goods below their intrinsic "economic" value while causing the price of labor to rise above its market value create incentives for producers to economize on labor even though labor is the most abundant national resource and there is widespread unemployment. A social benefit/cost calculation would undoubtedly dictate that a more labor-intensive technology be utilized. But since most decisions in developing nations are still based on private rather than social calculations, the net result will be a misallocation of resources from a national point of view.

In the case of education, a proper functioning reward and cost structure would be one that develops and allocates human resources

14

in accordance with the needs and opportunities in various segments of the economy. For example, the very high wage premiums paid to workers in the modern urban sector in conjunction with the lock-step process in which scarce jobs are allocated on the basis of ever increasing educational attainment leads directly to three obvious misallocations of human resources. First, the output of the educational system being greatly in excess of that which the economy can absorb, many emerge from it seeking jobs for which they may be educationally qualified but that have been preempted by others with even more education. They become temporarily unemployed for whatever period is necessary for their aspirations and status requirements, partly perhaps instilled in them by the educational system itself, to adjust to the stinging realities of the modern sector. "Frictional" unemployment of this kind may in the aggregate be both substantial and growing as the numbers and durations involved increase and represents a serious waste of a nation's educated human resources. Indeed, some analysts speak of the educated unemployment problem almost exclusively as a manifestation of "great expectations."

Second, those who adjust their sights downward and secure modern sector employment normally must take jobs for which they are "overeducated" in terms of the number of years spent in the educational stream. Those who fail to get modern-sector jobs at all swell the ranks of the permanently unemployed or become self-employed in the traditional sector with little opportunity to contribute productively to the society that invested so heavily in their education. The combined effect of the overpaid and thus overeducated employed and the impoverished and unproductive educated unemployed represent, in our opinion, a serious misallocation of scarce national resources. For example, the resources spent on expanding the educational system might have been spent instead on needed public works projects providing employment opportunities to the school leavers as well as those with less education.

The third misallocation associated with the education/high-wage bias of modern-sector employment policy relates to the built-in urban/rural distortion that this policy creates. Since almost all modern-sector jobs are in fact "urban" jobs, since these jobs pay vastly higher wages than the rural alternatives, and since education serves as an initial screening mechanism for access to these jobs, there is a natural tendency for those with more education to migrate to the cities. A recent study, for example, of rural-urban migration in Kenya clearly showed that (1) the average income earned by an urban migrant varies directly with levels of educational attainment, (2) the probability of securing a salaried urban job is higher, the higher the level of educational achievement and, as a result of (1) and (2), (3) the propensity to migrate to the cities varies directly with years of completed education—that is, there was a disproportionately large percentage of urban migrants with levels of educational completion in excess of average levels for their age group in the nation a whole.[2] The net effect of this phenomenon is the drawing away of young talent from rural areas where development needs are so great and where trained and educated manpower is in such short supply. This urban/rural middle- and high-level manpower misallocation is accentuated by the fact that much of this youthful talent is being wasted in urban areas as a result of limited employment opportunities and rising unemployment. However, as long as the wage structure continues to place such a premium on urban jobs, it will remain in the best private interests of the educated unemployed to stay in the cities in the hope of someday being successful in the "urban job lottery" even though from a social productivity outlook their contributions might be much higher in rural areas.

Manipulating the Supply of Educational Opportunities as a Policy Variable

In the preceding section it has been assumed that the supply of educational opportunities accommodates itself to the apparent demand for them. Indeed, the rapid expansion of educational facilities at post-compulsory levels during the 1960s concomitant with the growing numbers of educated unemployed suggests that the satiation of demand was the principal objective of education even though it was not usually fully realized in practice.

We think the reasons for this pattern of governmental behavior are essentially self-evident and in the circumstances practically irresistible. Given heavily subsidized or free education on the one hand and unrealistic income differentials between the modern and traditional sectors on the other, a substantial gap between the demand for education and the supply of employment opportunities is inevitable. Manipulating the supply of educational opportunities within these limits is not likely to close the gap, though, for reasons we have given, its accommodation to demand is likely to widen it.

The manipulation of educational supply instead changes the visible nature of the problem confronting governments without altering materially its basic dimensions or underlying causes. If governments opt for educational policies that seek to satisfy demand, as they apparently do, they leave for themselves the problem of rationing job opportunities in the modern sector among the many who are educationally qualified. So far this problem has seemed to be politically tractable though as the average educational level among the unemployed rises and their numbers grow, as they are almost certain to

16

do with present policies, the size of it may overwhelm the rationing mechanism commonly employed.

That rationing mechanism is the educational system itself. Jobs in the modern sector typically are allocated to those with higher levels of educational attainment, those less fortunate educationally being relegated to the unemployed or dispatched to the fringes of the modern sector or the search for subsistence in more traditional settings. The rationing device has the appealing political merit of being apparently objective, relatively untainted by obvious favor, and patently dependent for its operation on many private as well as public decisions. But its operation does not relieve unemployment or improve the allocation of resources beyond ensuring that those most overeducated are indeed employed. So the magnitude of the problem is left to grow, and an apparently fair rationing mechanism is unlikely to provide political cover for an increasingly explosive situation.

But the need to ration employment seems to be preferred in developing countries to a scarcity of school places and a consequent need to ration educational opportunities. As a result, educational supply increases rapidly, swelling enrollments and proliferating instructional activities. The pressures for expansion that stem directly from the burgeoning demand for education would in the extreme lead toward open education, which undoubtedly has merits in advanced countries with full employment and incomes high enough to justify on social grounds the demand for education as a consumption good. It tends to equalize opportunities and to eliminate private and political favor as criteria for educational advancement. But the cost of such effects in poor countries with inadequate job opportunities, low incomes and essentially free education as privately perceived is enormous financially and economically, and politically as well if unemployment grows more rapidly as a consequence.

In addition to forces on the demand side that stimulate overall expansion, there are pressures from alternative suppliers of education, which lead public education to proliferate the activities for which it is responsible. Many types of specialized education and training that might more efficiently be given in or near the work place may nevertheless find their way into socially expensive vocational training schools or polytechnic colleges. The private business sector and public enterprises that might better perform these services to tailored needs may favor socially inefficient public institutions simply because a poorer-quality product at zero private cost is preferable to a better one whose full costs must be borne privately. If, in addition, the public institutions overproduce, as we have argued, the misallocation of resources to public education is increased.

Does this dismal picture of growing unemployment and overblown educational systems suggest that another built upon an educational supply adjusted to employment opportunities would be substantially happier? Probably not, in the extreme, though educational overqualification for the limited jobs available should diminish, and more jobs could indeed be created with the funds saved on education. So long as education remains essentially privately free and modern-sector jobs are relatively lucrative, the demand for education must be excessive. The problem of rationing severely limited educational places is an enormous one and even if it could be and were accomplished objectively, the mechanism would be open to charges of favoritism. Moreover, the demands of those locked out of the educational system at every stage beyond literacy would likely be politically influential, even if the limitation of supply has economic advantages.

Clearly the unsettling conditions associated with either extreme of educational supply policy when it is the only policy variable are cause for alarm. Within these extremes, however, and as compared with the educational supply policies most governments appear to be pursuing, we feel that greater reluctance to expand education in response to demand is in order and would have a number of beneficial effects. Such a policy would reduce the gap between educational supply and job opportunities by reducing the former and releasing some resources for the expansion of the latter, slowing the rates of increase in the degree of overeducation for jobs and the numbers of educated unemployed. The widening of the gap between the demand for and supply of educational places would bring pressures on governments to reconsider their rationing devices and hopefully to increase the share of educational costs that must be borne privately, particularly by those seeking education at higher levels. It should be recognized, however, that giving greater weight to prospective employment opportunities in planning educational expansion can only be a partial solution since it does not come to grips with what we perceive to be the basic issue—namely, that the demand for education continues to outrun opportunities for productive employment.

There is simply no solution to the imbalance between educational demand and modern-sector job opportunities to be found in the manipulation of educational supply alone. The pressures must build until policy attention is turned to the more fundamental issues of tempering demand to more realistic proportions and generating more modern-sector employment opportunities.

Some Policy Considerations for Governments

We have alluded at several points thus far to the desirability of excluding from our considerations education to the level of literacy.

We regard the minimum verbal and quantitative skills associated
with literacy as essential for (1) informal self-learning, (2) further
formal education, and (3) communication and the transmission of
basic technical, economic, social, and political information. It is
thus a fundamental basis for national cohesion, internal mobility,
family health, and effective self-employment in traditional settings.
The economic productivity of universal education to the level of
literacy is itself persuasive justification for such a policy. We do
not, however, argue that it need be free for all; indeed school fees
may be a strong force influencing family size where the desire for
education is strong. But we do argue that once the basic skills for
communication and self-learning have been provided, formal public
educational opportunities should in the circumstances of poor countries be geared more closely to the minimum educational requirements of the jobs that can be created. For such a policy to be effective it must be supported by constructive efforts to curtail excessive
educational demands on the one hand and to expand productive employment opportunities on the other.

To temper the demand for education toward more realistic
levels, we suggest that governments of developing countries should
strive to bring the private calculations of the benefits and costs associated with education closer to the social benefits and costs by the
following means:

1. Making the beneficiary bear a larger and rising proportion
of his educational costs as he proceeds through the system as the
most effective means of rationing available places. There are three
principles in this recommendation. First, the share of educational
costs borne privately should be substantially larger than is typically
the case in developing countries today. This would have the effect
of reducing the demand for education beyond literacy across the
board. Second, the rate of educational subsidy should decline as an
individual advances in the educational system. Thus the private
demand for education would be curtailed more at higher levels where
it is socially most expensive and where most of the overeducation
in terms of educational requirements for jobs takes place. A policy
of declining subsidies would also respond to the valid criticism that
current programs involving rising subsidies are antiegalitarian and
in fact represent a subsidy of the rich by the poor. Third, the private
share of educational costs should, insofar as possible, fall on the
beneficiary, not on his family or friends. It is his future earnings
that will be increased. Ideally, he should pay for his education out
of those future earnings. This suggests, of course, that private
educational costs should be financed directly out of a student's own
resources or indirectly through loans repaid either by financial levies
against his future income or by social contributions of his expertise,

19

such as service in rural areas. We feel that such arrangements are especially desirable and feasible at all levels of education beyond secondary. Below those levels the burden of private costs would likely continue to fall on the family, in which case a system of subsidizing the able poor would be necessary.

2. Reducing income differentials between the modern and traditional sectors and within the modern sector to ensure a more realistic appraisal of the prospective benefits of education. It would carry us too far from the field of education to consider means in detail here. We only note that these means are much more extensive than direct, sharp, and unrealistic cuts in modern-sector money wages and include more time-consuming processes of holding the line on average and minimum wages in the modern sector while productivity and prices adjust upward, purposive efforts to change the terms of trade between the modern and traditional sectors, and greater attention to rural as opposed to urban infrastructure needs.

3. Ensuring that minimum job specifications do not overvalue education. Students should not be encouraged to seek levels of education that overqualify them for the jobs they can realistically expect to obtain. It is essential for that purpose that the economic system not exaggerate educational prerequisites to employment. Governments can take direct action on this matter within the civil service, where a large share of modern-sector employment is to be found.[3]

4. Ensuring that wages are related to jobs and not to educational attainments. If the other policies are effective, this becomes essentially an interim measure. So long as overeducation is increasing and those emerging from the system must accept jobs that realistically require progressively lower educational qualifications, the tendency, particularly in teaching and the civil service, to tie salaries to levels of education simply increases rates of overpayment, stimulating even more students to follow the same socially misguided path.

To increase the supply of modern-sector job opportunities, we suggest that governments should do the following:

1. Reduce wages relative to the price of capital as these enter into employment decisions in both the public and private sectors.

2. Give more careful consideration to improving rural infrastructure and to the possible location of new modern-sector activities in areas where wages have not yet reached the distorted levels typical of established urban centers.

3. Allocate a larger share of development budgets to productive employment-creating activities as opposed to education than has been the pattern in the last decade.
This is not to say that funds spent on education do not create employment but only that some of the funds so spent in the past might have been more usefully allocated to other activities that were both more

labor intensive and more productive. Education beyond literacy should compete for funds on these criteria, not on the notion that it is a privileged activity exempt from such considerations.

We feel that, over the next decade at least, reasonable efforts along these lines will leave a residual rationing problem in education of substantial magnitude. Dealing with this on the basis of merit rather than favor will be a continuing challenge to the governments of developing countries. We do not deal with it here.

Proposed Guidelines for International Donor Agencies

The past policies of international donor agencies with respect to educational expansion were for the most part well grounded and responsive to the diverse manpower needs of developing nations. However, circumstances are changing rapidly, and donor postures must now be framed in the light of needed national policies such as those identified above. Shortages of educated manpower are rapidly being overcome and a general extension into the future of present rates of growth in educational supply will surely produce new and hopeful school-leavers greatly in excess of the new employment opportunities for which they must compete. Consequently it is now a matter of urgency that donor agencies reexamine their educational assistance policies. Rates of future educational expansion appropriate to realistic appraisals of manpower needs can for the most part be met out of national resources. Moreover, substantial outside support even for lower levels of education where expansion continues to be justified may simply free national educational resources for the less economically justifiable expansion of higher levels. In short, donors should assist developing countries to do what is socially wise rather than what seems to be politically expedient in the field of education.

To the extent that developing countries can and will finance needed educational expansion of traditional kinds out of their own resources, donor agencies are given an opportunity to be more selective and innovative in their own contributions to educational development. We would give priority to the following kinds of activities.

1. Intensified and expanded applied research, particularly in the developing countries themselves, on alternative educational and informational delivery systems appropriate to the diverse employment needs and opportunities of these nations. Special attention should be given to those opportunities outside of the modern sector, a sector toward which Western-type industrial training and higher educational systems are presently oriented.

2. Systematic and controlled pilot experimentation with educational innovations emanating from research efforts. Given the risks

21

and costs associated with experimentation, it is unlikely that developing nations will be able or willing to bear the cost of systematic experimentation.

3. Selective assistance to overcome unanticipated manpower scarcities and bottlenecks.
The extent to which the various international aid agencies can associate themselves with these kinds of activities will undoubtedly vary, but we feel that they merit serious consideration.

Notes

1. For the most up-to-date review of cross-country data on unemployment and underemployment rates in developing countries, see D. Turnham and I. Jaeger, The Employment Problem in Less Developed Countries—A Review of Evidence (Paris: OECD Development Center, June 1970).

2. M. P. Todaro, "Education and Rural-Urban Migration: Theoretical Constructs and Empirical Evidence from Kenya," Conference on Urban Unemployment in Africa, University of Sussex, September 1971 (mimeo).

3. The recently published ILO mission report on employment problems in Ceylon contains a number of interesting and innovative suggestions for avoiding tendencies toward excessive education by, in effect, prohibiting certain categories of students from proceeding beyond a given level of education. Matching Employment Opportunities and Expectations: A Programme of Action for Ceylon. See ILO, Geneva (November 1971).

EDUCATIONAL POLICY AND THE ECONOMICS OF
EDUCATION: SOME PRACTICAL LESSONS FOR
EDUCATIONAL PLANNERS IN DEVELOPING COUNTRIES
Mark Blaug

The economics of education is a young subject: It emerged as
a separate branch of economics only toward the end of the 1950s and
the beginning of the 1960s. One would be surprised, therefore, if it
were now capable of furnishing clear, practical advice to public investors in education. Nevertheless, it is evident that much of the
research in this field has been inspired by the hope of providing
answers to policy questions, and it is also evident that the drift of
this research tends to support certain policy positions and to undermine others. My purpose in this section, therefore, is to derive
some of the practical guidelines that have emerged from recent work
in the field. At the same time, I will mention some questions to which
there are as yet no answers, suggesting lines of inquiry that should
be further pursued if the economics of education is to make its maximum potential contribution to educational planning.

The Optimum Shape of the Educational Pyramid

The single, most striking presumption to emerge from the
burgeoning literature in the economics of education is that almost
all developing countries suffer from persistent underinvestment in
primary education, hand-in-hand with persistent overinvestment in
higher education. As is well known, ever since 1950, or thereabouts,
higher education the world over has been the faster-growing sector
of the educational system, whether measured in terms of enrollments
or in terms of financial outlays. In the 1950s and early 1960s the
principal rationale for the rapid expansion of higher education was
the practice of manpower forecasting: All the figures that emanated
from long-term manpower forecasts in Africa, Asia, and Latin
America revealed enormous "shortages" of secondary and higher
educated manpower. In the last few years, however, a sense of
disillusionment with manpower forecasting has gradually spread
through the world, in part because of the absurdly rigid view that it
implied of the capacity of the economic system to absorb school-
leavers into employment, and in part because of a growing fear that
it constituted an open-ended invitation to expand secondary and higher
education without limits. More important than all these, perhaps,
was the realization that manpower forecasting leaves the educational
planner with virtually no choices to make. Since the forecasting
methods employed are held to be inapplicable to the requirements

23

for primary-educated workers, and since the costs of education do not influence the final results, the typical manpower forecast necessarily commits the bulk of educational expenditures to the expansion of secondary and higher education. It is only after this first call on public funds is met that the planner can start thinking about such alternatives as quantitative expansion versus qualitative improvements, formal education in schools versus informal training in industry, and adult literacy versus schooling for children, but on all these questions he gets no help whatsoever from manpower forecasts.

In retrospect, it is all too easy to see why manpower forecasting swept the world, and its intuitive appeal is such that it will probably linger on for many years to come. The mounting evidence that an amazing variety of manpower structures are compatible with identical levels and rates of growth of national income has still not been adequately assimilated.[1] Similarly, there has been some reluctance to accept the fact that the ability of economists to forecast the future is severely limited. Because of the length of most educational cycles, manpower forecasts that attempt to be useful to educational planning are impelled to look ahead at least 5 to 10 years. No one is surprised to discover that perfectly accurate forecasting is impossible over such lengths of time. Nevertheless, the wild inaccuracies of virtually all manpower forecasts of the long-term variety are such as to render them almost indistinguishable from wild guesses in an upward direction.[2] Fairly accurate predictions can be made for two- or three-year periods, and these are undoubtedly useful for an "active manpower policy" that provides information for training programs, labor placement services, vocational guidance, and the like. In time, by continuously evaluating these short-term forecasts, we will learn to predict better in the medium and long term. But over the next decade or so there is little point in arguing whether educational systems should be geared to long-term manpower requirements because it is a simple fact that they cannot be.

Fortunately, there are other ways of doing educational planning even when we are only concerned with narrow economic objectives. The leading alternative approach is cost-benefit analysis, sometimes labeled rate-of-return analysis. This has its problems, too, but it does have the merit of getting us started on the right foot: When we decide to spend another dollar on education rather than on some other activity, or on one kind of education rather than another, we do so in the belief that, for a given cost, some stated goal can be more effectively achieved; when the goal is an economic one, we must be saying in effect that the contemplated action will result in greater economic benefits per unit of costs than any other. Cost-benefit analysis, therefore, is surely the appropriate framework for thinking about educational planning for economic ends.

24

In practice, the benefits of education in rate-of-return analysis are taken to be the extra income payments that typically accrue to people with additional education, and many commentators have drawn attention to the so-called externalities or neighborhood effects of education that are not reflected in personal income flows. This is only a serious objection, however, if we are making ambitious comparisons between expenditures on education and expenditures on, say, health or transport; it is much less of a problem when we are comparing expenditures between different levels of education, unless of course we have reasons to know that higher education, for example, generates more externalities than secondary education. We know very little about the externalities of education, and there is not even agreement as to what form they take; it would be a bold planner, therefore, who could claim that certain levels of the educational system generate greater neighborhood effects than others.

A deeper question is whether the higher earnings of better-educated people really reflect their superior productivity; perhaps the structure of wages and salaries is a matter of social conventions, having little to do with the contribution of individuals to national income. But if so, this consideration affects the price of steel as much as it does the economic returns to education, and yet few planners would use it to deny the value of calculating the expected rate of return on a new steel factory before constructing it. It is perfectly true that the rate of return on educational investment in a country is a meaningless figure if the pattern of earnings bears no relationship to the relative scarcities of people with different skills. For that reason, rate-of-return studies in developing countries increasingly couple analysis of the economic value of education with a study of the operations of the labor market.[3] In other words, a rate-of-return calculation only creates a presumption of how resources ought to be reallocated within the educational system, but it cannot by itself prove that they are misallocated.

Some sociologists have wondered whether the higher earnings of better-educated people is simply a reflection of their superior home background, in which case we are attributing to education effects that are due to social class origins. On the available evidence, it must be said that this is a wild surmise: People with more education earn more on average the world over even when family background factors are held constant. Most of the evidence, to be sure, derives from developed countries, but for a few developing nations there are now similar data to show that lifetime career opportunities are not rigidly determined by circumstances of birth.[4] Home background and length of education are of course correlated, but the correlation is nowhere as high as is sometimes suspected.

With these caveats, we can now ask what rate-of-return analysis reveals about investment in different levels of education in the third world. We have relevant data for 10 developing countries, and in most of these (Brazil, Malaysia, and the Philippines are exceptions), primary education yields higher social rates of return than any other level of education.5 As between secondary and higher education, however, the situation is more mixed: In half of the developing countries, secondary education also ranks above higher education, but in the other half the ranking is reversed. The one general lesson we can draw from these results, therefore, is that there appears to be underinvestment in primary education in almost all developing countries; that is to say, given the existing quality of education, too much is being spent on the higher levels and too little on the lower levels of the system. I must emphasize the fact that this is a conclusion about quantities: Existing rate-of-return data cannot tell us what would happen if the content of primary schooling were radically altered; they cannot even tell us how far to carry the reallocation of resources because rates of return only provide signals of direction, not statements of actual amounts to aim at. However, the discrepancies in rates of return to the different levels of education are, in most cases, so large that even huge shifts of resources over a period of 5 to 10 years would not suffice to close the gap.6 It is sometimes said that, insofar as the causes of dropouts in primary education are largely a matter of poverty and deprived home background, there is little the educational authorities can do to increase attendance rates in primary schools. But free meals, free uniforms, busing at subsidized rates, and so on can do much to increase enrollment rates, and all these measures would compete for budgetary funds with the rising outlays on higher education.

The argument in favor of shifting expenditures toward primary education is probably strengthened by introducing the vexed question of "externalities," and it is further strengthened by considering noneconomic objectives for education, such as equality of educational opportunity or political stability. The point is, however, that even if we take a much narrower view of the instrumental ends of education, there is now a nice harmony between the views of most economists and most educators.

The Vocational School Fallacy

Some years ago, Phillip Foster set a cat among the pigeons with an article entitled "The Vocational School Fallacy in Economic Development."7 Arguing from Ghanaian evidence, he denied the validity of the belief that vocational training provided inside formal

26

educational institutions could ever become an effective method of accelerating economic development; he further denied that general education and vocational training are ever substitutes for each other, the former being indeed a necessary foundation for the latter, and the latter being generally more efficiently provided on the job rather than inside schools. He conceded, however, that there was an argument for "special vocational institutes being created in particular cases where their endeavors can be closely meshed with on-the-job training and with the actual manpower requirements indicated by the market for skills." Since then, a good deal of evidence has been forthcoming from other countries that threatens even this slender foundation for a vocational school strategy in educational planning.[8]

The problem is essentially that of the degree of inaccuracy that inheres in the art of manpower forecasting. If we could more or less accurately forecast the requirements for specific skills, there would indeed be a case grounded on economies of scale for training people on a full-time basis to acquire these skills. But even the most enthusiastic manpower forecasters agree that medium- and particularly long-term manpower forecasts cannot be expected to do more than to distinguish the needs for people with general academic education from the needs for those with scientific and technical preparation. Since formal educational institutions, either at the secondary or at the tertiary level, invariably commit themselves to a two-to-three-year cycle, the inability of manpower forecasters to make accurate, detailed predictions of skill requirements over the medium-term would seem to be fatal to a vocational-school strategy.

Let us be clear about what the argument is. Everyone agrees that vocational schools are expensive; that vocational school teachers ought to be both well-trained teachers and persons with industrial experience, but that such are few and far between; that the equipment of vocational schools is liable to be either outmoded or so advanced as to have little relevance to the country in question; and that it is virtually impossible to simulate the actual rhythm and discipline of factory work in the classroom. Nevertheless, if vocational schooling made good sense, these would merely constitute surmountable difficulties. Unfortunately, vocational training in formal educational institutions makes little sense on either educational or economic grounds. It is impossible to foresee accurately the requirements for specific skills in an economy two to three years hence; for that reason, vocational training on a full-time basis must necessarily impart general skills, at which point it ceases to be "vocational" in the sense in which that term is usually understood.

We are not denying the case for accelerated training courses provided on a part-time basis after working hours, or even on a full-time basis for several months in the year. Nor are we denying the

27

case for "vocationalizing" secondary school curricula if what is meant thereby is the provision of some work-oriented shop courses, combined with take-home projects of a practical kind. But to ask schools to prepare students to take up clearly defined occupations is to ask them to do what is literally impossible. The most that schools can do is to provide a technical foundation for on-the-job acquisition of specific skills.

It is worth adding that the popular clamor for vocational schooling among politicians in developing countries, much encouraged by the so-called business-like attitude of the World Bank to educational finance, implies a patently naive interpretation of the economic value of education. Schooling makes people more productive not just by imparting cognitive knowledge but also by "socializing" them in various ways: punctuality, achievement motivation, the willingness to take orders and to accept responsibility are no less vocationally useful skills than the ability to turn a lathe or to read a technical instruction.9 The notion that there is one kind of education, called general education, which has nothing to do with the world of work, and another called vocational education, which is firmly geared to the "needs of a growing economy," is part and parcel of the rhetorical folklore that continues to impede rational educational planning in developing countries.

Private Costs and Social Costs of Education

Perhaps the chief merit of rate-of-return analysis of educational investment is to have emphasized dramatically the enormous gap that prevails in almost all countries between the private and the social costs of education. Private rates of return to education everywhere exceed social rates of return despite the fact that private rates only take account of personal earnings after the deduction of income tax, whereas social rates are calculated on earnings inclusive of income tax. The reason for this is simply that the total resource costs of education everywhere exceed the costs that students and parents must bear themselves. It is a striking fact, of which few educators were aware before the advent of the human investment revolution in economic thought, that the abolition of tuition fees does not suffice to make education free to students: In almost all cases, indirect costs in the form of earnings forgone while studying constitute a larger proportion of the total costs imposed on students and parents than do direct costs in the form of fees, books, and travel. Furthermore, indirect costs are nowhere subsidized by the state. Since the opportunities for gainful employment increase rapidly after the age of 12 in most developing countries, the failure to compensate parents for the forgone earnings of their school children constitutes an effective bias against participation in secondary and higher education for the poorer classes of the community. Given the other built-in educational biases against children from poor families, it is hardly surprising therefore that, as we move up the educational ladder, the survivors are drawn increasingly from well-to-do families. In the light of these considerations, the excessive investment in higher education in most developing countries takes on a new significance. Quite apart from the objective of maximizing the rate of growth of national income, the policy of allowing higher education to grow at its own natural rate is steadily undermining the goal of equality of educational opportunity. In short, far from these two goals being necessarily in conflict, I believe there is now evidence to show that both economic and social objectives would be served by redirecting resources in favor of the lower stages of the educational system.

The brief discussion of costs is sufficient to show that this can be accomplished in a number of ways: A portion of the educational budget could be reallocated from higher or secondary to primary education, leaving the cost structure of the educational system unaffected; alternatively, a larger share of the total costs could be shifted to students and parents in higher education, say, via a system of student loans coupled with a rise in fees, the sums thereby released being devoted to primary education. The money could be reallocated to bring about a change in enrollments at the various levels, or it could be used to convert quantitative reductions at one level into qualitative improvements at another level; only piecemeal experiments can tell us which is the better method. The possible courses of action are much greater in number than is usually imagined, and, in particular, there is absolutely no reason to exclude the costs of education as one of the policy instruments.

Cost-Effectiveness Analysis

The tenor of these remarks suggests that rate-of-return analysis or cost-benefit analysis is in fact only a species of a much larger genus that can be used to evaluate any activity, however many objectives that activity aims to satisfy. I label the genus "cost-effectiveness analysis," but some practitioners prefer to describe it as "systems analysis" or "management science." Whatever it is called, the method in application to a number of alternative "projects" consists essentially of three steps: (1) specify each of the multiple objectives in such a way that they can be scaled, preferably in cardinal numbers, but possibly in ordinal numbers; (2) in terms of that scale, measure the effectiveness of all projects per unit of costs for each of the objectives; and (3) choose the "best" project by applying the planner's "preference function," that is, a set of weights or order of priorities among objectives without which it is impossible to choose among a series of possible conflicting cost-effectiveness ratios. This is cost-effectiveness analysis, but it is also the explicit formulation of the logic of rational decision-making. Its intimate association with program budgeting (PPB) techniques should be obvious; PPB in fact consists of steps (1) and (2), leaving step (3) to be decided "politically."

In principle, all this is no doubt unobjectionable, although in practice it may be difficult to work systematically through every step. Nevertheless, it has the great advantage of showing not only that all educational decisions involve value judgments but also precisely where the value judgments enter. Steps (1) and (2) are positive social science, since one does not have to like a country's objectives in order to formulate them operationally, or to quantify the degree to which its educational system effectively achieves these objectives. Step (3), on the other hand, is obviously normative social science and raises delicate questions about how one is supposed to elicit a government's "preference function" without actually imposing one's own.

Educational planning in the round must go beyond cost-benefit analysis to cost-effectiveness analysis. We know that it is difficult to give an unambiguous interpretation of the economic development goals of a nation. How much more so is this the case with social, political, and even purely educational goals. The fact that one can still encounter statements in the literature that profess to advocate something called the "social demand approach" to educational planning—by which is meant either that country A should spend the same proportion of gross national product (GNP) on education as other countries do, or that all students in country A who want an education should have it subject to prevailing standards and prevailing costs, leaving unexamined both standards and costs—is proof enough that non-economic goals have hardly begun to be operationally formulated. Radically different educational policies can be justified in terms of "equality of educational opportunities," depending on what we mean by that objective. It would be easy to multiply examples for some of the other goals. Suffice it to say that the concept of educational planning for economic objectives may be an untidy mess, but it is a paragon of order compared to educational planning for social, political, and educational objectives. Is it perhaps that sociologists, political scientists, psychologists, and educationists have lacked a framework of decision-making in which their positive findings may be fitted? If so, cost-effectiveness analysis is such a framework, which would permit social scientists other than economists to make their contribution to the subject.

Concluding Comments

It would be absurd to pretend that recent work in the economics of education adds up to an impressive list of concrete recommendations to educational investors in developing countries. What it does provide is some general presumptions, such as those in favor of investing in primary education and, in general, opposed to vocational schooling. Beyond that, it offers some suggestions resting ultimately on the inherent uncertainty of the future and the limited capacity of social scientists to reduce the level of uncertainty by accurate forecasting. Decision-making under uncertainty leads, of course, to different kinds of decisions from those of decision-making under certainty: The irreducible uncertainty of the future argues in favor of teaching general rather than specific skills; of late rather than early specialization; of part-time rather than full-time education; of expenditure on the provision of information, if necessary at the expense of facilities; and, in general, of postponing all "lumpy" decisions as long as possible. In the last analysis, however, recent work in the economics of education warns us to keep rigidly distinct the question of the goals of education from the question of achieving these goals more or less effectively. It offers us, in short, a paradigm of rational planning in the field of education.

It must be remembered, however, that we still know very little about the learning process in schools and even less about why schooling is so highly rated in the labor market. Indeed, our appalling ignorance of the functioning of labor markets in developing countries is undoubtedly the Achilles heel of the economics of education, which continues to sow seeds of doubt about its major findings. It is clearly the problem area on which future research ought to be concentrated.

Notes

1. Some of this evidence is to be found in R. G. Hollister, A Technical Evaluation of the First Stage of the Mediterranean Regional Project (Paris: OECD, 1966) and OECD, Occupational and Educational Structures of the Labour Force and Levels of Economic Development (Paris: OECD, 1970). It is further discussed in M. Blaug, Introduction to the Economics of Education (London: Penguin Books, 1972), ch. 5.

2. See B. Ahmad and M. Blaug, The Practice of Manpower Forecasting (London: Allen Lane, Penguin Press, 1972), which consists, among other things, of a detailed appraisal of the forecasting experience of eight countries, of which three are developing countries.

3. See, for example, H. H. Thias and M. Carnoy, Cost-Benefit Analysis in Education: A Case Study on Kenya (Washington, D.C.: International Bank for Reconstruction and Development, 1969); M. Blaug, R. Layard and M. Woodhall, Causes of Graduate Unemployment in India (London: Allen Lane, Penguin Press, 1969).

4. The evidence is discussed in Blaug, Introduction, op. cit., pp. 51-54, 227-30.

5. See G. Psacharopoulos, The Economic Returns to Investment in Education in the Process of Growth and Development (London: Allen Lane, Penguin Press, 1972). For a quick review of the findings, see the same author's "Rates of Return to Investment in Education Around the World," Comparative Education Review, February 1972. The developing countries in question are Mexico, Venezuela, Colombia, Puerto Rico, Chile, and Brazil in Latin America; Malaysia, Singapore, the Philippines, Thailand, India, South Korea in Asia; Nigeria, Ghana, Kenya, Uganda, and Zambia in Africa; and Greece and Turkey in Europe.

6. For some examples of "sensitivity analysis" to show how rates of return in certain countries will change in the future, given specified changes in enrollments at various levels, see C. S. Dougherty, "The Optimal Allocation of Investment in Education," Studies in Development Planning, ed. H. Chenery (Cambridge: Harvard University Press, 1970) and M. Selowsky, The Effect of Unemployment and Growth on the Rate of Return to Education: The Case of Colombia (Cambridge: Center for International Affairs, Harvard University, Report No. 129, 1969).

7. In Education and Economic Development, eds. C. A. Anderson and M. J. Bowman (Chicago: Aldine Publishing Co., 1966), reprinted in Penguin Modern Economics: Economics of Education 1, ed. M. Blaug (London: Penguin Education, 1968).

8. See E. Staley, Planning Occupational Education and Training for Development (New Delhi: Orient Longmans, 1970).

9. For an elaboration of this theme, see M. Blaug, "The Correlation between Education and Earnings: What Does it Signify?" Journal of Higher Education, vol. 1, no. 1, 1972.

THE CONTRIBUTION OF THE ECONOMICS OF EDUCATION TO AID POLICIES: A CRITICAL COMMENT
Michel Debeauvais

The Evolution of Ideas Since 1960

In 1960, the economics of education began to affirm itself as a new domain of economic analysis, whose progress would make an essential contribution to the elaboration of education policies.

Theoretical notions of human capital, of the investment represented by the cost of education, of the economic return to education, seemed to confirm scientifically the political recommendations favoring an increase in resources marked for the expansion of educational systems. This extension of the economic analysis to the realm of education opened the way for research whose results have had a wide import: Educational progress explained a very important part of economic growth; the return on the cost of schooling revealed itself to be much greater than the return on material investments; techniques of economic planning could be applied to the realm of education, which would allow priorities to be determined and resources to be used in the most effective way; new methods of predicting the needs for qualified manpower would assure the harmonization of the economic objectives of education with those of the economy.

The thesis presented here could be summarized as follows: After a period of perhaps exaggerated confidence in the effectiveness of economics as applied to the realm of education, we are now going through a phase of critical reevaluation of methods and concepts recommended since the early 1960s. The theoretical hypotheses concerning the relations between the economy and education have not been confirmed by the research of the past few years; the methods of planning for "human resources" have been revealed to be neither as certain nor as effective as had been thought; education and manpower policies have been shown to have little influence on the evolution of learning and of the job market.

Of course, these points of view have various nuances, and moreover they do not meet with the unanimous agreement of economists; they are basically personal viewpoints and are therefore subject to discussion.

The Politics of Aid to Education and the Politics of Education

One might ask if aid to education constitutes a field of study distinct from that of the development of education within the national frame of reference. The political questions of aid to education are found where questions of external aid strategy and those of national educational policies intersect. In principle, the main objective of the policies of donor countries is to contribute in the most effective way possible to the development of the recipient countries. However, it is possible to identify the unique national objectives of each country or donor agency, each with its own specific strategy. Here, one will admit that the goals of external aid are no different from those pursued by the national politics of the recipient country. However, even with this simplified hypothesis, there is still a problem peculiar to aid; that is, the global distribution of aid by a donor country (or agency) between the different developing countries, as well as the fact that aid to education is included in aid to different economic and social sectors. At present the choices seem to be dictated more by political considerations than by economic criteria, and their analysis depends more on political science than on economics. In any event, international comparisons mentioned hereafter may provide elements useful for appreciating and clarifying these problems of allocation of aid.

Three Points of View to Distinguish

To present the contribution of the economics of education to the realm of external aid to education, it would seem useful to distinguish three levels of analysis: (1) the economic theory, whereby certain relatively recent developments have extended to the realm of education several concepts and methods of economic analysis to form a subheading, currently labeled the economics of education; (2) economic planning techniques, which have been applied to the educational sector for about a dozen years; and (3) development policies: One has tried to formulate and to place in operation national educational policies, applying to "human resources" a strategy with a value comparable to that advocated in the economic domain.

It is important to make these distinctions, which correspond to three different points of view. For economists, it is important to elaborate the criteria of choice that would allow the determination of the most effective theoretical solution. Their principal concern is the advancement of knowledge, without according a decisive importance to available facts or to the realism of theoretical situations studied previously. The planners (who are often limited to planning technicians, in the sense that the plans are, in many countries, elaborated by a small group of technicians) must propose decisions, no matter what the degree of advancement of theoretical knowledge and use the available facts. They have a tendency to emphasize the most easily applicable techniques, and the methods that they use

do not always rest on a satisfactory theoretical base. With regard
to politicians in power, or to administrators (without going further
in differentiating points of view), they accord a privileged importance
to that which is "feasible," and their criteria are those of action.

The type of question asked by each of these three interlocutors
has no direct response. For the "policy-maker," the contribution
of the economics of education may be judged as follows: Are the
results of research sufficiently certain and concordant to allow the
determination of more favorable decisions? Are the proposed solutions realistic? The planners tend to pose a different type of question:
Are the theoretical decisions applicable within the present state of
available information? If the economic theory does not appear useful
in a given concrete situation, can one extract from the present facts,
historical examples, or international comparisons, statements that
are sufficiently precise and stable to serve as a basis for the future?
The economists are more interested in the theoretical significance
of these statements, in trying to find a rational base for their decisions,
independently of their conditions for application.

Foremost amongst these points of view is the implication of a
deliberate orientation toward "utilitarian" judgments provided by
the contribution of the economics of education to educational aid
policies. This is obviously only a partial view, and it would be dangerous to generalize: Research may contribute to the progress of
knowledge, even if the results only lead to discussion, or if they
contradict the results of previous research; in other respects, a
forecasting technique can be utilized advantageously even if its
theoretical foundations are weak or nonexistent; even when decisions
are made in terms of tradition or of non-economic criteria or when
certain social objectives are not (yet) quantifiable, that does not
signify that the theoretical research is useless.

Knowledge does not progress in a linear fashion, nor in terms
of the demands of action. Divergencies among the three points of
view are inevitable, and it is neither possible nor desirable to make
them disappear, as each is an essential element of the social dialogue.

Relations Between Education and the Economy

According to the theoretical plan, the economics of education
had the merit of bringing into evidence the ties between the educational system and the economy and proposed a method of analysis
for the study of the economic and financial aspects of the educational
sector as well as of clarifying the interrelationships between the
diverse branches of the economy. From this came two directions
for research: (1) the economic analysis of the school system: how

to apportion the resources among the various parts of the system? and (2) interactions with the economy: What portion of the national resources must be devoted to the educational sector? What are the consequences of education on the productivity of workers?

Many concepts drawn from economics have been utilized in replying to these questions:

• Education is not only a precondition of economic development, but also a factor in growth.

• The expenses of schooling must no longer be considered in an indifferent way; one must realize its structural and qualitative characteristics, especially levels of training and professional qualifications.

These notions have been widely acknowledged among economists and have known a great public success. Each is founded upon research, and one may trace the evaluations of each in a comparable manner: In the first phase, simple and obvious correlations are found between economic and educational development; but the research that followed gave divergent results and often led to the rejection of the first conclusions.

Worldwide Relations

The notion of education as a factor of growth gave way to two types of research. The first consists of looking for a direct relation between the level of educational development of different countries and the level of their economy. One studied the correlations between the level of literacy and the per capita income (A. Anderson and M. J. Bowman, 1965),* or between the level of schooling (primary, secondary, and higher education) and the GNP (F. Edding, 1962), or between a variety of indicators of economic and social development (Harbison and Myers, 1966: United Nations Research Institute for Social Development [UNRISD], 1968). Numerous significant correlations have been obtained, the highest being those that relate educational costs per person to per capita GNP (Blot and Debeauvais, 1966). One can connect to these studies research that tends to construct synthetic indices by combining the greatest number of quantitative and qualitative facts about the educational system and the labor force. Harbison and Myers (1966) were satisfied with a balanced

------

*Parenthetical references are given in full in References section, p. 44.

average of two levels of schooling to define the level of educational development of different countries. For several years, UNESCO has undertaken the analysis of a greater number of statistics with the aid of a "taxonomical" method suggested by Z. Hellwig (1969), with a view to identifying groups of countries presenting similar characteristics or similar levels of development (F. Harbison and J. Marhunik, 1970: J. Silvio, 1971) or analogous historical evolutions (J. Galtung, 1969).

UNRISD calculated a series of average indices for different groups of countries defined on the basis of per capita income, each set of "points of correspondence" presenting the characteristic profile of the group considered.

Synthetic Indicators

Also undertaken was the analysis of correlations between indices with the aid of different forms of factorial analysis, notably the analysis of principal components in order to point up social factors of development (Niewarowski, 1965) or the analysis of connections (Benzcery Lebar, 1966: D. Blot, 1972).

Relation between the Qualitative Structure of Manpower and the Economy

One may also compare the comparative research based on the educational (or professional) characteristics of manpower relative to the levels of productivity. In effect, the dependent variable in this case is made up of that portion of the labor force having a certain level of education, or a certain level of qualification, that is, the stock of education incorporated in the active population: The independent variable is more often the production per worker, which considers the levels of per capita income relatively unimportant differences due to the differences in the level of activity.

The majority of correlations thus obtained are significant (Layard and Saigol, 1966: OECD, 1970 and 1971) but also rather low: More than half of the differences established between the countries must be attributed to other factors not included in these studies. When one determines the limits of confidence with the help of standard deviations, the deviations are too large to use the regression equations for conjecture (M. Debeauvais, 1971). Further, universal or global statements are those that give the highest correlation: Accordingly, when one considers the most precise and homogeneous categories (economic sectors, levels of instruction, or professional categories), statistical relationships become less significant (M. Debeauvais, 1970). When supplemental variables are introduced into regression equations (Horowitz and Zymelman, 1966; OECD, 1969), correlation coefficients are augmented at the same time, which situation denotes a pronounced colinearity among all independent variables.

Another difficulty encountered in these analyses is that the results do not give a univocal indication in the sense of causality: Is education the cause of economic development (effect of investment) or only the consequence (effect of consumption)? As one knows, correlations measure only the degree of interdependence between variables, and regression equations may be calculated both ways just as easily, with analogous results. Even with a time-lag (M. Debeauvais, 1969), the results do not present any significant differences.

Diachronic Relationships and Longitudinal Studies

Further, one may ask oneself about the significance of observed correlations at any given moment, if one wishes to compare the stages of temporal development of a given country. Spatial correlations, even when repeated on several different occasions with analogous results, can reflect historically determined relations, which are susceptible to evolution over the course of time. This seems to be the case with educational expenses: On the whole, each country presently carries on efforts proportionate to its economic resources (which is reflected in the proven high correlation between educational expenses and national income), but this effort has grown in all countries in analogous proportions, which explains the differences established among the temporal elasticities (very great) observed on the basis of historical series for each separate country, and the spatial elasticities calculated for all countries at a given time.

Moreover, considering the rate of growth of the educational system (and not the present levels, which reflect as much historical evolution as present efforts), the characteristic differences established between countries do not seem related to economic rates of growth, or to the level of economic development, or to any universal economic variable (M. Debeauvais, 1971).

From an educational policy viewpoint, one can dismiss the various research efforts mentioned above, as it does not seem justified to consider the development of the educational system as a factor of growth in all cases. This remark may be particularly applied to the quantitative priorities that were recommended at the start of the 1960s, in national as well as international plans. International experience has not provided the criteria to permit the determination of a "percentage of the GNP," which should be devoted to education as a requirement of economic development.

Education as a Factor of Economic Growth

The studies mentioned above rest on debatable theoretical bases, as the research on universal and direct relationships between educative and economic variables is based on an extreme simplification. In education, not only does one consider mainly those factors that are most universal and quantifiable (rate of learning, number of years of study, or total educational expenses), one doesn't consider the role of capital, whereas in economics the better part of the research efforts have been devoted to discovering the most effective combinations between capital and labor. Other research originates in confronting economic theory, notably of the production process, with data drawn from observing the world economic systems.

Research conducted in the 1950s on economic growth over a long historical period, observed in many industrial countries, has shown that the economic factors considered up until then accounted for only a fractional amount of the total expansion. Among the different explanations put forth in an attempt to identify this "residual factor," the one that cites education as the "third factor" of growth has had the greatest success (T. W. Schultz, 1960). The increase in the "stock of education" of the working population is interpreted as a qualitative amelioration of manpower, expressed in a higher level of productivity among the work force.

Results of calculations showed that education was contributing importantly (occasionally even preponderantly) to the increase in the national product. This point of view has not been universally admitted, and other economists (including Kendrick and Solow) prefer to consider that the "unexplained residue" can be explained by the progress of knowledge, which essentially is incorporated into the capital in the form of increased productivity: We are dealing here with an element that E. Denison considers to be residual, while he considers education to be the transmission of existing knowledge, and not as the producer of new knowledge.

E. Denison (1962) has thoroughly examined these growth studies in trying to measure the respective influence of a larger number of factors (he identifies more than 30) capable of explaining economic growth in the United States. In the results obtained for the two periods 1909-29 and 1929-57, he finds the role of education to be considerably diminished but still very important, as he attributes one-fourth of long-term U.S. growth to the raising of the level of instruction of the working population.* But the extension of his

---

*Not taking into account any negative factors (such as reduction in working hours), educational progress involved, for the period

TABLE 1

Contribution of Education to Growth Rates of National
Income, Per Person Employed
(in percent)

Area	1950-62	1950-55	1955-62
United States	22	19	25
Northwest Europe	6	5	7
Belgium	17	17	17
Denmark	6	9	5
France	6	6	6
Germany	2	2	3
Netherlands	7	6	9
Norway	7	7	8
United Kingdom	17	22	14
Italy	7	8	7
Peru (1962-67)			4.5 to 5.0

Note: The contribution of education to growth is evaluated in the following manner: The increase in the number of years of schooling of the working population is balanced by a series of "qualitative indices," each level of studies being affected by a weight corresponding to the relative salary; the author further supposes that three-fifths of the salary differences are due to education, and the rest were attributable to other factors such as individual aptitudes, professional status, and parents' education. For Peru, the evaluations were obtained by using analogous methods of calculation, where statistics would permit.

Sources: Edward E. Denison, "Why Growth Rates Differ" (Washington, D.C.: Brookings Institution, 1967), Tables 15-3, p. 192, and 21-1 to 21-20, pp. 298-317); Peru: "Libro Blanco de la Productividad," Centro Nacional de Productividad, Lima, 1969.

research to the economic growth of eight European countries (Denison, 1967) showed that the portion of growth attributable to education was much smaller than that of the United States, as shown in Table 1.

1929-57, an average annual increase of 0.67 percent, a growth in actual national income of 2.93 percent, or 1.6 percent per employee, the contribution of education to growth being 25.8 percent in the first case and 41 percent in the second.

It is noted that education "explains" less than 10 percent of the economic growth in 5 of the European countries examined: Only in Belgium and the United Kingdom (both of which have the lowest rates of growth) does the role of education approach that observed in the United States.

Certainly, these figures should not be considered as factual data showing that education would be more "profitable" in one country than in another: The method used in making these calculations may be open to several criticisms, and the results may be interpreted in many ways. But in any case, they serve to refute the often repeated argument that attributes the largest part of growth to educational progress.

The Economic Profitability of Education

The important contribution of microeconomic analysis was that it allowed the application of methods of costs-benefits analysis to the clarification of the criteria of choice concerning education, from either an individual or a collective viewpoint. If one accepts that different salaries are the exact measure of each individual's contribution to the social product, the comparison of "rates of return" on marginal increases of education discloses the disequilibrium between the educational system and investments in other sectors or permits the determination of priorities among different levels and types of schooling.

In a comparative research study, as yet unpublished, G. Psacharopoulos (1972) has recorded about 40 educational-rate-of-return studies in 25 countries. One may make the same observation as previously.[1] The first results (H. P. Miller, 1960; T. W. Schultz, 1961) have reinforced the opinion that in all cases education constitutes a very profitable investment, from an individual viewpoint. But subsequent research has led to interpretations with more subtle nuances. In numerous cases, the internal "rates of return" are not revealed as being superior to market rates, sometimes being even lower or zero. In 12 out of 23 countries, the rates of return on higher education are less than 10 percent. Such is the case for higher education in Colombia (M. Selowsky, 1968; T. W. Schultz, 1968); in India (M. Blaug, 1969); in Northern Nigeria (S. Bowles, 1967). In other cases, one may establish for the same country notable differences among different authors. In the most detailed studies where the basic data are the most certain, such as the investigation of electrical construction in Great Britain (L. S. E., 1969), in which five types of technical and scientific instruction are distinguished, 15 rates of return (social) out of 16 are less than 10 percent, 5 of which are less than 5 percent. Compared with the B.S. degree, even the Master's degree has a negative rate of return.

41

May one conclude that in the case of returns that are inferior to the market rates, economic analysis shows the desirability of slowing down the growth of the educational system (or of certain branches of the system) in order to correct the imbalance?

Economists are far from being unanimous on the subject of practical conclusions that can be drawn from this research. Among the criticisms formulated against this mode of cost-benefit analysis are the following: (1) the extraprofessional satisfactions that the individual may draw from education are not included in these calculations, nor are the indirect benefits to the entire community, such as the progress of knowledge; (2) by using average salaries for the different levels of study, there is a tendency to greatly overestimate the effect of education on salary disparities, without taking into account their dispersion at each of these levels, nor of other factors capable of influencing them; (3) the present rates of return are those measured in these studies, whereas the future returns are those that must be considered for guiding choices in educational matters; and (4) the hypothesis of a "perfect market" for salaries, where income disparities indicate individual contributions to production, seems difficult for many to admit, particularly in the case of developing countries.

Whatever the positions adopted by individuals on these different points, one can admit that this research has often posed interesting questions concerning the relationships between the educational system and the job market. We can mention, for example, the generally higher rates characterizing primary instruction, contrary to an opinion often attributed to economists, according to which it would be economically preferable to give priority to secondary instruction to the detriment of primary instruction; the relatively weak return on higher education, including when one analyzes the different disciplines separately (Layard et al., 1971); very low, zero, or negative rates for postuniversity training, which could also be interpreted as a sign that the principal benefits expected by these studies are found in the general progress of knowledge and not in productivity gains directly measurable in salary levels.

The disparities found between individual rates of return and those of the community (due primarily to the public financing of educational expenses) correspond to the imbalance established between the "individual demand" for education (which is often termed the "social demand") and the absorption capacity of the labor market.2 But this deals only with hypotheses, whose range is limited by the value placed on the objections mentioned above and which also holds for the deficiencies in the available data on salary structure, for the methods of calculation utilized, and for the not-too-realistic hypotheses founded on these calculations. It does not seem to be indicated that in the present state of research, the decisions of educational policy or aid are based on the "signals" furnished by comparing rates of return.

Forecast of Manpower Needs

One has often attributed to all economists the methods of forecasting the needs for qualified manpower that have been used to connect educational planning to economic planning. The Mediterranean Regional Project (1962-64) was the best-known example of these studies of "human resource planning." Without going into the details of this methodology, which has been covered in numerous other works,[3] we must stress that one of its principal weaknesses is the difficulty in quantifying the relationship between the professional structure and the economy, without taking into account the possibilities of substitution between professions or different levels of training.

Sensitivity analysis undertaken by R. Hollister and R. Trajtenberg (OECD, 1967) on the forecasts of the Mediterranean Regional Project, are not conclusive, due as much to deficiencies in the method used (analysis of factors of change of the professional structure) as to difficulty in interpreting the results.

Further, the comparative analysis based on the population census of 53 countries (OECD, 1970 and 1971) showed, as an overview, that the statistical relationship between economic and structural manpower variables were not as limited as one had supposed, based on former applications, and that the economic interpretation of the correlations obtained were not very satisfying. One sometimes invoked, to explain the mediocrity of these results, the theoretical weakness of macroeconomic models putting human capital and production into direct relation, without taking into account the entire group of production factors in a systematic way. But the results of the sector study on electrical construction in Great Britain (P. R. G. Layard et al., 1969) are even more negative, while all the characteristic variables concerning manpower, capital, the production process, and the type of products were taken into consideration.

Must one conclude that the economics of education does not contribute usefully to the elaboration of educational development policies? It does not seem to. All questions asked in the preceding pages are pertinent, and the development of research on the economics of education has posed them. Regarding the replies furnished, they are deceiving only for those who place excessive hope in the possibility of directly tying together systems as complex as education and the economy by several easily calculated parameters.

The phase of critical reevaluation in which the majority of theoreticians and practitioners presently find themselves was explained during the course of a recent seminar.4 This reevaluation must, in our opinion, open up new research areas; a precondition of such progress is, in our opinion, the gathering of data in greater amounts and of a greater significance than presently available on the educational and professional structure of the labor force, and on salary structures, in order better to understand the effective functioning of the graduate job market; another condition is the analysis of the actual conditions in which individual choices and collective decisions on matters of educational policy are made—using experimental observations of behavior prior to the formulation of new models of choice.

Notes

1. It must be noted that these are the author's personal interpretations and do not reflect those of G. Psacharopoulos.

2. M. Carnoy and H. Thias (1969) calculated, for Kenya, an individual rate of return on higher education of 20 percent for a social rate of return of 9 percent.

3. See especially R. Hollister, "A Technical Evaluation of the First Stage of the Mediterranean Regional Project," OECD, 1967.

4. Seminar on Methodology of Human Resources Planning in Developing Countries (Evaluation and Future Prospects), OECD Development Centre, Paris, September 1971.

References

(following the order in which the authors
are mentioned in the text)

Bowman, M. J., and Anderson, C. A. "Concerning the Role of Education in Development." Old Societies and New States, C. Geertz, ed. Glencoe, Ill.: Free Press, 1963.

Edding, F. "Internationale Tendenzen in der Entwicklung der Ausgaben fur Schulen und Hochschulen." Kieler Studien No. 47. Kiel: Institut fur Weltwirtschaft und der Universitat Kiel, 1958.

Harbison, F., and Myers, C. A. Education, Manpower and Economic Growth. New York: McGraw-Hill, 1964.

United Nations Institute for Social Research and Development. "Compilation of Development Indicators (for 1960)." Geneva, 1969.

Blot, D., and Debeauvais, M. "Educational Expenditure in the World: Some Statistical Aspects," in Financing of Education for Economic Growth. Paris: OECD, 1966.

Hellwig, Z. "Procedure of Evaluating High-Level Manpower Data and Typology of Countries by Means of the Taxonomic Method." UNESCO Working Paper, 1967, mimeo.

Harbison, F. H., Maruhnic, J., and Reswick, J. R. Quantitative Analyses of Modernization and Development. Princeton, N.J.: Princeton University, Industrial Relations Section, 1970.

Pomenta, J. Silvio. "Analyse des disparités régionales dans les domaines économique, social et éducatif au Venezuela" (Unpublished PhD. dissertation, Université de Paris, 1971).

Galtung, J. "Diachronic Analysis of Relationships Between Human Resources Components and the Rate of Economic Growth in Selected Countries." UNESCO, 1970, mimeo.

Niewiaroski, D. H. "The Level of Living of Nations: Meaning and Measurement." Estadistica, Interamerican Statistical Institute, Washington, March 1965.

Benzecri. "Analyse factorielle des correspondances." Institut de Statistiques de l'Université de Paris, 1968.

Lebart. "Introduction à l'analyse des données," in Consommation, vols. 3 and 4, Paris, 1969.

Blot, D. "L'origine sociale des étudiants européens et leur répartition par discipline: une application de l'analyse des correspondances." Ongoing research, to be published by OECD, 1972.

Layard, P. R. G., and Saigal, J. C. "Educational and Occupational Characteristics of Manpower: an International Comparison." British Journal of Industrial Relations, vol. IV, July 1966.

"Occupational and Educational Structures of the Labour Force and Levels of Economic Development—Further Analyses and Statistical Data." OECD, 1971.

"Statistics of the Occupational and Educational Structure of the Labour Force in 53 Countries." OECD, 1969.

Debeauvais, M. "Forecasting Highly Skilled Manpower Needs: Applicability of International Comparisons to Mexico." OECD, December 1970, mimeo.

Debeauvais, M. "L'expérience récente de l'OCDE dans le domaine des ressources humaines." OCDE (Centre de Développement), 1969, mimeo.

Horowitz, M. A., Zymelman, M., Herrnstadt, I. L. Manpower Requirements for Planning: an International Comparison Approach. Boston: Northeastern University, December 1966.

Debeauvais, M. "Comparative Study of Educational Expenditure and Its Trend in OECD Countries since 1950." Background Study No. 2, Conference on Policies for Educational Growth, OECD, May 1970, mimeo.

Debeauvais, M. "Educational Expenditure and Economic Development: an International Comparison." OECD internal paper (to be published in 1972).

"Aid to Education in Less Developed Countries." OECD, Doc. C(70)150, Nov. 1970, mimeo.

Coombs, P. H. The World Educational Crisis: A Systems Analysis. London: Oxford University Press, 1968.

Pearson, L. B., ed. Partners in Development. Report of the Commission on International Development. New York: Praeger Publishers, 1969. According to the Pearson's report estimates (p. 199), foreign aid to education amounted in 1967 to $600 million, "mostly in grants representing a total of over 40,000 educational experts and the training of close to 70,000 students and trainees." Difference from subsequent OECD estimates for 1968-69 are partly due to a real increase from 1967 to 1968 and 1969 and partly to a more systematic evaluation of aid from private sources in OECD survey.

Khoi, Le Thanh. "L'enseignement en Afrique Tropicale." Paris: Collection Tiers Monde, PUF, 1971.

Schultz, T. W. "Investment in Iran: an Economist's View." Social Service Review, June 1959.

Solow, R. M. "Technical Change and the Aggregate Production Function." Review of Economics and Statistics, August 1957.

Denison, E. F. "The Sources of Economic Growth in the U.S. and the Alternatives Before Us." Studies in Income and Wealth, vol. 19. Princeton, N.J.: Princeton University Press, 1957.

Denison, E. F. "Why Growth Rates Differ." Washington, D.C.: Brookings Institution, 1967.

Psacharopoulos, G., and Hinchliffe, K. "The Rate of Return to Investment Comparison—An International Comparison." Ongoing research at the London School of Economics.

Glick, P. C., Miller, H. P. "Educational Level and Potential Income." American Sociological Review, June 1956.

Schultz, T. W. "Capital Formation by Education." Journal of Political Economy, December 1960.

Selowsky, M. "On the Measurement of Education's Contribution to Growth." Quarterly Journal of Economics, August 1969.

Schultz, T. P. "Returns to Education in Bogota, Colombia." Rand Corporation, 1968, mimeo.

Blaug, M.; Layard, P. R. G.; and Woodhall, M. The Causes of Graduate Unemployment in India. London: Allen Lane, Penguin Press, 1969.

Bowles, S. Planning Educational Systems for Economic Growth. Cambridge: Harvard University Press, 1969.

Layard, P. R. G.; Sargan, J. D.; Agen, M. E.; and Jones, D. J. Qualified Manpower and Economic Performance. London: Allen Lane, The Penguin Press, 1971.

Thias, H., and Carnoy, M. "Cost Benefit Analysis in Education: A Case-Study on Kenya." IBRD, Report EC-173, November 1969, mimeo.

Hollister, P. A Technical Evaluation of the First Stage of the Mediterranean Regional Project. OECD, 1966.

A "GUIDE" TO INVESTORS IN EDUCATION WITH SPECIAL REFERENCE TO DEVELOPING COUNTRIES
T. W. Schultz

A guide to an established path is one thing, but how to proceed where there is no known path is the burden of my assignment. The terrain appears hazardous, concealing many unknowns. Under such circumstances, the appropriate instruction is to probe and to learn as one proceeds. In a nutshell, this is what each developing country must do as it proceeds to invest in education. There is no program planning model that will make a country rich in education. The computer with all of its capacity cannot print the instructions that investors in education require. What is possible and perhaps worthwhile is to think in terms of probing and learning from experience under the dynamic conditions that characterize the developing countries. This will be my approach in this section.

Let me begin with the key terms of reference. By "education," I mean those "teaching" and "learning" activities that contribute to the acquisition of useful abilities. Being useful implies that these acquired abilities have some social value and since they are scarce they have some economic value. These activities may be either formal or informal. I shall use "schooling" and "education" interchangeably. On-the-job training is also a form of education. By "investment" I mean making current sacrifices in order to acquire future satisfactions and returns. Parents sacrifice by forgoing some current consumption in order to provide schooling for their children. So does a community or a country because it too forgoes some alternative investments or current consumption whenever it allocates resources to education. I shall use the concept of "developing countries" to mean a dynamic process that entails modernization as these nations achieve wider economic opportunities.

My plan is, first, to call attention to three critical attributes of the economy that investors in education must take into account in probing for new information on where and how much to invest in education. Next, I shall point out what to look for in gauging the prospective real costs and benefits of education. Lastly, and most important, I shall present four propositions to indicate the approximate boundaries of the investment opportunities in education.

The three economic attributes of developing countries that investors in education must reckon with are the high cost of capital, the dynamics of development, and the lags in adjustment.

Capital scarcity. It is of course obvious that developing countries do not have the luxury of an abundance of capital. On the contrary, the supply is meager, and as development proceeds, the demand for additional capital increases markedly. Thus, a basic constraint is the high cost of capital. In rich countries there is a ready market for school bonds at 5 to 6 percent or even less, inflation aside, whereas the real price of capital in countries that are achieving development tends to be much higher. Because of the alternative demands for capital, the rate of return to investment in education "must" be higher in poor countries than in rich countries in competing for funds.

Moreover, this constraint is reinforced by the fact that the capital markets in poor countries are in their infancy and subject to many imperfections that limit severely both public and private financing of education. The fundamental human condition is that most of the people in these countries are really poor, their incomes are very small, and food and shelter absorb most of their personal income. For these reasons, in education as in other activities, the additional capital that can be had must be used sparingly.

Dynamics of development. Development brings hope wrapped with frustrations. It constantly rearranges all manner of economic options. The best new investment opportunities have pay-offs that are very high—for example, tube wells often produce 30 percent rates of return. Thus, development increases the over-all demand for capital. Although it also adds to the supply of capital, the net effect is that the opportunity cost of obtaining funds to invest in education rises as a consequence of development.

Moreover, the dynamics of development is anything but placid. It is the source of many economic fluctuations. Economic disequilibria abound, and they are for many people as frustrating as are the rapid growth years for teenagers. Firms, households, industries, sectors, and regions within the country get out of balance with each other. The educational sector is not spared. However much investors in education may dislike it, economic disequilibria are an inescapable attribute of the dynamics of development. They can be minimized, but they cannot be eliminated.

Lags in adjustment. If all people had perfect foresight about all of the necessary adjustments that are associated with development and if they had the capacity to make each and every adjustment instantaneously, there would be no lags. But there is no more point in dreaming about social and economic behavior that is impossible than it is to dream about our earth being free of gravity. Public bodies and private persons must reckon with these lags. Some of these adjustments can be made more efficiently than is often the case. But even so, there will be lags.

One of the consequences of development is that traditional skills are no longer sufficient. As traditional agriculture undergoes modernization and as cottage industries are superseded by modern industries, new skills are required. In responding to these demands for new skills, it takes time for people to discern, interpret, and act to acquire the more valuable new skills. It follows that the interactions between more schooling and more development are beset with all manner of lags. Neither planners nor the rank and file of the people are blessed with perfect foresight.

A developing economy is constantly subject to change. It implies risk and uncertainty for those who make investments, whether they be in education or in any other form of capital.

In looking for evidence on the economic value of education, it is necessary to examine both the costs and benefits of education. These costs and benefits are in large measure determined by the rate of economic growth and the resulting scarcity of capital. Thus, much depends on the state of the economy. As already noted, economic growth is not an equilibrium state, but a dynamic process beset with all manner of lags in adjustment. For the purpose at hand, growth implies responses to investment opportunities in acquiring additional income streams at a price lower than the equilibrium price. In terms of investment decisions, whether in physical capital or in human capital including education, economic growth is a consequence of the allocation of investment resources in accordance with the priorities set by the relative rates of return to alternative investment opportunities. Formally, the reciprocal of the highest-rate-of-return option is, in theory and in fact, the lowest price of additional growth.

Investment in human capital in the form of education, on the one hand, occurs as a response to the demand derived from growth and, on the other, contributes to the growth of the economy. In this context, the new economics of education directs attention to the interactions between economic growth and education. As developing countries succeed in improving their economic lot, three important interactions have been identified and substantially quantified.

1. The accumulation of human capital represented by education occurs at a higher rate than that of nonhuman capital.

2. Although the difference in the relative earnings between workers with a little education and those with much, decreases, the absolute difference in earnings tends to be sufficient to warrant further increases in the level of education.

3. As economic growth proceeds, the inequality in the distribution of personal income shows signs of decreasing. Increases in education and in on-the-job training appear to be important explanatory factors.

Investors tend to prefer industries the growth of which exceeds that of the economy. Education qualifies. Most societies prefer both higher earnings and less inequality in personal incomes; they are both associated with investments in education. Yet, despite these favorable interactions between economic growth and education, the costs and returns (benefits) that are specific to education must be taken into account. But here a serious difficulty arises because those who have a special interest in education are inclined to underestimate the real costs and to misspecify the benefits.

With respect to costs, earnings forgone while attending school are conveniently omitted both here and in the developing countries. Whereas in rich countries earnings forgone are important at the higher levels of education, in the developing countries they are as a rule also significant at the upper part of elementary schooling, all of the talk of chronic unemployment nowithstanding. They are real costs that are borne by the families with children because already at the tender age of 10 to 14, children are called upon for useful work in agriculture, which is the dominant sector in most developing countries.

Moreover, in the context of economic growth, the value of time rises, and as this occurs the earnings forgone by students rise as a consequence.

Nor are earnings forgone a trivial part of the costs of education. The available evidence suggests that they are half or more of the total real cost of higher education, upward of half of the real cost of secondary schooling, and in developing countries, earnings forgone may account for a third or more of the total real cost once children reach the fifth grade in their elementary schooling.

In accounting for the benefits from education, it is not sufficient to look only at the higher earnings associated with more education. There are private satisfactions associated with education. It is appropriate to think of these as cultural satisfactions that accrue to the student over his lifetime. Although they are nonpecuniary rewards that defy estimation, they must nevertheless be kept in mind. Meanwhile, much is made these days (especially by the proponents) of more higher education of the social benefits of such education. It is increasingly clear, however, that most of the social benefits are unsubstantiated. The real benefits that come from higher education accrue predominantly to the students. There are, however, two exceptions, neither of which appears on the list of these proponents. The first consists of the social benefits that are associated with the education of females. It is revealed in Head Start that children benefit from their mother's education; thus this particular social benefit enhances the educability of the subsequent generation. The other social benefit that is not on the list I shall refer to as the allocative benefit, meaning the observed increases in ability associated with the rise in education in decoding and interpreting new technical and economic information pertaining to production and consumption; and, as a consequence, the more educated adjust their behavior more rapidly (with a shorter lag) than do the less educated.

51

In production, under competition, it follows that the productivity gains from new techniques are transferred to consumers more rapidly than would otherwise be the case. Economists refer to this class of gains as a consumer surplus.

Both the Head Start gains that accrue to children from the education of mothers and the allocative gains, as specified above, are not restricted to higher education. They are important social benefits associated with elementary and secondary schooling as well. I shall elaborate on both of these in the next section.

Seeing the alternative demands for the very limited supply of investment funds in developing countries, what is the ranking of education as an investment? What are the priorities among the educational options? The following four propositions indicate the approximate boundaries of the educational investment terrain.

1. Among the educational options, the highest private rates of return in most of the developing countries are to be had from additional investments in elementary schooling, mainly from completing the fifth to the last elementary year.

2. When account is taken of the benefits bestowed on the next generation, the highest social rates of return are to be had from investments in the education of females.

3. The efficiency of the schooling investment process tends to be the highest where there is a general framework of public rules concerning school attendance and granting equal treatment in receiving public funds, designed to maximize the domain of family and local community decision-making.

4. Given 1, 2, and 3 above and given a successful development process, the rates of return to schooling tend to be fully as high as they are on the better half of the investments in nonhuman capital.

There is substantial support for these four propositions from the new economics of education. It is most telling with respect to the first.

In terms of rates of return, higher education ranks far below elementary schooling. The rate of return on completing the elementary years is as a rule the highest. The apparent reasons for this result are as follows: (1) For a person to remain literate over his lifetime, more than four years of schooling is usually required. (2) The economic value of having the ability to read and write is much enhanced by the opportunities that are forthcoming in a dynamic economy; this is the ability to decode, interpret, and act efficiently in taking advantage of technical change and new economic information. It is this particular ability that is the source of the "allocative benefits" referred to in the preceding section. It is true that these allocative benefits continue to increase with more education. However, when the total real costs of the additional education are reckoned, the rates of return tend to be highest for the fifth and subsequent elementary years in most of the developing countries. (3) Among the educational options, there is in most countries a longstanding bias in favor of higher education. Educators tend to nurture this bias. Universities, like steel mills, are symbols that enhance national prestige. The influential classes want their children to acquire a university education, preferably at public expense. Thus the stage is set in favor of higher education relative to the lower levels of schooling for the rank and file of the population. Moreover, this bias is evident not only in Colombia, Mexico, and other developing countries but also in the United States and other rich countries. Leaving the economic value of university research associated with graduate work aside, the rate of return to undergraduate instruction continues to be far below that for the lower levels of education.

The support for the second proposition listed on page 52 comes largely from recent studies made possible by the extension of economic theory in analyzing the nonmarket activities of the household. Seeing the earnings forgone that enter into formation of human capital, the stage was set for development of the "allocation of time" (Becker's classic 1965 paper). This paper represents an important new development in economic thinking; it treats time as the fundamental unit of cost in individual allocative decisions with respect to both labor and consumption. Analytically, this development is a major new economic approach to the nonmarket household activities, especially so in accounting for the economic value of the time of women. We now see that each consumer commodity has two prices attached to it—a money price, as in traditional consumer choice, and a time cost in acquiring, processing, and consuming the commodity. The bearing and rearing of children are also an integral part of the economics of the household.

For the purpose at hand, it is the wide array of effects of the education of females that the investors in education in the developing countries can ill afford to overlook. The organizational efficiency of the household and its contribution to family consumption appears to depend in substantial part on the level of the schooling of the woman. Most women in the developing countries are poorly equipped in terms of the schooling that is required to manage their households skillfully in taking advantage of new technical information with respect to nutrition, health, and child care. Another favorable effect of the schooling of women is the improvement in their ability to decode, interpret, and successfully adopt the new, superior contraceptive techniques. The acquisition of more schooling by females tends to raise the age of marriage, a potent force in reducing fertility. Thus, the implications of compulsory school attendance for more years than has been traditional (many females presently do not attend school at all) is strong and clear with respect to reducing fertility. The most important effect of the schooling of females may well be the social benefit that arises out of the marked advantage that children derive from being reared in homes where the mothers have this schooling. There is a growing body of evidence in support of the inference that the level of schooling of mothers is most important in accounting for the quality of the inputs they provide for their children. It is this class of social benefits that argues strongly for more public investment in the education of women. Whereas in the case of males, the gains in productivity from more schooling accrue predominantly to those who acquire the schooling, in the case of females there are substantial benefits that accrue to society. It is this particular social benefit that accounts for the relatively high social rates of return to the investment in the education of women featured in the second proposition listed at the outset of this section.[1]

As for the third proposition listed above, thinking continues to be confused, and clarifying evidence is hard to come by. The longstanding controversy on the role of the private self-interest of families in the schooling of their children versus the role of public and professional bodies in deciding the content and the amount of schooling is still with us, as it was when the classical economists divided on this issue. It is a difficult issue because each of its three interrelated parts—that is, standards, information, and incentives— requires fine tuning in order to approach an optimum allocation and utilization of resources devoted to education.

Standards. In providing funds for education, public bodies must establish standards that are to govern the utilization of such funds. A government or any public agency would be irresponsible if it did not do so. The unsolved problem, however, is twofold: (1) These standards have to be acceptable politically, and (2) for the resources to be used efficiently, they must combine a minimum of central control of schools consistent with a maximum of family and community involvement in decision-making with respect to the schooling. Most countries and especially the developing countries tend toward over-centralization of their educational systems. Thus, the standards that are established thwart local involvement, and private self-interest and initative are blunted. The recent "revenue-sharing" controversy reveals how difficult it is for Congress to agree upon standards that are politically acceptable. In turn, the controversy about the merits of "school vouchers" suggests how hard it is to get acceptance of the allocative role of the private self-interest of students (families) in matters pertaining to education.

Information. With respect to earnings forgone, students (families) are well-informed. But with regard to the benefits that will accrue to them from schooling, the state of information is far from

54

optimum. How much more are they likely to earn with more schooling? Will they be less subject to unemployment? (In the United States, lifetime unemployment is substantially less for the more educated. But what are the facts on this point in the developing countries?) The normal life span is increasing. But there is a long lag before the importance of this favorable development for investment in education becomes known to most families. But worse still is the lack of information on the value of the different components of education and on the differences in the quality of the instruction.

Incentives. It is not difficult to specify formally the desired properties of these incentives, but it is very hard to achieve them in practice. Formally, they should be efficient both socially and privately; they should also be clear and strong in order to mobilize the private self-interest of students (families). A major difficulty arises out of the fact that they tend to be inefficient because they fail to provide students (families) with socially appropriate scarcity signals so that students (families) can make socially efficient choices. The key argument in favor of student vouchers is that when public funds for education are thus allocated they would become efficient incentives both privately and socially. There are, of course, all manner of compromises, each with its price, and the price is relatively high in developing countries, where capital is very scarce.

My fourth proposition rings a bell that is pleasing to the ear of investors in education. It announces that there are investment opportunities in education that will enhance the future economic well-being of a developing country fully as much as the better half of the investment opportunities in nonhuman capital—that is, in structures, equipment, inventories, and land improvements. But the conditions that I have set forth in presenting this proposition must not be overlooked. The fifth and subsequent elementary years of schooling rank very high; from a social point of view, if we look to subsequent generations, the education of females also ranks high. The proper organization of public provisions for and private utilization of funds including the earnings forgone and other resources of students (families) is exceedingly important. But there is still another essential condition—that is, successful development. If the country is not embarked on modernization, if it is not acquiring and adopting new superior techniques and other inputs but is coasting along in a traditional manner, there will be little or no pay-off on additional investments in education. If the development is sluggish and sporadic, the rewards for more schooling will be low and subject to much uncertainty. But as the dynamics of development become strong and continuous, the additional skills and abilities associated with more schooling are in demand and the rates of return to the investment in them become high and as favorable as the best alternative investment opportunities.

Let me reaffirm what I said at the outset. It would be wishful thinking to believe that there is a well-marked path on which the investors in education can proceed. I have limited my comments to the probable boundaries of the educational investment terrain in developing countries. Surely, it goes without saying, the economics of education scrutinizes only one of the many facets of the educational diamond.

What are the implications of my "guide" for investors in education? Let me venture to suggest the following approaches in contributing to education in the developing countries.

1. Concentrate on the enlargement and improvement of elementary schooling, and thus give less attention to college and university instruction than has been true during recent years.

2. The schooling of females should be placed high on the agenda.

3. Ways and means of vitalizing local involvement in school affairs by parents and by local communities should be actively explored.

4. The new information that is required in pursuing these several objectives cannot be obtained from the development and applications of national educational programing models. These models are too aggregative, the substitution between different levels of schooling cannot be ascertained, the prospective demands for education are subject to too many uncertainties to be specified in these models and, above all, adequate data are lacking.

Less "heroic" analytical approaches carry much more promise; thus searching for microeconomic effects in terms of the costs and benefits of schooling is much more likely to provide useful new information for the purposes at hand.

5. The "allocative benefits" as they have been revealed by the work of Finis Welch and D.P. Chardhri[2] should be investigated in a wide array of different developing countries.

6. The new economics of the household in analyzing the non-market activities of households with special reference to the effects of schooling upon fertility should be encouraged and supported in the developing countries. In terms simply of enlarging our scientific knowledge of household behavior, the developing countries provide a unique set of conditions that need to be studied intensively, lest we rely on unwarranted conclusions drawn from the behavior of households in the advanced countries.

7. Throughout all of these endeavors, the commitment should be to engage in learning from the ongoing experience in the developing countries.

Notes

1. See T. W. Schultz, "Woman's New Economic Commandments," Bulletin of the Atomic Scientists, February 1972, pp. 29-32.

2. Finis Welch, "Education and Production" Journal of Political Economy (JPE) January-February 1970; and D.P. Chardhri, "Education and Agricultural Productivity in India" (Ph.D. dissertation, University of Delhi, 1968), and in his postdoctoral studies, University of Chicago, 1969, supported by the Rockefeller Foundation.

THE JUDO TRICK:
A PLEA FOR LESS CONCERN WITH WHAT TO DO IN EDUCATION AND MORE EXPERIMENTS (AND RESEARCH) ON HOW TO DO IT
Richard Jolly

Virtually every serious commentator agrees that major reform within third world education is long overdue.[1] In one way or another major changes are required: (1) to make the style and content at every level of education more relevant; (2) to control the overexpansion of formal education; (3) to encourage expansion of useful forms of technical and vocational education, informal education, and training; (4) to deal with escalating costs; (5) to find ways of modifying the inequality that the educational systems have tended to increase rather than to diminish.

In almost every third world country, one can find a library of international reports, government commissions, and plans recommending such changes. The problem, as we all know, is that so little action has taken place—less action, in many respects, than in many other equally important areas of government policy.

One explanation is that too much is being demanded of this education system or its administrators—too much and all at the same time. This line of argument emphasizes the scarcity of available resources, in terms of administration, qualified teachers, buildings, textbooks, and so on, and concludes with a plea for much more modest advance, to make haste slowly, and to forgo major reforms.

Toward the other end of the political spectrum is the explanation that the education system is locked by a rigid set of social forces and interest groups, which nothing short of revolutionary change will release. This line of argument often leads on to lack of concern with immediate policy prescriptions, since the existing situation is beyond redemption.

This section draws heavily on ideas arising in the course of work on the Ceylon and Kenya International Labor Organization (ILO) employment mission reports, Matching Employment Opportunities and Expectations (Geneva: ILO, 1971), and Employment, Incomes and Equality (Geneva: ILO, 1972). My thinking on the central points has been tremendously influenced by Ronald Dore, John Anderson, and Tony Somerset, who were each members of one of the above missions and have written much on similar themes elsewhere. They or others cannot, of course, be held responsible for the way in which I have interpreted or used their own ideas and conclusions.

The starting point of this paper is the belief that both these explanations—and a number of others—are directly at variance with the obvious facts of what has been occurring in the educational systems of the third world. Contrary to loose judgments about education systems being unchangeable, the education systems in most third world countries (as in most developed countries) have undergone dramatic changes over the last two decades, so great as to make them in many respects virtually unrecognizable by earlier standards. Primarily, of course, these changes have been of quantitative expansion, but at the same time—and remarkable because they have taken place simultaneously—there have been other changes, particularly in localizing the whole educational administration and in certain respects in localizing the syllabi and adapting teaching methods.

The sheer magnitude of this quantitative expansion in the majority of the developing countries is apt to be missed. Table 2 summarizes the figures and for comparison includes expansion in the developed countries over the same period—a period incidentally when most developed countries expanded education far faster than ever before. Yet the changes in the third world, in most countries, have far exceeded the changes in the rich countries.

The conventional reaction when faced with these experiences is to concentrate on how this expansion has inevitably led to rising expenditure and declining quality, with general constraint all around. Too easily one misses the point that in country after country expansion has far exceeded what most people—the local administrators,

TABLE 2

Annual Rates of Increase
in Educational Enrollments by Level, 1960-68
(percentages per year)

Region	First	Second	Third
Poor regions			
Africa	5.6	10.5	9.0
Asia	5.4	6.0	11.0
Latin America	5.3	10.8	10.4
Rich regions			
North America	1.8	3.1	10.0
Europe and USSR	1.9	4.9	8.2

Source: Learning to Be (UNESCO, 1972), Appendix Table 4.

teachers, international experts, even the politicians—thought was possible 10 or 20 years ago. In spite of the scarce resources, the limited finance and the shortage of skilled manpower, the planned rates of expansion were often far exceeded, even under the guidance of new administrators who were newly localized and had limited previous experience.[2]

Of even greater significance is the fact that this expansion has in various ways depended on the enormous and widespread use of individual energies and private resources and effort in support of public education as well as private. Literally millions of families have scraped together what was required to get another child or relative into school, or from primary school into secondary. Less significant quantitatively but often the critical contribution at the margin of expansion has been the community effort to build schools, to raise funds, and to recruit and pay teachers.*

Private firms and industry also devote a great deal of resources in support of training programs as well as formal education. It is difficult to tell on balance how this private contribution is influenced by government activities. The provision of general technical education by government probably discourages some of at least the larger firms from doing as much as they otherwise would. On the other hand, many countries have adopted training taxes for which firms can obtain rebates in respect of expenditure on their own training schemes.

No adequate documentation is available that encompasses, let alone measures, all this support. One indication of the magnitude, however, is the fact that in almost every country the education system has in one way or another involved more people directly than any other single nationally organized activity, not excluding public-sector employment or the military. Most of these persons are students, unpaid but often attending at some cost to themselves or their families.

---

*In addition to positive outlays, the sacrifice of work and earnings forgone by students can be a major cost of education—almost always borne privately. These opportunity costs are important even at the primary level in poor countries, particularly in the rural areas. (They have often been identified as an important cause for dropping out.) At secondary or higher levels, they can also be important, though the existence of widespread unemployment among the educated makes it difficult to estimate their magnitude. Recall, however, that opportunity costs of students' time in the United States was estimated by Schultz as 43 percent of the total costs of high school education and 53 to 55 percent of the total costs of higher education (see T. W. Schultz, "Capital Formation by Education," JPE, 1960).

Widespread change has thus been the rule, not the exception. Quantitative change has been remarkable by any standards. Qualitative change has been too little and often in the wrong direction. But the argument of this paper is that the currently desired qualitative reforms are no more impossible, in terms of scarce resources, than the quantitative changes that have already taken place—and taken place in spite of limited resources. The crucial thing lacking is not the additional scarce resources but understanding of how to mobilize existing resources, or better, how to restructure the system so that the energies and resources that have already been released in support of quantitative change can now be directed toward qualitative change.

(The crucial assumption here is that qualitative improvements depend primarily on changes in organization and the better use of existing resources, especially training and organization of teachers, rather than on vast additional inputs. Additional inputs are no doubt required, but they will be small, relative to the additional resources required for quantitative change at past rates. This assumption is confirmed from both micro- and macro-data. At the micro-level, few primary schools spend much on equipment and materials compared with expenditure on teachers' salaries or buildings. This is borne out at the macro-level. Public expenditure on education in the poorer countries rose by 11 percent per year from 1960 to 1968. To have devoted only a fraction of this increase each year to books, equipment, and other teaching materials would have doubled or trebled expenditure per student on these items. This is quoted not to suggest that teaching materials are the central issue or that such a move by itself would have achieved very much. The point is to show that the financial constraints on these aspects of qualitative improvement are a second-order problem.)

This is what one means by the judo trick. One is tackling an educational juggernaut of enormous size, accelerating but in the wrong direction. Can one identify the crucial points of balance at which to exert new forces, and thus to change the whole direction of its development? It's a simple metaphor. Is it relevant?

The literature on education planning has to date given very little attention to this problem:

(1) The manpower literature—and a great deal like it on human investment—has concentrated on what ought to be done, only rarely on how to do it.[3]

(2) The literature on education administration has concentrated mainly on the formal reorganization required for more efficient administration, largely of the government system, but also of private schools and agencies. It has included very little on how to motivate change among the millions of parents and students as

opposed to organizing the hundreds of administrators or even thousands of teachers.

(3) The rate-of-return literature has also for the most part concentrated on what ought to be done rather than on how to do it. But in one respect this literature has been concerned with motivation, namely in its calculations of private rates of return. At least in principle this literature has been focused on individual economic motivation of the student or his parents and/or his family (though it is usually not clear which). From an empirical treatment of motivation, this literature suffers serious weaknesses, since it has almost always assumed without investigation that individuals are solely seeking to maximize their discounted returns from future earnings made possible by education.* There has been scarcely any research into the questions of whether this is the focus of individual motivation, or the ways in which individuals perceive their selections and their accuracy in estimating them. Moreover, at the level of social returns, the rate-of-return literature has, like much other planning literature, largely neglected social motivation and concentrated on what is argued to be socially desirable.[4]

(4) Some of the sociological literature has emphasized individual motivation—but often primarily to explain the current situation rather than to change it. Philip Foster's much-quoted study of Ghana shows why the pattern of earnings creates incentives that made it—and no doubt still make it—rational for secondary school students to prefer white-collar to technical education. But Foster does not explore how changes could be made so that secondary school students, their parents, teachers, local politicians, and educational administrators would not merely prefer, but devote their full energies to, change.[5]

The common point in the planning methodology underlying most of this literature is the assumption that educational change is usually initiated by the formal body which has administrative responsibility for the school system—that is, government in the form of the Ministry

---

*Even assuming that people are primarily motivated by prospects of economic gain, it is by no means obvious that educational decisions are given by simple maximization. There are many analogies with peasant behavior where maximization of minimum incomes is a common reaction in situations of risk or where the distributive arrangements within the family lead to "nonmaximizing behavior" in the sense of nonindividualistically maximizing behavior. It is also noteworthy that rate-of-return calculations are commonly based on data for males only. Yet female enrollments have often been expanding faster than male enrollments in many places and at many levels.

of Education, or the private agency responsible. It is fairly rare in the literature to find the idea that change is often initiated by a combination of pressures from students, teachers, parents, and politicians and only in reaction, is partly and inadequately channeled or controlled by the ministries of education and other parts of the government bureaucracy.

(John Anderson's studies of the Harambee school movement in Kenya are a notable exception. The significance of the Harambee movement in Kenya was that it led to an outburst of nongovernment community schools after Independence, initiated by local communities interacting with local political leaders, usually scraping together sufficient resources to construct the building. The recurrent costs of hiring teachers and collecting textbooks were sometimes met locally, sometimes from various aid donors, almost always by hiring unemployed, less qualified teachers at low rates. After several years of struggle, sufficient pressure was developed to persuade the government program to take over such schools to make them part of the formal system and be responsible for their recurrent costs. There is no doubt in Kenya, at least, who initiated the vast program of secondary school expansion.)[6]

Structural Reform and Motivation

With this starting point, one can turn with new hope to the difficult problems of achieving change in education systems. In order to be precise and provoke some reaction, the framework for analysis and strategy will be posed somewhat starkly, though hopefully even this simplified structure will seem applicable to many situations.

1. Of the various interest groups closely involved with formal education (students, parents and relations, teachers, educational administrators, politicians), the interests of students and their immediate relatives set the pattern that, with variations, the other groups follow.

2. The main decisions and group pressures of students and parents are largely along directions set by their long-term economic interests, particularly with respect to education's role in providing access to the better jobs, status, and incomes.

3. Education's role in these respects operates primarily through four key points of its structure and the structure of the job market: (a) the system of selection at entry; (b) the system of selection and examination within the school system; (c) the system of selection for jobs; and (d) the structure of earnings and other incomes.

4. Successful change depends primarily on making changes at these key points in the structure, so as to realign the lines of force of the main interest groups, in ways that will assist the other changes desired.

5. The probability of achieving fundamental long-run reform will be the greater if one identifies and selects as the catalysts those forms of structural change that initially are the easiest, in terms of interest groups for and against this change and, to a lesser extent, in terms of the administrative requirements and the number of persons involved.

This model of motivation is by no means new, though it is somewhat broader than the framework of motivation that has been included in most earlier analyses. This framework is concerned not only with the interests of individuals but with the sectional interests of other groups directly involved in education. This framework focuses attention on those aspects of the educational structure that influence an individual's chances, rather than on the precise calculation of those chances. Finally, and most fundamentally, this framework emphasizes that it is the structure that must be changed in order to redirect any energies for educational reform, rather than making quantitative changes within an accepted structure.

The five points outlined above must not be interpreted too rigidly. In different societies, with different social systems, let alone different forms of government organization, the pattern of pressures and interests will no doubt differ. They are designed to illustrate a method of analysis that is hopefully relevant to a number of countries, not to put forward a universal system. It may be useful to emphasize how this framework of analysis differs from other analyses that have focused on the quantitative aspects of the different parts of the school system as opposed to the qualitative implications of the structure of the system. Earlier analyses have attempted to show that because of higher economic returns to white-collar education, people prefer white-collar to technical training. This explanation goes beyond this to concentrate on the forces that distort the content and style of education within the school system as well as the forces that encourage the growth of formal as opposed to informal education. Furthermore, methodologically the earlier explanations assume preoccupation with economic returns and put their effort into detailed calculations of what those returns are. This explanation is less concerned with the calculation of arithmetical rates of return than with the identification of which structural features of the system direct and determine the individual's incentives and in what ways.[7]

This method of analysis and approach in planning educational reform can be illustrated with a number of recommendations made in the International Labor Organization (ILO) mission reports for

Ceylon (Sri Lanka) and Kenya. The broad analysis of both these reports was structural, in the sense that the analysis was closely related to that of the structuralist school of economists. In a sense, the method of analysis for education proposed in this paper might be described as the structural analysis of education.8

In Ceylon, the same unfortunate features of education are found as exist in so many other countries: largely irrelevant curricula, overexpansion numerically, limited on-the-job training, high costs. There was evidence of considerable inequality, though less than in many other countries and modified by the welfare state policies of the 1950s and 1960s. The mismatch between work opportunities and job expectations had by 1971 reached the point when there were some 550,000 persons seeking work, roughly a third of whom had completed secondary education or more and another third who had only completed primary. In Kenya the picture was much the same and in some respects more extreme: greater inequality, even smaller proportions in technical education, a greater sense of unreality of the curriculum in relation to the economic activities of the population, nine-tenths of which was rural. The rate of educational expansion at all levels had been high, but particularly that of general secondary schools, where expansion had been spurred by the Harambee movement. Both countries have a long history of internally and externally produced reports recommending a full range of the usual reforms.

In both Ceylon and Kenya, the analysis of the ILO reports focused on the way key elements in the structure of the educational systems reinforced these tendencies to increasingly irrelevant expansion, in spite of growing unemployment among those who obtained the education. In both cases, the starting point was the way in which the examinations system operated as a vital link in the chain of cause and effect. Because educational certificates were used in selection for most of the best jobs, examinations became (as in so many countries for the same reason) the dominating focus within the school system, with disastrous effects.

The backwash effects of examinations within the school system worked through several mechanisms. Exams have to test examinable subjects—and in Kenya to test them in ways that can be codified in multiple choice questions and marked by computer. In turn, this meant that the school syllabi concentrated on examinable themes and led the teachers to concentrate on those parts of each theme for which preparation had a high pay-off in terms of examination results. Even when practical subjects were introduced into the curriculum, they were soon corrupted by the examination system. As one example, the agricultural curriculum concentrated on the book-learning aspects of agriculture rather than on lessons useful for practical farming. The Kenya primary education examination asks,

"A substance which is found in many fertilisers is a) humus b) nitrogen c) magnesium d) calcium." Thus even attempts to make education focus on useful topics can be corrupted by the backwash effects of examinations.

A deeper effect of examinations is their reinforcement of the view that to learn is to qualify rather than to learn to do or to understand or simply to enjoy. Professor Dore has written eloquently on the end result of this:

> On the bright boys, a "model pupil" shrivelling of the soul, a passive acceptance of the authority of Jovian examiners which not unnaturally produces the cautious official careful above all to avoid making mistakes, a ritualist who joylessly learns only because it is in the syllabus and who will eventually joylessly work only because it is in his job specification. On the less bright boys, a sense of failure; little pride in having become literate and numerate, because by the values of the school learning in itself counted for nothing when it did not qualify. Perhaps they also acquire a few other snippets of knowledge—the principles of the lever, for instance, so efficiently prepackaged for examination reproduction, so firmly belonging to the arcane world of scholarship, that no child would ever imagine it could have anything to do with the well-beam in his back yard.[9]

More broadly, the focus on examinations leads people to misinterpret the realities and contribution of informal education, informal in the sense of the whole range of activities by which people in practice learn how to do things—from home training, on-the-job learning, and simply picking up useful ideas and skills through experience. Probably a very high proportion of what all of us know and the skills we use in our daily work is in fact acquired in this way. But this reality is obscured by the fact that many of those who hold the best jobs are paid and selected for these jobs on the basis of their formal education certificates. The tragedy is that this very process leads people not merely to ignore but to despise and neglect informal education whose potential contribution is so great.[10]

Analysis on these lines led in both the Ceylon and Kenya Missions to very specific proposals for structural reform of the educational system. In Ceylon, there were three central points of the strategy for educational reform. First, it was proposed that intelligence tests should replace achievement tests in order to eliminate the backwash effects of the examinations. The logic of this proposal was that because intelligence tests could not be prepared for, an individual's chance of being promoted to the next level of education would be seen as unrelated to the subjects he studied at that particular level. It was argued that this would break the link between choice of subject and prospects for promotion and, instead, stimulate individuals to concentrate on those subjects that they thought would be most useful for later work (particularly because only a small proportion would go on to higher study, the majority leaving school).

The second proposal was to make entry to almost all forms of postsecondary education exclusively through employment. After secondary school, everyone would spend at least three years in employment. Those who performed sufficiently well in employment and had moved to a job or had definite prospects of moving to a job requiring postsecondary training and education, would be selected for such education and sent specifically to acquire it. It was argued that this would give postsecondary students a very specific sense of the skills and abilities they wished to acquire from higher education, which in turn would lead to pressures on the university to provide the relevant training. It would also lead to a considerable reduction in the pressures for expanding higher education, since university places would be provided in relation to employment needs.

Finally, it was proposed that the first three years of employment in any form of wage-earning job would be paid according to national service wage scales. These were considerably below existing wages for persons with secondary or university qualifications and related almost exclusively to age, with no premium at all for education but with a small bonus for responsibility. The national service pay scales would involve a drastic reduction in the financial incentive to obtain formal educational qualifications. But, applying only to wage-earning employment, the pay scale would increase the relative attractiveness of self-employment. But perhaps the strongest argument in favor of the national service wage scale is in terms of implementation. By not affecting the wages of persons already in the labor force, implementation of the pay scales would be possible without arousing the united opposition of all persons in wage-earning employment—an interest group that time and again has caused the downfall of attempts at wage reform.

These three structural changes, together with a variety of other proposals designed to alter the overall employment position in the country and the prospects for future growth, are designed to alter the biases within the school system in ways that would release individual energies and group resources sufficient to complete the reforms and carry them further.

In Kenya, the core of the recommendations were again focused on the examination-selection systems and on pay scales. It did not seem appropriate to recommend intelligence tests, since the scientific basis for such tests in East Africa seemed weaker and the administrative and skill resources available to implement such a system were extremely limited. So a system of district and school quotas was proposed by which a fixed proportion of primary students in each district would move forward to secondary schooling with a small additional bonus quota for the better schools. Here the logic was again to reduce influence of examinations by replacing at least part of their influence by a predetermined quota. There would still have to be examinations to decide who would be selected within each school, but the proposed structure of quotas would significantly alter other directions of individual and group pressure. First, the bonus for each school would be awarded, not by performance in a national academic examination, but by performance in a local test in which individual students would prepare in their last year at school a study of some practical problem or topic of interest in his local area. Since schools would receive their additional bonus by how well and how relevantly their students undertook these projects it was argued that these projects would greatly influence the whole style and content of teaching.

Second, the Kenya Mission proposed that selection for jobs within the Civil Service should no longer be by level of education. Again, administrative weaknesses made it impossible to go as far as proposing that discrimination in hiring by education should be made an illegal offense, but in more modest ways, the need to sever the link between education and job selection was identified as a key point of structural change.

Finally, as part of an income policy, the Kenya Mission proposed that new recruits into the public services with secondary school or higher qualifications should be paid salaries for a specified period at well below existing rates, and the Mission suggested initially for five years at three-quarters of existing salaries. Again, this was a less dramatic proposal than in the Ceylon Mission but was motivated by a similar logic.

It is not the purpose of this paper to debate the pros and cons of these particular recommendations but to relate them to the framework of analysis given earlier. These recommendations can all be seen as particular examples of proposed structural changes within the framework identified earlier. The crucial point is that besides their particular relevance for Ceylon and Kenya, they illustrate how changes might be made in the structures that motivate and channel individual and social pressures on the school system.

Research and the Role of Donors

As a program for research, the validation or rejection of the hypotheses underlying the structural framework of analysis is a first priority. First, to identify and investigate further those key structural features of the school systems on which individuals and interest groups focus, which determine their perceptions of the advantages and disadvantages of different choices within the system and the strength of their relative preferences. Second, to explore more subtly this range of motivations at different periods on the process of expansion. Third, to explore with as much imagination as possible what variations are possible at the key points of structure within the school system and the advantages and disadvantages of each.

This research in many respects would be best as a program of experimental action rather than of academic theorizing. Wherever possible, to try out these ideas in practice would lead to a more rapid assessment of their practical value than to theorize more about them. Education systems in most countries of the world reveal too little experimentation, too much uniformity—which is particularly tragic since there is so much uncertainty about what changes are desirable, let alone possible.

Experimentation in this area, however, raises a fundamental problem. Since of the key points for structural change are those where only change at the national level will suffice for an adequate experiment, not change at the local level. If, for example, a major change in salary scales is made on the lines proposed in either Ceylon or Kenya, it ought ideally to be introduced nationally, if a loophole is not to be created, whereby individuals simply move elsewhere to obtain jobs at the old salary scales. To a lesser extent, this problem also arises with other radical changes in the school system, for example in the case of examinations or job selection or in changing the examinations or syllabi.

(This problem arises with respect to very many types of policy, however. In a world of differing national policies and possibilities of migration, it is at some level never totally avoidable. The brain drain is the most obvious example, both of the problems created by extranational influences and of the need to devise a variety of policies to tackle the problems that arise, given that a total prohibition of emigration is usually neither desirable nor possible.)

The proposals for research are also the priorities for changes in donor support, of third world support through financial aid and technical assistance. The number of manpower-dependent countries, in which massive support of mainstream secondary and higher education through the supply of teachers is required, is rapidly dwindling. Increasingly education systems should be self-sufficient, with aid

donors providing selective support to meet particular deficiencies
and encourage innovation. The deficiencies may be various, and many
are already well known to persons working in the field, but the innovations required are those experiments that will provide the experience and research evidence needed to perform the judo trick.
To identify the moves on this path to educational reform could be
one of the most significant contributions to educational improvement
in the last part of the 20th century.

Notes

1. Whatever else it said or failed to say, this certainly was
the message of the Faure Commission report, UNESCO, Learning
to Be, 1972. But see also Philip Coombs, The World Education
Crisis (London: Oxford University Press, 1970), or the education
section of almost any recent national plan or education plan of almost
any third world country.

2. I have analyzed why quantitative expansion need not made
be at the expense of quality in Planning Education for African Development (East African Publishing House, 1969), pp. 106-113. This
study also gives the statistics of quantitative change in African countries 1950-60.

3. See our own review of 38 African manpower plans: Richard
Jolly and Christopher Colclough, "African Manpower Plans: An
Evaluation," International Labour Review, August/September 1972.

4. Mark Blaug, P. R. G. Layard, and M. Woodhall, Graduate
Unemployment in India (London: Penguin Press, 1969), are among
the few rate-of-return proponents to have explored alternative "individual objective functions" (pp. 19-22). But their alternatives are
hypothetical possibilities, not the results of empirical investigation.
The only empirical attempt I know by an economist to assess how
individuals perceive and how accurately they estimate their future
income showed that even Harvard graduate students forgot to take
account of the effects of income tax on individual income. See H. G.
Grubel and D. R. Edwards, "Personal Income Taxation and the Choice
of Professions," Quarterly Journal of Economics, February 1964,
pp. 158-163.

5. See Philip Foster, "Education and Social Change in Ghana,"
(Chicago: University of Chicago Press, 1965).

6. For further details, see John Anderson, The Struggle for
the School (London: Longman, 1970) and more particularly John
Anderson, "The Harambee Schools: The Impact of Self-Help" in
Richard Jolly, ed., Education in Africa: Research and Action (East
African Publishing House, 1969).

7. Philip Foster's study—and by far the major part of the rate of return literature—assumes that the wage structure correctly reflects private marginal products and, within relatively minor margins, reflects social marginal products as well. It will be clear that my position starts from the viewpoint that the wage structures in most developing countries are so grossly distorted as to be only a marginal guide to productivity—though of immense significance for explaining individual incentives, particularly incentives for seeking formal-sector wage-earning jobs and the education needed to acquire such jobs. For Ceylon and Kenya, the data and evidence given to support this view is in the ILO reports. A more general statement of the argument is in A. R. Jolly, "Employment Wage Levels and Incentives" in I.I.E.P., "Manpower Aspects of Educational Planning," UNESCO, 1968.

8. This and later paragraphs draw particularly on Chapters 8 and 9 of the ILO Ceylon report and Chapters 14, 15, and 16 of the ILO Kenya report.

9. R. P. Dore, "Deschool? Try Using Schools for Education First. The Educational Impasse in the Developing World," Institute of Development Studies Discussion Paper no. 6, May 1972, p. 6.

10. This and the two preceding paragraphs echo many points that Ivan Illich has so passionately expounded (and very succinctly in his paper for the Faure Commission, "On the Necessity to Deschool Society"). For a broad critique of Illich's thesis, see Ronald Dore, "False Prophets: The Cuernavaca Critique of School," IDS Discussion Paper no. 12, October 1972. A brilliant empirical investigation of the actual operations of one poor country's examination system is given as technical paper number 25 of the Kenya ILO report "The Examination and Selection System as the Certificate of Primary Education." This shows that even in conventional educational terms the primary-school-leaving exam is a very poor selector of high academic achievers. This was the conclusion of an earlier study by the same investigator, H. C. A. Somerset. See his "Predicting Success in School Certificate: A Uganda Case Study," (East African Publishing House, 1968). These conclusions are of crucial significance for assessing what is lost academically by moving to quite different selection systems. The answer is, not much.

2

EDUCATION AND
SOCIAL JUSTICE

EMPLOYMENT IN THE 1970s: A NEW
PERSPECTIVE
Mahbub ul Haq

Ever since you asked me to make a presentation to this distinguished forum—on the very dubious assumption that since I was
associated with Pakistan's economic planning for 13 years, I ought
to know something about employment strategy—I became conscious
of a very deep responsibility. And despite all the gaps in my knowledge, I was determined not to let you down. So I went on a feverish
search of all the literature on employment strategy, all the theories
and policy prescriptions that the economists and the practitioners
in the field had to offer. And I came up with some distressing discoveries.

First, it appears to me that we are assembled here to discuss
a problem whose nature and dimensions we simply do not know. I
looked at various estimates of unemployment and underemployment
that had been prepared for the developing countries—even by that distinguished organization known as the ILO—and I was distressed to
find that estimates of 5 percent to 10 percent unemployment and 20
percent to 25 percent underemployment were tossed around with a
casualness that was simply frightening. There was no agreed methodology for measuring unemployment or underemployment, no definite
ideas or projections on what had happened in this field in the 1960s
or what might happen in the 1970s, and very poor knowledge about this
"vital" concern even in some of the largest and most affected countries like India, Pakistan, and Brazil.

Second, while we knew so little about the nature and dimensions
of the unemployment problem, we suffered from no modesty when it
came to definitive policy prescriptions. The favorite prescription
of the economists—besides the doubling or tripling of growth rates—
is to correct the price system, particularly exchange rates, interest
rates, terms of trade between agriculture and industry, and prices
of all factors of production. But has this faith in the price system
been tested empirically? When various developing countries cor-
rected their exchange rates or interest rates at various times, was
this followed by a great surge in their employment situation or merely
by better utilization of capital, larger output, and higher labor productivity? In any event, how large a segment of the economy does
the price adjustment affect when there is a large subsistence sector
in these countries and the modern industrial sector generally contributes less than 10 percent to total output? No one will dare suggest that price corrections will not move these economies in the right
direction. But are they decisive? Or do they make only a marginal

impression on the unemployment problem? We need far more empirical evidence before we can pass any overall judgments.

Third, there is a fashion these days to talk about intermediate technology, something that is supposed to be more labor-intensive and more suited to the needs of the developing countries than the technology presently used in the developed world. But where does it exist? I found very little evidence of it in the developed countries, which have no real incentive for fashioning special technology for the developing countries and which export a good deal of their technology under tied assistance. There are no great improvisations going on in the developing countries themselves and no major research institutes devoting their energies to the development of intermediate technology.* The only place where I found something resembling intermediate technology was in mainland China, but there has not been much transfer of it to the developing countries, as China's trade and aid are fairly limited at present.

Fourth, I found in the literature on employment abundant suggestions that the developed world should open up its markets to the labor-intensive products of the developing countries. Here, at least, the evidence is fairly clear: No one has detected any impatience on the part of any developed country to follow this prescription.

Finally, looking at the national plans of the developing countries, it was obvious that employment was often a secondary, not a primary, objective of planning. It was generally added as an afterthought to the growth target in GNP but very poorly integrated in the framework of planning. Recalling my own experience with the formulation of Pakistan's five-year plans—and I ought to know—the chapter on employment strategy was always added at the end, to round off the plans and make them look complete and respectable, and was hardly an integral part of the growth strategy or policy framework. In fact, most of the developments that affected the employment situation favorably, such as the rural works program and the green revolution, were planned primarily for higher output, and their employment-generating potential was accidental and not planned. There were endless numbers of research teams, our own and foreign, fixing up our national accounts and ensuring that they adequately registered our rate of growth; there was not a fraction of this effort devoted to employment statistics.

The employment objective, in short, has been the stepchild of planning, and it has been assumed, far too readily, that high rates of

---

*I was informed after my lecture that there is a small research institute in Britain, the Intermediate Technology Group, operating on a shoe-string budget, which is devoting all its efforts to this subject. I am sorry that I missed that.

growth will ensure full employment as well. But what if they don't ?
A sustained 6 percent rate of growth in Pakistan in the 1960s led to
rising unemployment, particularly in East Pakistan. And what happens
if the developing countries cannot achieve the high growth rates of
10 percent or more that it may take to eliminate unemployment and
are confined to 5 percent or 6 percent over the decade of the 1970s ?
Should they quietly accept rising unemployment, and the social and
political unrest that accompanies it, as the inevitable price for not
growing any faster ?

There were uncomfortable questions of this kind that led me
to a reexamination of the overall theory and practice of development.
And I found it to be even in a sorrier state than the literature on employment.

Has Poverty Decreased ?

Here we stand after two decades of development, trying to pick
up the pieces, and we simply do not know whether problems associated
with dire poverty have increased or decreased or what real impact
the growth of GNP has made on them. We do know that the rate of
growth, as measured by the increase in GNP, has been fairly respectable in the 1960s, especially by historical standards. We also know
that some developing countries have achieved a fairly high rate of
growth over a sustained period. But has it made a dent on the problems
of mass poverty ? Has it resulted in a reduction in the worst forms
of poverty—malnutrition, disease, illiteracy, shelterless population,
squalid housing ? Has it meant more employment and greater equality
of opportunities ? Has the character of development conformed to
what the masses really wanted ? We know so little in this field. There
are only a few selected indices, and they are rather disquieting.

A recent study in India shows that 40 percent to 50 percent of
the population has a per capita income below the official poverty line,
where malnutrition begins. And what's more pertinent, the per capita
income of this group declined from 1950 to 1970 while the average
per capita income went up.

In Pakistan, which experienced a healthy growth rate during
the 1960s, unemployment increased, real wages in the industrial sector
declined by one-third, per capita income disparity between East and
West Pakistan nearly doubled, and concentrations of industrial wealth
became an explosive economic and political issue. And in 1968, while
the international world was still applauding Pakistan as a model of
development, the system exploded—not only for political reasons but
for economic unrest.

Brazil has recently achieved a growth rate close to 7 percent, but persisting maldistribution of income continues to threaten the very fabric of its society.

These instances can be multiplied. There is in fact need for much more work in this field. The essential point, however, is that a high growth rate has been, and is, no guarantee against worsening poverty and economic explosions.

What has gone wrong? We were confidently told that if you take care of your GNP, poverty will take care of itself. We were often reminded to keep our eyes focused on a high GNP growth target, as it was the best guarantee for eliminating unemployment and of redistributing incomes later through fiscal means. Then what really happened? Where did the development process go astray?

Where We Went Wrong

My feeling is that it went astray at least in two directions. First, we conceived our task not as the eradication of the worst forms of poverty but as the pursuit of certain high levels of per capita income. We convinced ourselves that the latter is a necessary condition for the former, but we did not in fact give much thought to the interconnection. We development economists persuaded the developing countries that life begins at $1,000, and thereby we did them no service. They chased elusive per capita income levels, they fussed about high growth rates in GNP, they constantly worried about "how much was produced and how fast" and cared too little about "what was produced and how it was distributed."

This hot pursuit of GNP growth was not necessarily wrong; it only blurred our vision. It is no use pretending that it did not, for how else can we explain the worsening poverty in many developing countries? How else can we explain our own preoccupation as economists with endless refinements of statistical series concerning GNP, investment, saving, exports, and imports; continuing fascination with growth models; and formulation of evaluation criteria primarily in terms of output increases? If eradication of poverty was the real objective, why did so little professional work go into determining the extent of unemployment, maldistribution of incomes, malnutrition, shelterless population, or other forms of poverty? Why is it that even after two decades of development, we know so little about the extent of real poverty, even in such "well-planned" economies as India and Pakistan?

Besides the constant preoccupation with GNP growth, another direction we went wrong was in assuming that income distribution policies could be divorced from growth policies and could be added later to obtain whatever distribution we desired. Here we displayed a misguided faith in the fiscal systems of the developing countries and a fairly naive understanding of the interplay of economic and political institutions. We know now that the coverage of these fiscal systems is generally narrow and difficult to extend. We also know that once production has been so organized as to leave a fairly large number of people unemployed, it becomes almost impossible to redistribute incomes to those who are not even participating in the production stream. We have a better appreciation now of the evolution of modern capitalist institutions and their hold on political decision-making, and hence we are more aware that the very pattern and organization of production itself indicates a pattern of consumption and distribution that is politically very difficult to change. Once you have increased your GNP by producing more luxury houses and cars, it is not very easy to convert them into low-cost housing or bus transport. A certain pattern of consumption and distribution inevitably follows.

We have a number of case studies by now that show how illusory it was to hope that the fruits of growth could be redistributed without reorganizing the pattern of production and investment first. Many fast-growing economies in Latin America illustrate this point. In my own country, Pakistan, the very institutions we created for promoting faster growth and capital accumulation later frustrated all our attempts for better distribution and greater social justice. I am afraid that the evidence is unmistakable and the conclusion inescapable: divorce between production and distribution policies is false and dangerous. The distribution policies must be built into the very pattern and organization of production.

Where does all this lead us? It leads us to a basic reexamination of the existing theories and practice of development. It is time that we stand economic theory on its head and see if we get any better results. In a way, the current situation reminds me of the state of affairs in the developed world in the early 1930s before John Maynard Keynes shook us all with his general theory. Since existing theories fit none of the facts in the real world, they had to be discarded. Keynes provided us with a fresh way of looking at economic and political realities. His theoretical framework was not very elegant, but his ideas had a powerful impact.

The developing countries today are seeking a fresh way of looking at their problems. They are disillusioned, and somewhat chastened, by the experience of the last two decades. They are not too sure what the new perspective on development should be, but at least some of the elements are becoming increasingly clear.

A New Perspective on Development

First, the problem of development must be defined as a selective attack on the worst forms of poverty. Development goals must be defined in terms of progressive reduction and eventual elimination of malnutrition, disease, illiteracy, squalor, unemployment, and inequalities. We were taught to take care of our GNP, because this would take care of poverty. Let us reverse this and take care of poverty, because this will take care of the GNP. Let us worry about the content of GNP even more than its rate of increase.

Second, and this follows from the first, the developing countries should define minimum (or threshold) consumption standards that they must reach in a manageable period of time, say a decade. Consumption planning should move to the center of the stage; production planning should be geared to it. And consumption planning should not be in financial terms but in physical terms, in terms of a minimum bundle of goods and services that must be provided to the common man to eliminate the worst manifestations of poverty: minimum nutritional, educational, health, and housing standards, for instance. There are two major implications of this strategy. One, we must get away from the tyranny of the demand concept and replace it by the concept of minimum needs, at least in the initial stages of development, since to weight basic needs by the ability to pay is outrageous in a poor society. It will only distort the patterns of production and consumption in favor of the "haves," as has happened in many societies. Two, the chase of elusive present-day Western standards and per capita income levels, which cannot be reached even over the course of the next century, must be replaced by the concept of a threshold income that each society defines for itself and that can be reached in a manageable period of a decade or so.

Third, the concerns for more production and better distribution should be brought together in defining the pattern of development; both must be generated at the same time; the present divorce between the two concerns must end. If the pattern of production (and exports and imports) is geared to satisfying minimum consumption requirements and to employing the entire labor force, higher production will itself lead to better distribution.

Fourth, and this is implicit in the third, employment should become a primary objective of planning and no longer be treated as only a secondary objective. Let a society regard its entire labor force as allocable; over this force, its limited capital resources must be spread. Let us reverse the present thinking that, since there is only a fixed amount of capital to be allocated at a particular time, a society can employ only a certain part of the labor force, leaving the rest unemployed, to subsist on others as hangers-on or as beggars, without any personal income, often suffering from the worst forms of malnutrition and squalor. Instead let us treat the pool of labor as given; at any particular time it must be combined with the existing capital stock irrespective of how low the productivity of labor or capital may be. If physical capital is short, skill formation and organization can replace it in the short run. It is only if we proceed from the goal of full employment, with people doing something useful, even with little doses of capital and organization, that we can eradicate some of the worst forms of poverty. With this goal, even the character and pattern of production will change, since better income distribution will also mean greater production of those goods that are less import- and capital-intensive and require more labor.

The Chinese Experience

These are only a few elements in the new perspective that is needed today on development. They are neither complete nor carefully integrated nor perhaps very original. I offer them only as an invitation to further thinking. And if some of this framework sounds fairly mad, let me invite you to study the development experience of the largest developing country in the world—mainland China. I visited it twice in the last few years and I must say that I was greatly impressed by its economic performance measured against ours in Pakistan. It was not obvious to me what the real rate of growth of China was, but it was obvious to me that they had looked at the problem of development from the point of view of eradication of poverty and not from the viewpoint of reaching a certain prescribed per capita income level. It appears that within a period of less than two decades, China has eradicated the worst forms of poverty; it has full employment, universal literacy, and adequate health facilities; it suffers from no obvious malnutrition or squalor. What's more, it was my impression that China has achieved this at fairly modest rates of growth, by paying more attention to the content and distribution of GNP. In fact, China has proved that it is a fallacy that poverty can be removed and full employment achieved only at high rates of growth and only over a period of many decades.

How has it accomplished this? Of course, its political system, its isolation, its great size, its ideological mobilization, all of these have contributed to the evolution of its pattern of development. But are there any lessons to learn, even when we do not subscribe to its political system? Is there not a practical illustration here of a selective attack on the problems of poverty, pursuit of a threshold income and minimum consumption standards, merger of production and distribution policies, and achievement of full employment with a meager

81

supply of capital? It is no use insisting that these results must have been achieved at tremendous social and political costs; people in the developing countries are often undergoing these costs without any visible economic results so that they look at the experience of China with great envy and praise. It is time, especially as China's isolation ends, that there be an objective and detailed study of its experience in place of the usual rhetoric to which we have been subjected so far.

In conclusion, let me say that the search for a new perspective on development has already begun in the developing countries. Many of us of these countries, who are essentially products of Western liberalism and who returned to our countries to deliver development, have often ended up delivering more tensions and unrest. We have seen a progressive erosion of liberalism, both in our own countries and among our donor friends abroad. And we stand today dispirited and disillusioned. It is no use offering us tired old trade-offs and crooked-looking production functions whenever we talk about income distribution and employment. It is no use dusting off old theories and polishing up old ideas and asking us to go and try them again. It is time that we take a fresh look at the entire theory and practice of development.

THE MEANING OF DEVELOPMENT AND ITS
EDUCATIONAL IMPLICATIONS
Ralph M. Miller

Looking at aid programs in the most favorable light and dis-
counting the political and economic motives of the donors, "development with social justice" might be offered as the slogan for the effort
of the 1950s and 1960s. As such, the effort embodies a contradiction
that amounts to a denial of history. Development assistance has promoted an industrial model of development with the intention of ameliorat-
ing economic inequalities and relieving dangerous social pressures.
Historically, industrial development in the Western nations has increased economic inequalities and has even led to dislocation of previous social and economic patterns and the increase of social tensions
and human suffering. Formerly, a price has been paid for development. The hope expressed in the idea "development with social justice"
is that we can program development so as not to exact the accustomed
price.

The political motives prompting development assistance, the
intention to maintain or strengthen political alliances by promoting
stability accord with the fond hope of "development with social justice."
Prosperity was assumed to be the basis of social order, and a pro-
grammed increase in the level of economic activity was taken as the
key to prosperity.

Whatever the motive for development assistance, the programs
have been predicated on a Western model of development with the
intention of modernizing agricultural economies so the new nations
might have greater access to the modern international economy. In
spite of planning efforts greater than any that accompanied the early
phases of industrialization in Europe and North America, no alternative pattern of development is emerging. Nothing radically different
from the "free enterprise" view of development is apparent* and it
seems the entrepreneurship and individual initiative that were crucial
to the broad advance of Western development must equally play a

---

*Even the emphasis on centralized planning in India has not yet
achieved a functioning pattern of development that, in terms of efficiency, stands as an alternative to the usual Western model. Moreover, smaller developing nations have nothing like the internal demand
to support industrial activity that can be found in India. Nor can the
entrepreneurial and commercial spirit in Indian society be overlooked;
it gives incalculable support to new developments. This last point is
most vividly illustrated by the penetration of Indian merchants and
businessmen into many other developing countries.

part in contemporary development efforts. If so, must there not also be the same inequalities, rivalries, and unexpected disruptions? The essence of enterprise is to seize the advantage, to exploit the possibility that others fail to see; and such exercise of individual inventiveness leads to developments that are simply unpredictable and whose consequences cannot be taken account of in advance planning.

Even in the "green revolution," which only modestly applied technology to agriculture, there has been significant dislocation as the more enterprising farmers have sometimes increased their landholdings and thus created a more severe disparity between the successful and the landless. Such a process of "rationalizing" (reorganizing) agriculture by concentrating it in the hands of the most efficient farmers is completely defensible in conventional economic terms, but in countries where urban areas are already thronged with unemployed the release of more people from the land is no boon. It does not compare to the urbanization that accompanied the industrialization of Europe and America.

If the histories of the industrialized nations thus suggest that development, insofar as we are able to foster it through international cooperation, is not likely to promote social justice and, indeed, must inevitably introduce disruptive elements of change, what of the hope that development will lead to stability? The thesis that development leading to prosperity produces stability seems all the more dubious in view of the cycle of wars, including the two world wars, proceeding from political and economic rivalries among the industrialized nations. Whether the development of Europe could have been accomplished without conquest and recruitment of resources from colonies is at least a moot question. The growing sense of social crisis within the United States and other prosperous nations suggests that the highest levels of prosperity do not even assure internal stability.

If there is some level of general prosperity that is conducive to stability, that level would seem to be the product of a "mature" economy that has not only achieved relatively high prosperity but has had time to diffuse prosperity through most levels of society. The climb to such maturity is fraught with dislocation and tensions, and what we are concerned with under the heading "development" is really the most precarious part of the climb.

Development is now less often referred to in such simple economic terms, but has a significant change of heart accompanied the change of rhetoric? A great exponent of manpower planning, Frederick Harbison, has lately been urging a "human resource" approach to development. Yet Harbison's approach remains essentially economic in such assertions as ". . . employment must take its place, alongside GNP—and of equal prominence—as a central object of concern in development planning and an essential criterion in the examination of

84

progress in development."[1] For Harbison, "human resource" development is no more than a broader approach to preparation of a labor
force, including nonformal education and rurally oriented programs.
He flatly admits, "Education has other and broader purposes than
human resource development. No educator would consider that his
sole function is to prepare people for the labor force."[2] Harbison
apparently will leave it to educators, or others, to determine and
accomplish these broader purposes, for his exposition of a "human
resource" approach deals only with training a greater variety of
workers in more diversified programs and with stimulating employment in sectors that have been neglected.

If growth in GNP is not an adequate criterion of development,
neither is the creation of employment. Both are essentially economic,
and they equally suggest development should be toward a cash economy
wherein the work role is the key to individual status and participation
in the goods of society.

It has been emphasized that the industrial, Western concept
of "employment"—more pointedly, "unemployment"—is irrelevant to
conditions in developing countries. My objection is more fundamental:
The experience of North America and Western Europe—or of Japan—
cannot serve as a guide and standard for the newly independent nations.

The Western, industrial system is a minority system in relation to world population, and its growth needed enormous resources
in relation to population and further required economic thralldom for
nonindustrial nations. Though this thralldom becomes more enlightened
over time, a program of Western-type economic development for the
third world is really asking these nations to commit themselves to
a system in which they are already the losers. The worsening of the
terms of trade as between primary producers and manufacturing nations is one of the striking evidences that the new nations have lost
ground, in economic terms, even during the decades of concentrated
development efforts.

The basic question is whether all nations can be winners, or
even come close to breaking even, in the world trade game as carried
on under competitive conditions. We still assume that it is competition and the hope of getting more that makes the mare go. Basically,
nations that have the advantages under the present system and have
achieved their high standards of living through high levels of trade
and business activity must agree to press their advantages less vigorously and to make concessions to the disadvantaged nations. Whether
they will be willing to go very far in this direction, whether they will
go nearly far enough, seems doubtful in view of the hard bargaining
and the determined pursuit of self-interest in evidence at the meetings
of the big 10 in the face of monetary crisis.

It seems remarkable that, for all the economic emphasis in development thinking, so little attention has been paid to fundamental issues. Already the wastefulness and resource-hunger of the leading industrial nations are becoming painfully apparent in the problems of pollution, energy, water, and raw materials. Considering that the economic well-being of the industralized nations has steadily depended upon increasing per capita consumption that has reached the point where planned obsolescence and fashion changes are essential to maintaining the volume of business, can it seriously be maintained that the road to well-being for the new nations is along this same route?

It is in the spirit of these fundamental questions about the global utility of an economic approach that has consumed vast quantities of resources to maintain the well-being of a fraction of the world's population that it is possible to challenge the "human resources" approach as no better than sheer emphasis on GNP. It is not stupid to ask, "Why should everybody work?" The question is pertinent in strict economic terms when the most efficient technologies are steadily less labor-intensive and where the highly organized work of the best operatives can produce more than is needed by all. What use is universal employment if it is achieved through spreading work and is for the purpose of making jobs rather than achieving higher production? The answer to some of the dislocations previously noted as endemic to the Western pattern of development has usually been to urge labor-intensive technologies, especially in the rural sector.

What we have not recognized is that work has three distinct functions: (1) as an element in the productive process, (2) as the means whereby men qualify to share in the goods produced, and (3) as the means of establishing a man's function and status in society. While there has never been a perfect balance between the productive and sharing functions of work, this century marks the first time when human muscle has been seriously in oversupply. So long as we hold firm in venerating work and in distributing the necessities of life (as well as the luxuries) according to ability to work, we shall continue trapped in a situation where the struggle to create jobs for all undercuts the utilization of technologies and economies of scale essential to achieving success in international competitive markets. In other words, to generate the production and income to create jobs, the less developed countries must embrace technologies that are inimical to creating the largest number of jobs.

Can there be an answer to this dilemma so long as development is argued in essentially economic terms? Is attention to rural development and nonformal education, in itself, a significant shift from the economic conception of development? Harbison is much interested in rural development and in nonformal education, but his view is that

"Broadly based rural development, in short, means the transformation of stagnant, traditional societies into productive, dynamic rural economies."[3] A typical measure of the success of rural development programs is the increase in cash flow or the extent to which the rural sector can be brought into the money economy.

Another dilemma resulting from the economic conception of development concerns the loss of meaning. One advantage of traditional societies, as compared to modernized technological societies, is that traditional societies have various ways of conferring status and a variety of social roles that give meaning and satisfaction to the people in those roles. While there appears to be great role diversification in technological societies, the differences in jobs obscure the fact that status is measured in monetary terms so that the meaning of a job is largely reduced to the salary it commands. The decline of some former authority figures, such as clergymen, who don't measure up in terms of income, is the best evidence of this emphasis. If a man's activities produce high levels of income, be that man Billy Graham, Arnold Palmer, or Frank Sinatra, there will be prestige for him while high-quality work gets little respect unless it is accompanied by the only conspicuous accolade a technical society can bestow. With increasing numbers of people in developing countries obviously failing to gain places in the wage economy, their meaning, as persons, is jeopardized as it would not be were they marginally employed or underemployed in a village.

Once we question the utility of trying to create jobs for everyone, we must seriously ask, "What else is there to life if people may not have regular employment and may not buy many of the things they desire?" On this question the Western world is likely to be mute, since our way of life has centered on the ownership of things and we tend, increasingly, to assign status in society in relation to income and control of wealth. Here we must try to respect the experience, not simply of "traditional" societies, but of all human association, of all relations among men not directed to material ends. Surely we do know that human friendship, the security from mutual help, and the stimulation of a variety of responsibilities in relation to other men are ultimate sources of human satisfaction. Instead of pursuing the futile objective of development in our (economic) terms, we must try to become more sensitive to possibilities in other environments and ways of life. The "uneconomics" of such an approach to development is summed up in a possible answer to the preceding question: "If it is wasteful to create jobs simply so people may qualify to share in the material goods of life then we must arrange society so that they share on some other basis."

More generally, a broader approach to development will be "uneconomic" in that it will not aim primarily at economy and efficiency.

It will not be deliberately wasteful, but it will take as its objective
the welfare of human beings and will recognize that human welfare
does not simply depend upon increased cash flows or greater success
in international markets. What people can learn to do for themselves
is something that they will not have to pay others for doing, and much
can be done in such matters as nutrition, sanitation, and child care
so as to improve life without requiring much paid work or the introduction of hired extension services on a large scale.

It might seem strange if we said our objective was not development, but life. Yet, surely, this is the issue. That the alternative
of helping men to live, and to have life more abundantly, could seem
strange only indicates how much we are locked within a particular
view. Living more abundantly cannot be measured in the familiar
terms of loans and grants and the value of resource transfers from
country to country. It certainly cannot be reduced to the kind of balance
of payments support that bulked so large in the Pearson proposals.
It must be, most of all, a closer working together of people. Donors
will have to listen more carefully and must be prepared to work in
more humble and smaller-scale ways. We have simply got to give
up the notion that development is a matter of setting up administrative
units to dispense technological solutions prescribed by Western, industrial development theory.

Educational Implications of a Broader
Conception of Development

Recognizing that formal education systems in developing countries are foreign intrusions and that their function is selection and
vocational preparation for the modern sector, it is apparent that education systems and almost all of educational assistance are bound up
with the pattern of development that is under question in this section.
The "formality" of these systems, in the strict sense, is an outcome
of the vocational emphasis and the close linkage with the modern
sector; formal education requires a curriculum, or a schedule of
skills and knowledge, that it is assumed can be taught under certain
conditions of instruction and then applied in out-of-school situations.
Given the very limited research, or even systematic questioning,
into the relationship between curricular content and job-and-social
functions, education systems become more formal as they justify
their content and methods in terms of tradition and long-standing
definitions of the "educated man." This tendency is apparent in the
educational practice, in developing countries, of justifying their school
programs by comparing them to allegedly international academic
standards—frequently the standards of the former metropoles of
colonial days.

The educational implications of any broader conception of development are primarily four:

1. Education must become less formal.
2. Education must be freed from system restrictions and be developed through a variety of specific projects on a smaller scale.
3. Education projects must be recognized as experimental and must be monitored so that we may find out what works in specific situations.
4. Education must become more of a service within a complex of development efforts and less of an instructional program for the sake of instruction.

The first implication follows clearly from what has been said about the formality of education in the strict sense. Curricula can be worked out in detail and a long-range investment in teaching materials can be undertaken on a national basis only when there exists a well-established vocational pattern with some sort of job specifications and employment qualifications that afford guidance to the school system. Regardless of whether the fit between the curriculum and the vocational system is actually very close, it is maintained in a purely formal sense by writing the qualifications for public-sector employment in terms of school certificates. The moment we suggest that education is not simply a preparation for this vocational system, all illusions about the adequacy of curricula must be given up. We are no longer talking about designing a system to prepare pupils for roles already established.

Education must then become less formal in the sense of taking account of local conditions and assisting people in a process of development that includes working out new roles for themselves. Much of this educational pioneering should go on in rural areas simply because that is where most of the people live. Moreover, any effectively "new" education in relation to a broader conception of development requires breaking away from the ritual of education, as well as from the idea that the only real purpose of education is as an escape route to the urban modern sector.

In spite of the warnings offered by C. Arnold Anderson and Philip Foster about the futility of trying to "ruralize" education, we must seriously ask what contribution education can make to rural living. Perhaps the urban drift cannot be stopped, but even more certainly the modern sector cannot expand fast enough to absorb the rural-urban migration.* If people are to find meaning in their lives,

---

*An interesting comment on the failure of modern sector growth to keep abreast of population growth and the urban drift was offered in a remark by Raoul Prebisch on the basis of his studies for the

unless enlisting among the urban unemployed be accepted as meaningful, they must be encouraged and helped to find new possibilities in rural living. Education alone certainly cannot revitalize rural life; it can only be a part of the total effort. But if we accept that education can accomplish nothing in this respect and that the only education people will accept is that aimed toward modern-sector jobs, then we must confess the utter irrelevance of education to current development imperatives.

It is only schooling—education carried on under the familiar ritualistic forms—that is irrelevant. What we need to turn attention to are alternative forms of education that are developed in relation to local needs and that utilize local skills. Local initiative must be emphasized, for the nonformal educational models of the developed world are often wildly inappropriate to conditions in developing countries. Extension services, for example, developed for the literate and technically sophisticated farmers of the United States, were not effective models for Nigeria, according to the Consortium for Nigerian Rural Development. Similarly, an emphasis on capital support in educational aid and a preference for supporting technical education schemes that afford the donor the security of using familiar budget and planning procedures may mean that we are committing ourselves to the support of projects guaranteed to be irrelevant. From the donor side, it takes much more effort, more man-hours, and higher administrative costs to spend a given amount of money in a diversity of small projects, rather than in a large, heavily capitalized project. However, donors must accept that inconvenience if they are to support the variety of educational undertakings suited to conditions in particular regions that will be necessary if education is to assist in bringing about new patterns of development.

Thus, the first implication, making education less formal, leads directly into the encouragement of small-scale projects, adjusted to local conditions and not confined within the requirements of any national, or other widespread, systems.

I do not suggest that hordes of aid workers be turned loose on the countryside to develop novel projects. The first thing to realize is that much of the effort of finding a more appropriate form of

---

Economic Council for Latin America. Prebisch estimates that an annual growth rate of 8 percent in the industrial sector will, by 1990, create enough jobs to regain the balance between the number of urban employed and the total population that existed in Latin America in 1950. He was emphasizing that population has been outstripping even the hopeful 6 percent rate of economic growth suggested by the Pearson report.

development and giving it appropriate educational support must come from the indigenous people. The entire role of outside planning of educational assistance must be revised, and I can think of few procedures less appropriate to the development of various small-scale educational efforts than the employment of the typical IBRD-UNESCO educational planning mission. This point must be elaborated. C. Arnold Anderson is entirely correct in entering ". . . a strong judgement that proposals 'to plan' more adequate systems of this kind of training are misjudged and would prove dysfunctional. Indeed, I would argue, first, that few countries possess any sets of officials capable of suggesting, let alone operating, a useful set of 'out-of-school' programs."[4] While Anderson was referring to out-of-school programs of vocational education and was making the case for proprietary education, his skepticism about the possibility of planning applies as much, or more, to any attempt to foster educational diversity outside the modern sector.

Therefore, rather than offering assistance through support of large projects and system development, educational assistance must be made more flexible and more swiftly responsive to small project requests. With the approval of host governments, aid donors must find ways of responding to that sector that is least able to articulate its needs. There is a development paradox here in that the budgetary and planning requirements of typical aid agencies pretty well limit them to responding to requests from the most developed sectors and institutions in the less developed world because it is just these sectors and institutions that have mastered the art of preparing aid requests. In effect, donors must become less formal and give up the security of planning and budget procedures, which, in any event, have often created a false impression that we knew what we were doing. There will be risk in responding more swiftly to small-scale requests, for not every local project is going to take off. The aim should be to support a variety of local programs and, without burdening these programs with outsiders, to monitor them so that we may learn about the efficacy of specific educational strategies in relation to specific regional conditions and aspirations.

Thus, we come to the experimental implication, for a genuinely experimental approach to support of small-scale programs is the only way of developing more effective educational programs. This approach requires giving up the notion of exporting complete educational technologies, though we should always be alert to see how specific technologies—instructional procedures, devices, materials, and so on—may be utilized within a developing program. We cannot tell in advance what may work and what may be necessary when specific educational efforts are undertaken in support of particular development projects. We may assist others in their own efforts to initiate new programs, and we offer them the benefit of some of our experimental techniques and some specific resources. We cannot design and develop the projects for them, for we have very limited experience in such undertakings, as is attested by our fumbling efforts to develop educational programs for minority groups or for the native peoples of North America. Recognizing that we must attempt not only a different kind of education but an unknown kind of education that is also to have a new functional relation to development, we must also incur the risks of experimentation.

Turning attention to the service function of education within a complex of development efforts means admitting the futility of merely giving instruction in how to develop; one must begin by attempting the development itself, and the instruction comes in as specific technical problems are identified. Education then becomes but one ancillary service for people who are trying to do something for themselves. Donor assistance to such projects may not be possible in "pure" educational packages and may be more a matter of finding out how to render material support to development in ways most conducive to helping people learn to do more for themselves. Here, simple notions of efficiency may have to take second place to exploiting the learning possibilities of development projects.

I do not say we must forthwith abandon all support to formal educational programs, but I do say we should put up risk capital in support of schemes that are not "bankable" in the usual sense. In all, I am urging an experimental attitude to find out what kinds of educational programs can contribute in what ways to local development efforts. We will need, at the very least, a much broader conception of education, including attention to nonliterary educational materials and programs. If education is really to assist persons who are going to stay rural, it may have to focus upon the young adult group and it will certainly have to start giving instruction without going through the preliminary of teaching reading.

I do not think the Western world has many people skilled in rendering such basic instructional service, but if we cannot render such assistance we may find our established patterns of educational assistance increasingly irrelevant to the needs of development.

Finally, I think the human component of such an experimental and service-oriented educational program must be fully appreciated. The essential nature of such a program is to help people do things for themselves, to assist them in tackling immediate problems in food storage, sanitation, village organization, and so on. It is of vital importance that the people gain confidence so that in confronting the difficulties and possibilities of their situation they see themselves as doing something about it. Typical educators and typical lessons do not often have this effect, especially when they are bringing technical good tidings (usually in symbolic form). What are needed are versatile people able to render practical assistance, to achieve understanding of local problems and local customs, and to offer instruction only when it is needed. Indeed, "instruction" may be too strong a word, and they may have to settle for seeking out occasions to exemplify what can be done and how it may be done. Clearly, the long tradition of recruiting foreign educators for service in developing countries is not appropriate to such practical living and learning. We shall have to find, again by experiment, just what roles foreign personnel can fulfill. I need not go into that problem now. I raise this final point simply to emphasize that, if we seriously consider the nature of educational activities appropriate to a changed conception of development, we have actually to reconsider the nature of the programs and personnel that have so far constituted aid to education in developing countries.

Notes

1. Frederick H. Harbison, "A Human Resource Approach to the Development of African Nations" (Washington, D.C.: American Council on Education, 1971), p. 17. In making this remark, Harbison is quoting from an ILO paper, "Towards Full Employment."

2. Harbison, op. cit., p. 8.

3. Ibid., p. 7.

4. C. Arnold Anderson, "Reflections upon the Planning of 'Out-of-School' Education," International Institute of Educational Planning, December 1971, p. 14.

EDUCATION AND DEVELOPMENT
Joseph Ki-Zerbo

In the economic battle that is thrust upon each underdeveloped country, which of the three principal factors of production—I mean, natural resources, capital, and men—is the most decisive as a strategic weapon? I think we shall agree that it is the social labor of man, for it is this work that subdues, domesticates, and mobilizes the other elements of progress. Accordingly, I consider that the most significant variable in the development of these countries is indeed the quantity and quality of human labor. An African proverb says that "when the stomach is full the foot is fast," emphasizing the interdependence that exists between the limbs of the human body and bringing back to mind Aesop's well-known fable. I believe that is also true in the field of education, even when education is a luxury reserved for a small minority and even if, unfortunately, other groups in the society are overburdened through a discriminatory division of the social labor to assure the privileges of the minority. This was the relationship between the coolies and the mandarins, the Greek slaves and the free men, and also in the United States between the black slaves and the plantation owners.

This inhuman labor imposed upon certain categories of men is mitigated today by machines that have taken the place of physical labor. But in a type of revolution, a third or second industrial revolution, the machine has come to take the place not only of physical labor but also of intellectual labor. What better proof for us that education is truly an investment in the strict sense of the word! I have even come to measure the value of this investment by comparing the earnings of an educated man to those of the uneducated man. Of course one must take into account the time tied up in people's education, but one must realize that education gives to those who benefit from it the power of catalysts upon their environment.

Education at the same time also fashions the producer and the consumer, and I believe that even taking into account the amount of time spent in education and knowing that the length of active life is several times that of schooling, I think that one can consider education as a real investment. An American professor by the name of Becker has calculated that the annual earnings of the male population in the United States is equal to 11 percent of the total expenses involved in their education. Capital invested in instruction for their education was thus amortized in nine years, which is not bad at all.

In former years, when it was suggested to them that they send their children to school, many African chiefs preferred to send the sons of slaves or grillots. Today they bitterly regret having done so because this represents a lost investment.

94

Finally I shall simply mention the revenues that are taken in by a number of countries like Switzerland solely through the sale of letters patent whose ownership is defined by collective agreements and by international law. I shall also mention that research is more and more integrated into economic progress within the framework of businesses.

In other words, brain power is the engine of progress, above all in underdeveloped countries, where the relative difference between the point of departure terminus a quo and the progress achieved is even greater than in developed countries. I think it would be good to assert this forcefully at the start, for in many underdeveloped countries the Department of National Education is considered solely as a "budget-devourer," a barrel of the Danaides that is never filled. But can one deduce from this proposition that education is an investment, that it will be adequate to educate people in order to ensure almost automatically that development occurs? It is exactly there that another problem arises. The size of the educated classes grows, and yet progress does not always follow, thus leaving us with the question, What type of school for which society? In other words, we believe that it is a product of today's school that will sketch the design of tomorrow's society, and the dilemma arises: Will we have a school generating social energy or a cancerous school that will grow monstrously over a carrying organism while waiting to destroy it? It is this fundamental problem of our times that I should like to examine in rough outline with respect to the underdeveloped countries in general, with respect to Africa in particular, and even more particularly with respect to Upper Volta.

In the first section, which will be essentially descriptive, we shall discuss the nature of the socioeconomic and cultural school of underdevelopment.

Then, in the second more difficult and dialectic section we shall seek to establish what a creative school of development should be.

The School of Underdevelopment

I should like to start out with the following proposition: The school in many underdeveloped countries is a reflection and a fruit of the surrounding underdevelopment, from which arises its deficiency, its quantitative and qualitative poverty. But little by little, and there lies the really serious risk, the school in these underdeveloped countries risks becoming in turn a factor of underdevelopment. I should like to demonstrate this with a few ideas.

First, the financial aspect of the present school. In particular, the Conference of Ministers of National Education at Yaounde examined this problem of the cost of education. Although certain expenditures fall on local collectivities or upon parents, in Upper Volta the annual cost of educating a student in primary school is CFA 16,000. In secondary school, it is CFA 50,000. And this in a country where the annual monetary income of a peasant, even a peasant family, does not exceed CFA 8-10,000. In other words, a secondary school student for whom the state assumes responsibility requires six times the annual monetary income of a peasant family.

From a point of view more macroeconomic, shall we say: For every CFA 10 billion of the national budget, expenditures on national education amount to more than CFA 1.5 billion; that is about 17 percent or 18 percent of the budget. Five percent of the gross national product. And for what? To educate all the children in Upper Volta it would take several times the national budget. And with the rate of population growth that has been verified in the underdeveloped countries, about 2 percent per year, one asks oneself sometimes if the rate of schooling should not be decreased. One must also realize that the gross domestic product in these countries does not grow more than 1.6 percent annually. This is a first qualitative aspect of the problem.

The second aspect, that of the school's output, is also alarming: that is, the number of students retained within the limits of the normal course of study. In Upper Volta, out of 1,000 students who enter the CP 1 (cours premier), only 600 reach the CM 2 (cours moyen) and 120 pass the entrance examination into the sixth grade. In general, 20 percent of those who start primary school finish it and 12 percent of those who begin secondary school complete it successfully. A considerable number of students repeat grades, and it has been estimated that in general one-fourth of the total student population are repeaters, a fact that in addition falsifies considerably the academic statistics on the rate of schooling. These losses are due to the poor quality of available materials, and I could quote you passages from letters that directors of primary schools in Upper Volta sent us for an inquiry that I had launched and that could easily fit into an anthology of black humor, so catastrophic are the descriptions they present.

The overlarge size of classes should be discussed equally. There are sometimes 100 or 150 pupils in one first grade of a school. Of course at that state one is in charge more of a nursery than of a real class. And finally, there is the cultural environment, which does not encourage the students' intellectual progress, at least within the framework that has been determined for them. In particular, school vacations discharge with an important loss of the capital amassed during the academic year.

Thus, despite the efforts made by states, the rate of schooling remains stationary at 9 percent or 10 percent—and this after 10 years. One can say that the increase in population multiplies illiteracy faster the poorer a country is, and this population growth in my country makes the student ranks grow each year by 12 percent although the population grows only at a rate of about 2 percent. Someone was surprised that illiteracy cannot be wiped out quickly. He was forgetting that these rates are not based upon the same absolute quantity. In the second case, the rate of schooling, this is based upon 120,000 children who are educated, but one forgets that there are 5 million people in the country, consequently the rate of population growth is based upon much more important quantities.

The education of all, dreamed about by many good souls and worthy hearts, remains, I believe, an inaccessible mirage for most undeveloped countries. One thinks of the character in an African story who was condemned to run after his shadow. To succeed on a similar terrain we would have to mobilize resources equivalent to those amassed by the rich nations for ultramodern weapons. Another dream that we better not play with. Let us get back to earth. We can establish, then, that almost all the nations of Africa and Asia experience a greater and more rapid growth in their expenditures on education than in the growth of their national income and the total of their public expenditures. In Morocco, for example, national education has absorbed 60 percent of the total increase in the budget. We are therefore at a critical threshold, and very weak economic growth does not allow us to go much further ahead. Private savings, as you know, are extremely limited in Africa, and a lot of effort is put forth for very meager results.

The analysis becomes even more bleak when we address ourselves to the qualitative aspect of the problem, which I shall do now.

I often say that today's school is an "insular" school. The school in the underdeveloped countries is generally the school of B A BA— that is, of crude schooling without a predetermined, very precise orientation. To understand that, one must go back to the colonial period when industrialization hardly existed or was totally absent, when we were engaged in extensive, subsistence agriculture, and when the agricultural yield, export agriculture, was produced on the basis of communal labor, which was very cheaply paid. At that time the school was made to furnish a handful of assistants for the administration, an administration with very extensive links. In other words, I think that the colonial school was not a Malthusian school in the sense that it squared exactly with the needs of the time. I also think that the colonial school was not so "insular" as the present school. Students were subjected to periodic manual labor (although the result served above all to butter the table of the teacher or the district commander). But today the school has sometimes aggravated certain faults in the colonial school without preserving some of its qualities.

First, physical insularity: Today's school has sometimes been compared to a sacred forest into which enter only a certain number of the initiated, charged to perform esoteric rites, escaping from everyone. Even without a fence one senses that there is an invisible enclosure that keeps out the laymen, and often even if the classes are clean, the yard is a sort of waste ground where one leaves to the sun the job of burning the weeds. In the same way the building material, the style of construction, is often inappropriate in relation to the local surroundings. It is the temple of knowledge, accessible only to the neophytes, and those who enter from the start go on a type of interplanetary trip: They meet strange scenery, peasants made up by brochures of travel agencies (which, happily, are becoming more and more Africanized). Here, it is a beech tree in its autumnal plushness that contrasts cruelly with the hairy, genial Baobab that one sees inadvertently when one looks out the window. There, it is a Breton cow that sits enthroned on a wall with the air of having been the first to be enthroned there. Surely it was Plato, I think, who said that astonishment is the first step toward knowledge, but when there is no more than that, I think the child loses ground. And that is why I speak of the "insular" school.

A school also of uprooting. This ivory tower school, this ebony ghetto school, if you will, is a little like a single hair in the soup, or a dangerous cyst, a tumor whose diagnosis reveals too often that it is cancerous.

First, social uprooting. A child is elected from among thousands of others. At the reopening of school there are epic squabbles and the teacher must sometimes break through the waiting line that has formed during the previous night. People spend the whole night awaiting recruitment. But once chosen, one is considered by one's own parents as a sort of raw material that should leave at the end of the assembly line as types of very clean, very considerate bureaucrats. And the mentality of the student himself also changes. Two years ago, we asked young pupils in Upper Volta who started the sixth form to tell us a little about their first impressions when they arrived in the capital. These were really exquisite morsels of spontaneity, the naiveté of the observations, a sort of wonder before this discovery, as many of these children had never seen houses of more than one storey, which they described as houses one on top of the other. They had perhaps never slept in a bed, as you and I are accustomed to do. The same applies to running water, which they had never seen—or electric light. In an African bush village there is no electric light. So that all this was a wonder for them, a considerable displacement, but four or six years later it is routine, they are used to it. This is the point of no return.

I shall also stress the curriculum, about which there is much
to say. Great progress has been made in history and geography:
You know that for a long time the syllabuses were the same as those
in France. I shall not remind you of a well-known phrase on this
subject, but I consider that history is like the collective memory of
people, and as memory is necessary for all the operations of the
mind, so if one took away a person's memory, that person would lose
his personality since he would recognize neither his father nor his
mother nor his house. He would completely lose his mind. He would
be, one would have to say, alienated, depersonalized. Likewise, when
one deprives children of their historic roots, one risks depersonal-
izing the people. It would be the same for the problem of language,
which I shall come back to, and for that of the texts studied by students,
which still condition success in examinations. Recently a school in-
spector told me about the texts of Mme. de Sévigné commented upon
in an African country, and he told me how these texts aroused little
enthusiasm, to say the least, from the African student lost in the bush.
Indeed, what interest should he find in the gossip, the tittle-tattle of
this good lady of the 17th century, who talks about a society so far
from the Bobo, the Dogon, and the Zulu ?

Therefore I think that there is a task to be done, and I personally
remember a competition at the technical lycée of Ouagadougou where
the subjects were sent from France. The subject of the competition
at the technical lycée as well as at the home economics school was
the following: "To Prepare a Sole Meunière." And as there are no
sole in the Ouagadougou dam, they were specially ordered by air in
order to make the competition possible. The result of these aberra-
tions, which no longer exist in this grotesque form but which persist
in other forms, is that the students accustom themselves, they adopt
a defense system, and they retreat in actual fact into rote learning.
They learn the dictionary by heart. Sometimes a student knows how
to read the texts of Tacitus, but he is not able to chat at home with
his own mother.

I shall finish by speaking about the last characteristic of this
school—that is, the school as an economic dead end and social powder
keg. In 1967 in Upper Volta, there were 9,580 candidates for the
CEP (Certificat d'Etudes Primaires) and 6,268 for the exam in the
6th form. The capacity of secondary institutions was very low despite
the efforts we had taken toward "nonresidency." They thus went from
the dormitory lycée to the classroom lycée. Despite that, there were
only 1,560 places available, and these places were taken by the best
students: in other words, by one-fourth of the candidates. Three-
fourths were left on the seller's hands. And among these three-fourths,
perhaps two-thirds will be retrieved by their families for work.

In the same year, there were 1,715 candidates for the BEPC (Brevet des Etudes de Premier Cycle); only 870 Voltaique students passed. There were only 420 places in the second form. We began a competition for entry into the second form, and the result was that 450 students who held the BEPC were thus rejected. Adding on those who could not repeat the third form, there was a total of 900 young people in 1967 alone who were let loose on the job market. And what kind of question will they be asked on the job market? They won't be asked, "What do you know?" but "What do you know how to do?" Well, these young people don't know how to do anything with their two hands. And as Molière said, "Vaugelas hardly knows how to make soup well."

This is a very serious situation. The statistics reveal at least 1,000 graduates in 1969, and soon there will be several thousand, who are still mouths to feed. In Dahomey, we are told, they are beginning to have persons with baccalaureat degrees who, unless they agree to become taxi drivers, are unemployed. When one compares this situation to a committed effort, everything takes place as if one were spending money to give oneself burdens, and I consider that the handful of academic people who are the upshot of this system neither legitimize nor justify it.

One could ask whether the school does not pose more problems than it resolves. It is the school that is at the root of this general exodus that one observes in the underdeveloped countries, particularly in Africa. This exodus derives, I think, from the hardship of life in the countryside, but perhaps also from the students' ignorance of the countryside. They are afraid of the unknown. Certainly in the eyes of someone who is very well educated, the scholastic baggage of these African students could seem very light, but for them it is the change from zero to infinity. And they construct for themselves an idea of the possibilities open to them according precisely to the idea they construct of this infinity.

Thus they compare the salary of a city orderly, CFA 10,000, to the income of an average peasant, which cannot exceed CFA 8,000-10,000 per year.

Thus this general exodus: The primary school graduate goes to the small town, the secondary graduate goes to the capital, and the college graduate goes to the rich countries. The rural areas bore the expenses of education in order to submit finally to a serious puncture that reduces their strength and their capacity to progress and even to survive. Well, in these cities the people become wreckages; they are uprooted; they resemble trees that are uprooted without being replanted elsewhere; they are literally felled and descend with the current of a river that offers no harbor. The recent movements of students are nothing, in my opinion, in comparison to what could happen when the stomping feet, if I may say, of the unemployed intellectuals take the leadership of the medinas of Africa.

Finally, the school is becoming, in my opinion, more and more antidemocratic. In fact, the school, seen as source of social ascent, is desired by everyone, but there is a budgetary limit from which arises the monopoly by the sons of bureaucrats, of people who are already educated. There is a serious disparity in the rate of schooling. According to the region, this rate varies within the interior of the same country. For example, for Upper Volta they say that 9 percent of the children receive schooling throughout the country, but that varies from 40 percent in Ouagadougou, 33 percent in Bobo, to 4 percent in Kaya, and 3 percent in Titao. As for the school in rural areas, where it exists, it is often reserved for the sons of rural people, and this tendency, I assure you, is likely to increase further, in proportion even to the rate of schooling, thus creating a social powder keg in so far as the school becomes the preserve guarded by a minority.

This is a pretty serious picture that obviously does not take sufficiently into account the flow of innovation that exists here and there, about which I shall talk in a little more detail in the second part, but I think that it was not bad to make this horizontal cut, which reveals all the same the principal defects of today's system, defects that call for urgent remedies.

Toward an Educational "New Deal"

I should like to end this essay with the second issue I just announced, namely, the problems of a new type of education, a creative school.

First, I shall emphasize the urgency of an educational "new deal." Given the picture I have tried to paint, one can ask oneself whether it is too late to redress the direction of education in African countries. I think not, but I do think that the time is now. Indeed, for several decades the effects of frequently aberrant practices have accumulated, and these practices tend to set up structures, structural imperfections that will be very difficult to correct later. Already one experiences difficulties, sometimes considerable, in changing something in education. Although traditions are not as old as in France, there is nevertheless the weight of habit, the ignorance of tomorrow on the part of many people, the lack of expectations. There are also egoistic interests and myths that are hatched, that are nourished like beloved chicks, if I may say so, but that most of the time are vipers. One arrives at a threshold of tolerance that will soon be exceeded. Indeed, this will take place when the school will have shaken up society in a fundamental way, when it will have unbalanced the economy without establishing a new equilibrium. Well, this moment, now, seems to me exactly like the most favorable time for a certain amount of innovation. Actually, certain illusions are now gone and outmoded.

You may remember that in 1961 UNESCO convened a conference on education for Africa at Addis Ababa. That conference had proposed that all these countries reach the goal of 100 percent schooling by 1980. At that time I had had the opportunity of making my contribution to the work of the conference; I did not emphasize the quantitative aspects of education, but rather the qualitative problems I believed were the priority.

At that time, I remember having said something like this: What is important to us is to know the direction of the rails before determining the power we must give to the engine. Indeed, we must know if it is leading us to a garage, or toward a station, or toward a precipice. Happily, the present direction has reversed the approach that was envisaged at Addis Ababa, and the Teheran Conference, about which you have certainly heard, chose the notion of functional literacy, as a function of social progress. For their part, the African state officials did experiments, sometimes bitter, and have come back from them. They touched with their fingers—I was going to say with their toes—the depths of certain precipices, and certain limits were revealed. I think that the redressing that is in process in genuine. But the process is long and slow. There are opposing currents.

The aim, then, is to change the school—returning to a phrase of Alain that I find very beautiful—"to change life." First, the appearance of the school and the students' physical environment should be changed. I think that the air-conditioned school in the Brazilian northeast or on the Mossi plateau would resemble more a space station emitting absolutely inaudible and undecipherable "beep-beeps" for the poor mortals who are, if I dare use the expression, on dry land. In the 17th century, too, there were the Ridiculous, Affected People who asked that the "conveniences of conversation" be brought to them, but during the same period certainly at least 95 percent of the people were illiterate, and besides that, as La Bruyère tells us, in the flat land of human beings there were also types of animals, as he tells us, male and female, bound to the earth and who, upon straightening, showed human faces. "In effect," he said, "they are men." The school that would remain totally detached from the surrounding reality would prepare for African countries situations of the type that were possible in the 17th century, but that today seem to me to be totally untenable.

Thus, bringing the school nearer to its surroundings, first by not giving it privileges in terms of architecture, with the qualification that a minimum of comfort is indispensable for the students, the same for furniture and decoration. I believe that that is essential for young people. Because the child reflects much more easily his surroundings than the adult, one must increase the local decor so as not to uproot the child too much. There are Bamileke boxes, masks, African dances of all types: One could make magnificent castings of busts of Benin art. Above all, one could ask students to contribute to the decoration of their classroom by drawing their inspiration from that which they see around them. I think that to live in beauty through one's own effort is the first stage of rooting.

As for the syllabus, the methods, and the structure, this is a huge subject, and as you know it is in primary education that the work began. Quite often reforms were then a little too superficial. Certain publishing houses, yielding to easy solutions, thought that in order to Africanize a textbook, it was enough to alternate Mistral and Camara Laye, or else Abraham Lincoln and Soundiata, or that it was enough to replace the apple tree with a mango tree and to put under the tree a little Traore instead of a little Dupont. I don't believe that this is the real way of adapting textbooks.

I should like just to survey certain disciplines that are essential in this field. First, the arts. There are now song texts that have been adapted well. I think you are familiar with the text, "Young Africa Sings" in which there are not only African folk songs, but also French, European, Hindu, etc. songs. In this field, the churches themselves have already made a choice and have exploited the prestigious capital that is the aptitude for rhythm and melody in African countries. Unfortunately, I think that there still persist in our schools a certain number of European songs that are untimely or deviant in relationship to the climate of the tropics.

In history and geography, the ministers decided upon considerable work in secondary education with the cooperation, one must admit, of our French colleagues who helped us create new syllabi in which about 30 percent of the credit timetable is devoted to the history and geography of Africa. I can tell you that I have lived through this experience: It was a veritable deliverance for our students, African pupils, who until then were forced to rack their brains in trying to follow the details of the geography of the Massif Central or the troubles of one Merovingian king or of Louis VI the Stout.

In French, the renewal has come later, but it is in process, and seems to me to be well under way. This renewal starts from the following proposition: French is not the mother tongue of young Africans. In that there is an obviousness that even now is no longer declared off-stage but that can serve as a corner stone for new methods. One can almost count on the fingers of two hands African students in whose homes an African language is not spoken. Even if the state is francophone, the society is not. In African countries, when 10 percent of the school-age population receives schooling, one can estimate

103

that 3 percent of the total population is literate. According to figures that were published at the Conference of French-speaking peoples at Niamey, one could number 1 percent to 5 percent of Africans who speak French correctly and 0.1 out of a thousand Africans who think in French. The colonial solution to this problem was strict and simple enough; it was cultural and assimilationist segregation. African languages were forbidden to the schools, and when you were caught pronouncing a phrase in an African language, the dunce's cap was put on you. Children were subjected to a pedagogy of repetition. The fact is that there was at that time scarce manpower to produce sufficiently good results. Of course the French that was thus mastered was always a little bookish, a little stiff, a little artificial, but in any case it was correct and reliable and some of those who went through classes at that time, the best ones, became well-known writers of talent. But the others? The others were bound to a type of servile imitation that went as far as copying the accent, the provincial accent of their teachers, whether it was the accent of Lille or of Perigord. One thinks of those Merovingian scribes who copied in Latin, who painstakingly imitated Terence or the legal writers in the era of Angustus.

But today the situation has turned upside down, and the school population is much greater. One cannot keep back the quantitative solution, the one that consisted of creating a contest for the children who are in school, while spreading literacy en masse, because after all that amounted to saying when we reach 80 percent literacy, we are certain that children will have a natural support for their schooling. We established, as a matter of fact, in the first section that this massive or total schooling is almost an unattainable objective.

From which we go to this second matter of fact: The African child is at least five years behind his French peer when he enters school because the French child learned his mother tongue by the most active and most effective method possible—that is, by means of life and activity. Thus elements of vocabulary, morphology, and syntax fall into place and the basic structures are totally absorbed without pain and even with pleasure since they are, so to speak, oozed out with a mother's milk, including the rhythm and melodic lines that are also very important in the spoken language, the down beats, the rests (everybody knows that the rests are also a part of music). But this backwardness of the African child arriving at school is not an absolute void; it is not a tabula rasa; there is something there; there is a "substratum," an arsenal of words, a network of forms, a small world of linguistic structures; consequently the point of departure is not the same: The incoming rails should not be the same; there must be a requisite shunting; one must reconnoiter the terrain, the substratum. I shall give an example: You can meet a young African child who will come and stand in front of you and who will say to you, "What's going on?" Of course "Que devenir" is not correct. It is simply the transposing of an African syntactic form. There are also contagious phenomena, not just with respect to pronunciation. There are phenomena that do not exist or that do not exist in the same form in African languages. I shall always remember that play that we were taught to perform and in which one of my friends had to start a reply saying "noble dame romaine" and invariably he made the following mistake "noble rame domaine." Why? Because he was Mossi and in the Mossi language the "d" and the "r" are interchangeable. Thus there is a difficulty that must be taken into account, there is a preventive measure that must be adopted, and I know that there are several institutes and linguistic centers like the Centre de Linguistique Appliquée de Dakar (CLAD) and the Bureau pour l'Information de la Langue de la Civilisation Française à l'Etranger (BEL) that are concerned with these problems. In other words, even for the mastery of French it becomes necessary to know African languages. Furthermore, I think that French should be considered not only as a language of culture but also first as an everyday, commonplace tool, a tool that should render routine services to the great majority of the people, as a means of communication, as a living foreign language, from which comes the method, the pedagogical approach that is more and more used, namely, to listen—first to listen—to speak, to read, to write— whereas before this method was not followed, and they started in directly with the written language.

Thus first: learn to speak. And, in this area, the problem of texts and the problem of the spoken expression is much more important than the problem of literature or literary history. And, in saying this, I think that it is not a matter of considering this as an anti-French choice. Far from it. We have established the futility of the competition for rates of schooling. Thus the alternative is as follows: Either one assures the essentials, like soldiers in a hard battle who regroup, who form squares in order to avoid disaster, and at that point one inculcates a practical mastery of the language up to a point where one crosses a threshold of no return in quality, in such a way that the surrounding erosion no longer has a hold on what has been acquired. Or one continues along the path of the automatic patchwork of French methods, and sooner or later will bring about a lingua franca more or less uneven that will also end up by crossing the threshold of nonreturn, but in the wrong direction, and at the end one will find himself with an autonomous language, a substitute for French.

If I have stressed this problem of the French language, it is because I think this subject is not so wide of the mark. Indeed, it is concerned with development. We have already emphasized the interaction between language and thought: When one does not master the idiom, one also does not master the thought, and if we want our students to have precise, correct, and accurate thoughts, like a good balance, I think it is absolutely necessary that they also master a language that has the same qualities. This is extremely important for future cadres, not only for writers but also for scientists. After all, if a philosopher uses indistinct vocabulary I think that at first his books without a doubt will sell badly, and the damage that he can do is quite diffuse and will only be revealed in time, perhaps creating some warped minds. But when it is a case of a bridge and highway engineer who makes his calculations on the basis of confused conceptual ideas, he puts the lives of his fellow citizens directly in danger.

The problem of using African languages is considerable. It is not a question here of treating this subject exhaustively. I shall say simply that the handicaps presented by the number of African languages has been exaggerated, by forgetting that very often in each African state today, there are sometimes two, sometimes three languages, and sometimes even one that is spoken by more than half the population. Sometimes two languages are spoken by 90 percent of the population. Thus there is a simplification that is not usually emphasized. There is also the problem of the richness of these languages, and it has been said that they are poor: In certain areas they are poor; in others, on the contrary, they are rich and can also be enriched by the addition of words pulled from roots common to all languages—for example, scientific terms. Moreover, let me point out that these African languages have been in the process of enriching themselves for decades since they had to face a certain number of necessities. For example, at home, in many African languages, a bicycle is of course not called a bicycle but an "iron horse," this being a term that has so much become a part of practice, that one no longer even thinks of the origin of the word. In the same manner, there is the "iron bird" for the plane. Or, to indicate the hospital or dispensary, one says "the house of cures" or the "house of the doctor." Or, again, to indicate the Centre des P and T, one says the "house of thread." These languages have enriched themselves a great deal, and they can do more. Nevertheless, there are obstacles. Although these obstacles are not permanent, they cannot be minimized, and difficulties remain: On the political side, because one must all the same have a choice, one must choose one of these languages: on the technical side, one must establish the writing of the languages; on the pedagogical side, textbooks must be reconciled, teachers must be trained, and there of course the difficulties are very serious, because suppose that we choose two languages for a country, it would be necessary moreover to recycle and train a great number of teachers in order that they can buckle down to the task.

Nevertheless I think that African languages must not be abandoned; they can already be used for adult literacy, because they simplify the difficulty; since the sound and the idea of the object are already blocked in, the only difficulty to overcome remains that of the sign. While in French literacy, the three difficulties are accumulated at the same time: the new sound to learn, the idea of the object, and the sign. I think that African languages can also be perfected by studies in university education, as the new syllabus envisages.

Lastly, I figure that even when the choice will have been made for one African language as the language of culture or the official language, this will not signify that languages of principal communication or culture like French will be abandoned, if only because they are bridges to the rest of the world. It is understood that at the Organization of African Unity (OAU) or the United Nations, it will be difficult to have Swahili or Hausa or Dyula adopted. Consequently French will always serve as the main language of communication.

In this connection, I should like to recall a sentence uttered by the French minister of National Education at UNESCO, two years ago: "The essential elements of thought and human feeling can only be expressed in French."

In this connection, I made it known that those who have tasted the language of Claudel, Baudelaire, and Racine up to the point of communion do not have the right to make such an assertion. Nevertheless, the French minister himself recognized that no language can claim to have at its command a wealth such that it can supplant all others. If humanity were suddenly reduced to one language, in my opinion this would be an insipid and sterilizing monologue, a cultural catastrophe from which the world would never recover. In reality, each language has something incommunicable. This is why African languages, which are a part of the common patrimony of man, must be saved, preserved, stabilized, written, and used.

Now I should like to pass on to the problem of sciences and technology. I think that a while ago it was suspected that Black African minds, in particular, were practically inaccessible to the sciences and mathematics. Today this prejudice has been erased since we have physical science and mathematics agrégés, students at the Ecole Polytechnique, and so on. And I remember the case of a child from the unknown bush of Upper Volta who was recruited practically by chance and who, in elementary mathematics, received very high honors. There is moreover a greater and greater percentage of science students among African students. It is my feeling that the man of the 20th century and even more the man of the 21st century must have a technical humanism, and I think that in our countries, for each newly recruited bureaucrat, one should have perhaps about 15 technicians who in short provide a counterbalance in the productive, technical sector.

107

But a debate has begun on this subject. Does one have to be liable for the creation of unemployed people while developing technical education, as has happened in the preceding phase, where one saw masons and metal-workers, for lack of job openings, turning finally toward other avenues to become clerks, constables, or policemen? I think that it is still necessary to train technicians in order to start the economic pump, since, while producing producers, by definition one is preparing people who will themselves invent solutions. But clearly all that must be planned, and this too is an imperative for the new school. I shall not press this point, although planning in Africa too often consists of declarations of intention because the verifiable variables are not sufficiently known and because the planner, moving in an extremely ambiguous and complex world that is difficult to test, resembled someone trying to interview the Sphinx.

I think, too, that it is necessary to step in and modify the relative weight of the educational cycles. There is the cycle of six years and that of seven years; isn't there a possibility of breaking all this up a little, anticipating for example an elementary school of four years followed by a "basic skills" school of four years, and lastly a formative school, already secondary, of five years. One can also disassociate certain disciplines that are frozen in the French system, or the opposite, which is what the Comité Africaine et Malgache de l'Enseignment Supérieure (CAMES) has accomplished with respect to philosophy, sociology, and psychology, which are separated in the French university system but which succeeded in being regrouped in Africa. We did not want philosophers who were not at the same time sociologists. The same applies to certain very elaborate specializations: cardiologists, extremely well-trained dentists. Perhaps we have a little less need of them in Africa than of general medical practitioners. Clearly this does not mean that I am against specialization, and I have had to defend this point of view at times when certain people tried to suppress purely and simply specialization. But I believe that specialization should be based on a choice of the party concerned, and, moreover, one should perhaps call in specialization after a certain period of positive work. Finally we must try to enlarge the base of selection while increasing the amount of manpower in basic education in order to functionalize the apparatus afterwards by careful and even rigorous selections.

The mentality that must be created among parents is a totally new mentality that is all the more necessary in Africa because the distance between the world of the parent and that of the school is much greater, in any case much greater than in France. It is necessary, as I have had the opportunity to emphasize, that parents interest themselves week after week in the work of their child, and not just when he is expelled. It is necessary, too that they follow the guidance of their children, since I have tried to tell them that to produce children is not a simple biological act for the perpetuation of the species; we must develop our children throughout life in order to make men of them. Similarly, by interesting themselves in the guidance of students, they are stating at the same time the problem of the general direction of education. Indeed in traditional Africa, the society that seemed withdrawn into itself was organized in such a manner that adults assumed the responsibility for the youngest children for a very long time, until an advanced age. Today disparate and sometimes virulent external influences bring all that back into consideration, and we are asking ourselves even today if we should not draw on the pedagogic methods used by means of oral transmissions in traditional African society, lessons for today's schools.

Thus if parents, teachers, and the public authority considered themselves all as passengers on the same ship, I think that the general guidance would be better adjusted.

What is there to say except that the school should be the concern of the whole village, and the village the concern of the school; it is in this way that we could put the school back in its place. By that I do not mean that we must drown the school in the complex of vicious circles or of misery that often affect the village. The school should remain a ferment, a leaven, consequently distinct from the mass but immersed and invested in that mass in order to act, and there I believe that we should in this way have the antidote, the antithesis of the insular school about which I have just spoken: It is a question of the community school. The CODIAM (Comité pour l'organisation et le Development des Investissements Intellectuels en Afrique et à Madagascar) has discussed these subjects so well that I would be ungracious to dwell upon them.

I think that education without social integration is necessarily mutilated and lacunary, and by integration I do not mean a simple going and coming between the school and the village, but the establishment of a new pedagogy, the key word here being the observation of the natural and social milieu and participation in that milieu. You know that the general attitude of the Black African does not aim at that. The black man now is in the world a little like someone swimming in water but who does not build a boat in order to master the water. There is a type of natural participation. The result is that at that moment one has more confidence in rites than in tools, and I think that that mentality should be changed. Magic and the belief in magic is even more frequently held: It must be removed to give way to an attitude that perceives the forces existing in the world, forces that can be analyzed, taken apart, put back together in order to change life around oneself by successive additions, not by a type of immediate and global change that would only be another magical attitude.

109

Therefore I think that the school must develop in our children critical attitudes, analytical and positive attitudes with respect to their surroundings, an attitude I would almost call aggressive, anyway a rational if not rationalist attitude.

Study of the milieu can thus become the axis of every experiment in the rudiments of science, language, reading, mathematics, and so on. One can size things up on the spot, and one learns not just with one's eyes and ears, but also with one's hands. Was it not said that man is intelligent because he has hands? Unfortunately, this is too often forgotten. I mean that one can even learn with one's feet, by walking, by bumping physically against objects, objects that henceforth will be actually known.

I also think that physical education should be developed. There I believe that the French system left us a not-too-brilliant situation, excuse me for saying it so bluntly. Perhaps it is not by chance that the civilization that produced Archimedes and Euclid is the same that created the Olympic games. There is in this expenditure of the body, in this body health an element of equilibrium that one recognizes more in the Anglo-Saxon system and that in the African case can be adapted, for example, by associating the African struggle with class curricula.

Manual labor, lastly, must create its own environment instead of submitting to it. However, one must not transform the school into an agricultural concern. Madagascar, from this point of view, opted for the solution of a common stream for four years at the start of primary school, a period after which there is an evaluation of students, a period of guidance. In Upper Volta, we chose two up-to-now almost parallel systems: The rural school is a short primary school of three years with one year emphasizing apprenticeship in the rudiments of language, writing, but also practical exercises to prepare modernized peasants. Clearly there would be more to say about this type of rural education; I would not want to dwell on it because I have already gone on long enough, but this does still pose problems because there is a risk of creating within the same country two types of schools that sooner or later will evolve in an antidemocratic direction.

If one wants the school, education, to be really a national education, it must concern itself with everybody without exception and not just with a successful elite. New types of teachers must be created, and very often we want to educate our children in the same manner as we have been educated. There is an Arab proverb that says that man is often more akin to his times than to his father. One should therefore educate children in the ways of their times and not in those of their fathers.

There are teachers who are engaged in rural education because they cannot do anything else, and they air their dillettantism and their boredom in this framework, as some of them who spend their time

110

flashing through the village on motorcycles with their transistor radios slung across their backs inundating the streets with the latest pop or rock tunes, which consequently constitute for students a veritable living counterpropaganda in relation to what they should teach. Thus I think we will need to train new types of teachers, as we are starting to do in the rural teacher-training schools.

And lastly we need a general civic education. Education must teach knowledge; that is to say, education must teach the fight against illiteracy, which otherwise lies in wait for all of us; education must also teach the way to earn a livelihood. Lastly, education in my opinion must teach self-direction, or if you will, being. In life, students will have just as much if not more need of character than of algebraic or physical formulae. We must not make of them robots who record a certain number of standard questions to which they furnish replies, or people who can only respond to the meaning of directions given by others but rather men in the full sense of the word—that is to say, creators and movers of society.

Thus it is a question—and this is essential—of placing a new human being in the world. Two years ago, the following question was put to students in an African school: "What are you?" And each time the majority of the students responded with a tribal affirmation, one saying "I am Mossi," the other, "I am Bobo." This is very important and shows the way in which each student situates or places himself in society. It signifies that the school has not succeeded in its curriculum, and personally I think that there is no civics without an element of geography and history in order to understand a little about the surrounding world. For example, the peasant or the African student who often enough sees a plane flying in the sky does not understand what it is because he does not grasp the concept of organized and differentiated space with a certain depth in its dimensions.

I also think that we should join this educational method with classical methods. School is not the only place for teaching, and in Africa you know that the radio, above all transistor sets, allow the great world news to be instantly known in the most remote corners of the earth. Sometimes when I am in an absolutely isolated village of Upper Volta I hear "This is Washington," "This is Moscow," and so on. This shows that the entire world is known to the entire world.

Movies and television also play an important part. I think, moreover, that movies in particular do not play a positive role in most instances. I shall always remember the scene I saw on the television at the information service at Ouagadougon (as there is no television in Upper Volta except for the city of Ouagadougou, there are only a small number of TV sets). I stopped to see what was being shown to the 30-old peasants who were watching. What were they looking at on the little screen? A showing of winter fashions by models in London and Paris! I want to tell you that such spectacles in countries as poor as Upper Volta seen by peasants whose standard of living I have just described to you are really regrettable. We must find something else to help them. I believe that, if we don't watch out, the movies will give Africans the false impression that the developed countries became developed with the stroke of a magic wand, simply because in the movies we are shown the most beautiful things, film stars dressed in the most elaborate manner possible. Africans who have not been to Europe will have the tendency to imagine that these countries were blessed and arrived on the scene like that. There is no historical perspective; they ignore Hercules' labors and the immense suffering that were endured in order to arrive at this paradise, which is, moreover, sometimes artificial. I fear that it is this which sometimes sets in motion the creation of certain attitudes on the part of young Africans, the formation of all sorts of clubs, of groups, of bands that surrender themselves to imitated, often adulterated forms of entertainment and borrow their names from the most shady sections of London or Chicago or elsewhere. I learned certain names, which I'll give you here: the "plunderers," the "razors," the "rockets," the "playboys," the "faces-to-faces," the "Cuban ambassadors," and other pleasantries of the same genre. There is a matter of escapism, an escapism that is costly to the nations in question. It signifies a sterile imitation that creates satellite minds and leads various peoples straight toward conformity.

In short, the type of mass education I evoke here is absolutely necessary because it can serve precisely as a support with reference to the new school. Continuing education is absolutely necessary as a technique, as a strategy below schooling, if we do not want illiteracy to sweep away for good the foundations of the school. Mass education allows us to speed up or rather to fall into step with today's world.

To sum up, I should like to recall the role of international cooperation in the establishment of such a new school. I believe that everything I told you could lead some people to think of a lessening, even a suppression of the cooperative assistance accorded the underdeveloped countries. The deception could lead certain parties to withdraw into their own shells, but today I think the world is too small for splendid isolation. I believe that development will either be interdependent or not at all—development, which Pope Paul VI said so strikingly, is "the new name of peace." I think one should not assist the underdeveloped countries in terms of one's own model of development of the school or of cultural development, but in terms of a model that should be fixed in an independent way on the basis of local realities.

On the other hand I consider that this cooperation will require going outside oneself in order to support the needs of others, since there is no cooperation without a sort of spiritual migration toward the other side, without a certain renunciation of oneself.

Lastly, we need to help countries to understand better their own needs, to understand the necessary qualitative changes. This is what is called the new pedagogy of the people, which is a preliminary to this discovery in the direction of a new school.

Thus it is necessary to concentrate efforts on the qualitative elements that will allow us to leave present structures in order to keep up with the new course of things: encouraging reform projects, training and recycling of teachers, every now and then purchasing new equipment, because sometimes qualitative equipment leads to a supplementary change. Thus in Upper Volta we thought of giving all secondary students training in typing before they knew how to do the least thing with their fingers. Of course, this posed the problem of furnishing typewriters.

In the development equation the school is an equivocal and ambiguous variable. Everything will depend on its content and its orientation, on the task it has been assigned. My friend Amédée Kahn, author of the book The Ambiguous Adventure, which you of course know, said "Man is born, man lives in a forest of questions, and every civilization is an architecture of answers."

If it is true that Africa must telescope two revolutions, the technical and the cultural revolution, the new school possesses in my opinion a great number of these answers, on the condition that it is not a cancerous school but an original and creative school, founder of progress, a school that, finally, will justify the profound words of the Wise Man: "The child is father to the man."

EQUITY CRITERIA IN EDUCATIONAL
PLANNING
John A. Smyth

The Demise of Efficiency Criteria

In recent years public discussion of the development of educational systems has included an increasing sensitivity to equity criteria in the selection of public policy alternatives. In developed countries, social class and ethnic inequalities in educational opportunities, achievements, and benefits have increasingly dominated debate on policy; in developing countries, rural-urban and interregional inequalities, among others, likewise have been salient. This interest in equity aspects of education has been due partly to heightened political awareness and intensified political pressure by disadvantaged groups, partly to the general cultural assault, particularly in developed countries of the West, on the utilitarian ethic, and partly to a growing public skepticism toward the intellectual coherence of "efficiency" criteria for investment in education. However, aside from particular causes, there may have been a certain inevitability in the demise of "efficiency" criteria, for reasons that will be explained.

"Manpower needs for development," which was once the most prominent efficiency criterion, now is widely discredited in nonsocialist countries, not only because so many educational plans based on manpower arithmetic have never been implemented for political reasons but also because it is viewed culturally as too primitive a concept, and scientifically as too flimsy. Without the apparatus of state socialism, manpower planning in principle is now seen to be unworkable anyway, and Western proponents of manpower planning, unable to reconcile the political reality of manpower/educational planning with the theory, have been increasingly drawn to structural and institutional reformism.

Other efficiency criteria have fared no better, even where they have been scientifically more plausible. The "social rate of return" criterion, for example, has had almost no direct impact on public educational investment policy in either developed or developing countries and has served mainly as an intellectual focus for skepticism about manpower planning. Unable yet to resolve satisfactorily problems of the quantitative scale of prospective educational investment,

---

*The views expressed in this paper should not necessarily be understood to reflect in any way the views of the author's employers.

which are the salient operational concerns of planning officials and which, it is hoped, have attracted the latter to manpower planning, devotees of the "rate of return" criterion have been increasingly drawn to free-market solutions and denial of a role for government altogether. However, like the "manpower need" criterion, the "rate of return" criterion is tarred with the same utilitarian brush, and in so far as the application of its logic also implies government activity— for example, for the purpose of manipulating social rates of return— it is operationally embroiled with the same problems concerning the role of the state in education, training, and manpower utilization that bedevil manpower planning.

Current interest in equity aspects of education, therefore, arises against an immediate background of political, cultural, and intellectual unease with efficiency criteria in education, in both developed and developing countries. Certain long-standing features of the institutional arrangements for the supply of educational services, in particular the sensitivity of these arrangements to what is broadly known as "social demand," provide the practical context for this feeling. However, there has not hitherto been much effort by educational planners systematically to reappraise either their preoccupation with efficiency criteria or the social, economic, and political analysis on which that preoccupation rests.

It is the dual purpose of this section, therefore (1) to suggest briefly why considerations of distribution probably will always dominate efficiency considerations in the supply of educational services under present arrangements for that supply, and (2) to discuss briefly some of the more obvious equity criteria and the possibility for consensus as to which, if any, are important. The article should not be interpreted one way or the other as making a plea for equity or efficiency criteria. That distributional considerations will dominate is seen not as something that ought to prevail, but simply as a fact arising from the conditions under which educational systems are presently organized. Much of the analysis depends on a view of what educational planning has actually achieved in various countries in recent years, rather than on what educational planners say they do or are trying to do. The degree to which the analysis applies to the socialist countries is not discussed.

The Role of Government in Education

That the state (here understood as a collective term for government authorities) is preeminent in education in developed and developing countries, socialist and nonsocialist, even where it is not preeminent in other spheres, is such an obvious universal feature of the institutional arrangements for the supply of educational services that its significance is often not clearly discerned. Indeed, it is frequently neglected even in the analyses of "radical" educational reformers and "innovators"—a curious neglect since somebody, or some institution, presumably is responsible for educational reform and innovation, even where it has been responsible for the mess to be reformed. That the state, rather than private corporations or individual educational entrepreneurs, dominates, and should continue to dominate, the supply of educational services in most countries undoubtedly has implications for the range of educational planning policy alternatives. In particular, it implies that distributional or, more loosely, "political" considerations probably will dominate educational investment policies. But this requires explanation.

Governments, of course, are not like the private corporations of classical or neoclassical economic theory. This is not to say that they are not bound one way or another by the laws of economics, but merely to note that their distinctive behavior in the market should be recognized for what it is, as some complex of economic and political rationality rather different from that of the private corporation. In the market for educational services, the demand can be viewed in standard economic terms as arising from a rational calculus by each consumer or potential consumer of the benefits and costs of purchasing these services—that is, as arising from the structure of private rates of return. In the aggregate, however, this demand does not confront the major supplier, the government, in the same way as it would a private firm: It confronts the government as a political imperative. Thus, educational services, while constituting a subset of all services that enter a society's economic behavior system, also constitute a subset of those services that enter the society's political behavior system, and in respect to the supply of which at any time there is an interaction between government and citizenry, of whom consumers and potential consumers of educational services constitute a certain (often privileged) subclass. In short, the educational consumer has both an economic and a political relationship with the supplier. There is a similar duality in the relationship between the teaching cadre and its employer.

It is, therefore, possibly naive to regard the activities of governments in respect to the supply of educational services mainly in "efficiency" terms, however desirable it might be that governments should administer educational systems more efficiently. Governments are preeminently political bodies. Indeed, it is not at all clear whether "efficiency" has any more meaning for governments other than as a measure of their legitimacy, which may or may not imply that in some sense they pursue "economically efficient" policies. In any case, "economically efficient" educational investment notably is a notion that has been urged on the third world by the main body of "development" specialists from the advanced countries of the northern hemisphere. Its status in advanced countries is rather weaker. "Manpower needs," for example, are things that poor African and Asian countries have, like the "need" for "responsible" administration and "planning" and belt-tightening generally. Questions of citizenship, opportunity, freedom of choice, discrimination, participation, and communication, if not regarded as frivolous, are believed to be rather beside the point, which is thought to be "development." A healthy Benthamite disdain for these expensive curiosities is thought to be the mark of a vigorous administration: Resources are limited, so they have to be optimally harnessed for "development," the argument runs; otherwise the country will never be "viable"; and if the supply of educational services is not determined by "manpower requirements" then resources are misallocated and "development" is retarded.

But ministers of education in poor countries, no more than in rich ones, do not willingly put on hair shirts. And, if after the past decade's exhortations, their attitudes toward the manpower plans drawn up for them still remain rather cavalier, if not entirely skeptical, they reflect at least a vigorous appreciation of what government is all about, if not of "development." Development assistance agencies in the West, such as the World Bank, the UN Development Program (UNDP), philanthropic foundations, and the like, therefore, in so far as they conceive their functions as being to provide aid to education on the basis of efficiency criteria only, are simply trying to square circles. And there exists no serious evidence that they have been successful in the effort. Governments go on doing what they always have done: trying to stay in power. And if that means paying lip service to efficiency criteria in order to get money and salve the donor's or creditor's conscience, then they will formulate the appropriate "assurances." What they do with the manpower plans and the like when the money is banked is embarrassingly well-known.

The Consequences of "Social Demand"

Educational investment planning clearly must be based on a recognition of the nature of the institution that monopolizes the supply of educational services and the nature of the relationship between that institution and the demand for education. The differential demands for educational services are political imperatives simply because the government is the government. As was indicated earlier, this does not mean there is no rational economic basis for "social demand"; on the contrary, the structure of private rates of return

117

probably is crucial. But it does mean that because private rates do not necessarily coincide with social rates of return (which constitute efficiency criteria), the government is politically hamstrung in its pursuit of efficiency objectives. How prepared a government will be to withstand social demand, say, for the purpose of achieving any particular efficiency objective, will depend largely on its power relative to the interests involved, and there is, of course, no reason to suppose in any instance that a particular objective will be feasible. Paradoxically, then, while to all intents and purposes governments "control" the supply of educational services, and an astonishingly voluminous literature and a thousand conferences have been based on the assumption that it is a pliable "instrument" for "development" in their hands, the reality probably is rather closer to the opposite. Governments, in respect to the development of education, are probably little more than instruments of the social demand for education and can hardly be otherwise. In this view, there is no surprise at the litter of abandoned manpower plans in the third world and elsewhere, or the frantic visions of an educational "crisis" among philosophers of "development." The fact of the matter may just be that, measured by what governments actually do and are able to do in education, not by what their planning officials say they ought to do, efficiency questions, as distinct from questions of distribution, just are not all that important.

However, in so far as the actual development of educational systems has been mainly a response to the structure of private rates of return (that is, social demand), with the public authorities continuously driven to expand the provision of places in education sectors with high rates and in other sectors providing access, and in so far as the pressure of social demand everywhere is distorted by the differential distribution of political power, the solutions actually reached to the distribution problem vary considerably in the degree to which different social groups participate in them. Since the structure of private rates of return typically is an inverse pyramid with the higher rates corresponding to higher levels of education, mainly because private costs apart from forgone earnings are held down by the tendency of public policy to minimize fees, the general effect of the pressure of social demand has been to cause most public authorities over time to shift more and more resources into the higher levels of education. Of course, this shift is inevitable once complete coverage at the lower levels is attained, but it is a striking phenomenon that throughout the third world, for example, the shift has occurred (and has been vigorously encouraged by external aid) even with significantly less than complete coverage of the lower levels.

The net result has been that at this juncture a great many countries now have large portions of their populations, chiefly the politically weak and excluded, who are without access to any educational services at all. A similar process operates in developed countries, although total exclusion is rarer there.

The operations of the market for educational services, therefore, while they ultimately produce a solution to the problem of distribution, produce only a pragmatic solution, not necessarily an equitable one. They do not necessarily produce either a universal minimum provision of educational services, even where this is a feasible budgetary burden, or an equitable distribution of educational opportunity, even where this is taken to mean little more than equiproportional enrollments by simple social category such as race or socioeconomic status. Even less, perhaps, do the operations of the market produce economically efficient solutions, except in terms of the parameters of the market itself as presently constituted. The resolution of the dilemma posed for efficiency by social demand has been so much dominated by pragmatic considerations of distribution that governments have even been prepared to tolerate high levels of unemployment among educated persons in order to enlarge the pool of access to the educational prequisities for whatever jobs are available and in the process have sunk manpower/educational planning without trace.

Measures of Distribution

Present arrangements for the supply of educational services do not necessarily produce either efficient or equitable distributions of these services but are not easily changed. Indeed, it is not at all clear whether they can be changed in their essential points at all. At least, any change less than that of getting government out of the education business altogether would be rather less than radical, let alone revolutionary. Short of that, it is clear that questions of equity have priority over questions of efficiency, if only because by its very nature the central concern of government in education must be distribution. To strike its own balance between conflicting interests and powers with respect to the present and future essentially is the problem of government, and this is plainly not essentially an efficiency, as distinct from distribution, problem, nor is it essentially a problem of more concern to rich countries than to poor ones.

Yet it is an obvious precondition for the resolution of the differential demands for educational services that there be a consensus on their equitable resolution. This does not necessarily mean that some groups will not be discriminated against one way or the other in the event but merely that equity is the only area in which a dialogue can occur. The problem of equity, therefore, lies at the heart of the settlement between citizens and state in respect to the supply of

119

educational services. A settlement, "efficient" or otherwise, in which there is no consensus as to its equity, simply is the rule of force and is potentially unstable for that reason.

Doubtless, the scope for purely subjective dispute about equity in education is rather large. If there is to be any constructive discussion, it will have to focus around objective measures, even though there be room for disagreement as to whether one or another measure is a better indicator of what is equitable. Essentially, there are two sorts of problems in reaching agreement upon an objective measure of equity in the distribution of educational services: The first is whether the equity focus is to be the distribution of educational services per se, rather than the distribution of things outside of but dependent in varying degree on education, such as income and wealth, citizenship participation, and so on; and the second is whether the equity focus is to be the concept of a minimum universal provision or some formal characteristic of the distribution itself, such as the mean years of schooling completed, or the coefficient of variation, or whatever. The two sets of problems constitute a useful matrix of measures for further discussion:

	Educational services per se	Education-dependent things such as income, citizenship participation
Minimum universal provision	for example, universal primary education, or compulsory schooling 5-15	for example, universal literacy, or income-poverty floor
Character of the distribution itself	for example, shape of the educational pyramid	for example coefficient of variation of incomes

It will be fruitful briefly to consider essential features of some possible measures in each of the four boxes in turn, beginning with the first column.

The Distribution of Educational
Services Per Se

The most common measure of an equitable minimum universal provision of educational services per se is, of course, universal primary education. In wealthy countries, universal secondary education is a more usual measure. Universal primary education is disputed by two sorts of "efficiency" critics: those who regard it under present arrangements as according primacy to schooling, which is considered an inefficient means of imparting whatever it is that is supposed to be imparted by primary education; and those who regard it, more primitively, as focusing on what is thought to be an education with only consumption, as distinct from investment, content. Recently, some critics of primary schooling have promoted the idea that such education is more appropriate for urban than for rural populations in developing countries, nonformal education being appropriate for the latter. Since much of the demand for education by rural populations probably is for an education similar to that provided to urban populations, this criticism raises equity problems of its own, particularly if universal primary education is a feasible burden for the government's budget.

Moving down to the next box, the shape of the educational pyramid is probably the most commonly recognized conceptual characteristic of the distribution of educational services per se. There is much room for dispute, however, as to whether one sort of pyramid is more equitable than another. For example, if the equity focus is access to basic education, a pyramid with a wide base and relatively thin enrollments at higher levels could be regarded as a more equitable distribution of enrollments than a pyramid with a narrow base and relatively wide enrollments at higher levels. If the equity focus is access to post-basic education, the latter pyramid might be regarded as a more equitable distribution of enrollments. In general, the equitable character of an educational pyramid is some function of the weights to be attached to the enrollments at the different levels of the pyramid relative to each other. Selection of the weights necessarily must be arbitrary; given equal weights, there is probably more consensus in favor of pyramids with relatively wide bases, on the grounds that greater access to basic education is to be preferred in equity to greater access for beneficiaries of basic education to continue to higher levels. The degree to which an educational pyramid is inequitable can be usefully, though arbitrarily, summarized by a single ratio if the unit costs of the different levels of education are taken into account: the ratio of total actual enrollment in the pyramid to the hypothetical enrollment if all students were given an equal amount of education within the same total budget outlay.

The educational pyramid, however, captures only one equity aspect of the distribution of educational services per se: the relation of enrollment at one educational level to another. But many critics of social inequalities in education are more interested in the equity of access to education, as between social class, race, region, and so on; equiproportionality, or "quota," measures would be their main concern.

The Distribution of Things Outside Education

The distribution of income and wealth is, of course, the main focus of most discussion about social justice, and some critics of social inequalities in education are more interested in the things partly dependent on education, like income, wealth, occupation, and so on, than in the distribution of educational services per se. Although it is difficult to draw a hard and fast line, these critics, with their concern for what people can or ought to be able to do with their education, are more inclined to an "instrumental" view of public policy and education than their colleagues whose focus is mainly on access to education. There is much dispute, however, as to how and in what degree things like income, wealth, and occupation are indeed connected to education, and some grounds for believing that the connection is weaker in developed than in developing countries.

A social problem that is possibly more salient in the latter than in the former is the simple capacity for citizenship, in particular the problem of literacy. If literacy is defined as one of the minimum prerequisites for meaningful citizenship participation, then a provision of appropriate educational services is implied. In recent years Western "efficiency" critics have vigorously disputed the literacy campaigns of the third world from the standpoint of a doubt about their ultimate "economic" benefits, particularly if the literacy education has not stressed what are thought to be "functional" (that is, economically productive) aspects.

In developed countries, the conception of a social minimum tends to be defined in terms of a floor minimum income, or "poverty line," and the like; and it used to be argued, though less frequently now, that such "floors" implied appropriate provision of educational services, on the grounds that the poor in the main could not be expected to lift themselves out of poverty without a basic educational preparation. This view has probably been one of the main rationales behind external aid to education in developing countries in recent years.

If the equity focus on income is not so much social minima but rather the character of the income distribution as a whole, the implications for the provision of educational services are very unclear. Much recent argument, particularly in developed countries, has been concerned to indicate that the connection between education and the distribution of income is "only" partial, whereas it used to be more commonly argued that the connection was "significant." Though this is rather like a dispute as to whether a glass is half empty or half full, the effect will probably be a greater skepticism toward the "instrumental" view of public policy and education, and more salience for a focus on the distribution of educational services per se, and, for that matter, more direct means of redistributing income. Such a movement among professionals actually would be little more than an adaptation to the prevailing circumstances of public policy, which in most countries has never seriously attempted to redistribute income through education or even through arrangements, such as fees, for bearing the costs of education.

Equity Criteria in Educational Planning

Since there are a variety of ways of looking at equity in the distribution of educational services—indeed the whole subject is obviously of continuing public concern and, for educational planners, full of potentially interesting methodological and technical problems—it is rather surprising that educational planning presently is mainly just embroiled with questions of efficiency. Doubtless, the emphasis on efficiency partly has reflected the bureaucrat's natural inclination and his distance from immediate political reality, but it has probably reflected also that manipulative view of education that has directed discussion of development and social change, particularly in respect to the third world in recent decades, and that has its philosophical origins in colonialism. Problems of distribution are of as much concern to governments of developing as of developed countries; indeed, they probably dominate in both. It is inevitable that the solutions will in varying degrees be "inefficient," and it may well be futile in the nature of things—the present arrangements for the supply of educational services—to hope that they will be otherwise. It is certain, however, that educational development plans that do not incorporate proposals for the equitable distribution of educational services, whether it is for common basic minimum provisions, less racial or regional discrimination, fair selection procedures, or whatever, will be entirely irrelevant.

NATIONAL RESEARCH AND DEVELOPMENT
CAPABILITIES IN EDUCATION
Francis J. Method

I. Education and Development

What we choose to call reform is necessarily determined by
our perception of the problem to be solved. The decision to reform
may be a decision to open up entry or to restrict it, to improve texts
or to do away with them, to extend conventional education or to develop
an alternative, to upgrade or to replace, to introduce new technology
or to go back to basics. These may be significant reforms or they
may only be changes. The term reform, as used in this paper, is
nearly synonymous with movement toward solution.

The process that gives direction to reform—that is, the process
by which understanding and consensus are achieved as to what the
problems are, may also be the key to getting reform moving. Once
there is consensus on the problems, the questions begin to suggest
themselves. Without such consensus, further research is likely to
be wasted effort—and may only serve to reinforce the problems.

If it was ever valid to consider that answers to the development
"problem" were to be found exclusively in the technologies and socioeconomic insights of the West, it certainly is no longer. Mahbub ul
Haq argues that "it is time that we stand economic theory on its
head and see if we get any better results" and points out that the
search for a new perspective on development has already begun
in the developing countries.

> Many of us of these countries, who are essentially prod-
> ucts of Western liberalism and who returned to our coun-
> tries to deliver development, have often ended up deliver-
> ing more tensions and unrest. We have seen a progressive
> erosion of liberalism, both in our countries and amongst
> our donor friends abroad. And we stand today dispirited
> and disillusioned. It is no use offering us tired old trade-
> offs and crooked-looking production functions whenever
> we talk about income distribution and employment. It is
> no use dusting off old theories and polishing up old ideas
> and asking us to go and try them again. It is time that
> we take a fresh look at the entire theory and practice of
> development.

It is apparent that education systems and almost all of educational assistance are bound up with a pattern of development that is

now being seriously challenged, though not as yet rejected in any but a few countries. Ralph Miller puts it bluntly: "Though this thralldom [to the Western, industrial system] becomes more enlightened over time, a program of Western-type economic development for the third world is really asking these nations to commit themselves to a system in which they are already the losers."

There is a ferment, a rethinking, and a self-assertion gathering momentum in the developing countries, and anybody who has his ear close to the ground in these countries can hear what Ki-Zerbo calls "the stomping feet . . . of the unemployed intellectuals [taking] the leadership of the medinas of Africa." This cannot be ignored, but more to the point, it cannot be listened to with a detachment that treats it as a phenomenon to be described and worked into a better articulated macroeconomic model. There is another voice, equally loud but less intelligible—hence less clearly heard by the leaders of the developed and developing worlds; it is the confused voice of masses of people being dragged out of a world that no longer sustains them into a world that doesn't understand them. If I may offer my some-what simple definition of the purpose of research and development, it is the need to understand the realities and perceptions of these masses of people and the dynamics of the modernizing processes that affect their lives, and thus to assist the development of policies and programs that at least begin to meet their needs and respect their desires.

Miller also argues:

The "formality" of these systems, in the strict sense, is an outcome of the vocational emphasis and the close link-age with the modern sector. . . . Given the very limited research, or even systematic questioning, into the rela-tionship between curricular content and job-and-social functions, education systems become more formal as they justify their content and methods in terms of tradition and long-standing definitions of the "educated man" . . . justifying their school programs by comparing them to allegedly international academic standards.

The injustices, structural imbalances, content irrelevancies, and learning obstacles of the educational system are often distorted mirror images of problems in the larger society. Consequently, one must consider that the possibilities of educational reform are limited by whether or not complementary reform is likely or concurrent in the larger social, economic, and political systems. Unless we are willing to argue that children should be educated to fit into unjust, discriminatory, and mean futures, reform must do more than refine

128

the pedagogy, improve the management, and substitute one content for another.

What point is there in even a good agricultural education when the child has little prospect of obtaining land or can't make an adequate living if land is obtained? What point is there in literacy when there are no books or newspapers in the villages? What point is there in teaching a child a language that is scorned in the "modern" sector? What point is there in instilling entrepreneurial dreams when wealth and opportunity are thoroughly controlled by a few families? What point is there in preparing a child for eventual professional training when access to the university is closed to all but the wealthy and privileged? What point is there in more humanistic teaching when employment is governed by certificates and examination passes?

If one is to argue for these and analogous educational efforts, one must also press for changes in the opportunities—in the labor market, in land tenure and farmer income, in the spread and impact of modern media and social services, in higher levels of education, and, ultimately, for very basic changes in the orientation of modernizing societies toward the majority of the people presently left behind and excluded. To do less is to encourage educators to prepare their students for the unattainable. Education must be planned in a realistic context and research leading to educational reform must look at the context as well as the educational system. It should be of great concern to educators that the current emphasis on developing and improving rural education systems seems to be proceeding much faster than are efforts to understand how rural societies actually work and what rural people already know and think they need to learn. A similar point might be made with regard to urban education.

Assistance agencies are, however, increasingly stressing "integrated" approaches that emphasize the close relation of education to other development efforts and focus on the development of nationwide learning systems. The U.S. Agency for International Development (USAID), for example, now observes that "there is a growing recognition in the developing countries that basic analyses of education are necessary, that piecemeal, marginal changes will not produce education of significantly better quality or larger quantity" and is concerned that donors "not encourage expansion of education without basic studies of the learning system in a particular country in terms of national goals and policies, and without the development of reasonable strategies." It is not so concerned that "education be defined as a 'sector' and studied as such, but rather that education be recognized as a vehicle for the realization of national goals, and that it be studied and restructured in these terms." Similar opinions could be quoted for most agencies.

Country programing and planning involving a wide cross-section of expertise and opinion seems to be becoming the rule rather than

129

the exception, both multilaterally with support from IBRD-UNDP-UNESCO and as a preferred policy of bilateral agencies such as USAID and the Canadian International Development Agency (CIDA). As evidence that this is not just idle rhetoric on the donor side, there is a growing list of countries that have been assisted in the process of fundamental reassessment of their national learning systems—Ethiopia, Kenya, Peru, Colombia, El Salvador, Nepal, Indonesia, Mali, Mauritania, Chile, Ceylon, and Tanzania constitute only a partial listing. The country programing and planning of education is now quite extensive, but it mainly governs the assistance planning of the respective agencies. In the fewer instances (such as those cited above) where this support has contributed to significant reassessment, there seems to have been extensive and prominent involvement of local educational leaders. The Education Sector Review in Ethiopia (assisted by IBRD and others, but conducted mainly by the Ethiopians themselves) is a good recent example. The involvement of a wide cross-section of Ethiopian leaders resulted in recommendations for fundamental restructuring of the basic education system, which now seem likely to be implemented.

Many argue that education should not be constrained by the dominant political and social values, systems, and realities but should strive to help children rise above them—challenging, questioning, and reforming them. One of the Bellagio participants in May 1972 suggested that the purpose of education should be to give people bad consciences. Paulo Freire argues for Concientizacao and a "Pedagogy of the Oppressed" and the Faure Commission argues for "Learning to Be." Others suggest that the function of education is to suggest alternatives, to employ a broader perspective and to supply a constructively critical voice that provides a counterweight to the dominance of bureaucratic and elitist interests.

There obviously are situations where the political forces have little intention of allowing education to serve any interests but those of their own segment of the polity. There is no use denying the existence of such situations, but they should be considered outside the scope of this paper, which assumes that assistance intended to foster educational reform will be directed to places where reform is in fact possible and desired. Though assistance will undoubtedly continue to countries not committed to egalitarian practices, there seems little reason to expect such assistance to result in reform.

But there is always a limit to the reformist role education can play, since it is basically the political system that funds public education. It will be necessary for educators to justify their role better and to recast the education system so as to fulfill it. If they are to maintain tolerance and support for free inquiry and questioning, they must increasingly show themselves capable of providing intellectual leadership and of contributing to solution of problems of concern to the larger society.

This is most true at the university level, the expensive capstone of the system. What is needed is not more contentious academic argument, but more leadership and the use of the forums of the educated to provide a voice for the inarticulate. National leaders often find their most vigorous opposition in the universities, and university advice and opinion should be weighed by whether it serves to assist the development of the whole society or to obstruct it and serve mainly the interests of the educated. If the universities and their elite product are to continue to be tolerated and supported they must become more service-oriented, both in the internal ethic with which they operate and in the external role they are seen to play through their various institutes, research and advisory groups, published works, and university service schemes. The Rockefeller Foundation and the Inter-American Development Bank (IDB) seem to be moving away from a concern with developing universities per se toward a concern with helping universities to work on problems of regional concern. Most donors seem to be shifting their support from general university development to support for individual scholars or groups of scholars, specialized institutes, and problem-oriented research projects.

The days when secondary education was justified on vague expectations that it was good for society and in some general way contributed to economic growth and social modernization seem to be coming to an end. Both a more activist mode and a more stringent justification of purpose are now being demanded (if only by the economic constraints), and educators will have to find ways of both broadening their focus and specifying their goals if they are to meet the demands of both their clients and their sponsors. Though there is growing assistance to the secondary level, and considerable experimentation, most attention seems directed to qualitative and efficiency concerns and to teacher training. One of the few current attempts to assess the role and impact of secondary education is the International Labor Organization program of education and employment studies.

Similar pressures seem to be confronting primary education. This is the level at which there is probably the most discomfort, disagreement, and uncertainty. There is a real conflict here between awareness that basic education is essential for any prospect of social equality, provides a foundation for social, economic, and political systems, and, in some sense, is an essential human right, and awareness that the present primary school system in most countries is extraordinarily expensive relative to national budgets, unconscionably wasteful and selective, and only minimally educative—and that often in dysfunctional ways.

The UNESCO-UNICEF revised policy issued last year has made this level the main focus for UNICEF: the study on "non-formal education for rural development" recently completed by the International Council for Educational Development (ICED), which was related to a similar study for IBRD, and a study in progress on functional literacy are two of its efforts in this direction. IBRD, Fonds d'Aide et de Coopération, Overseas Development Administration, USAID, Canadian International Development Agency, and Swedish International Development Authority are providing significant assistance at the primary level, but as yet there are only a few instances of support for major reform and experimentation with alternate forms of basic education. Some significant examples are the rural education efforts in Upper Volta (FAC-supported), efforts by USAID in Central America and FAC in Ivory Coast and Niger to utilize media, CIDA/IDRC support for the South East Asia Ministers of Education Organization (SEAMEO) initiatives in studying mass basic education, and UNESCO assistance in Mauritania, which is attempting to develop a basic education system based on Islamic education. The UNESCO functional literacy projects are perhaps the most extensive of these efforts.

Mass Education

Most would agree that it is useless to talk about equal opportunity unless everybody starts from some common ground, and there is a growing consensus that the movement for mass education must be supported, even though the financial means are not now apparent. It is necessary, it is just, and it is being demanded. The movement no longer seeks a simple expansion of what we now know as primary education (which mainly implies the preparation of the young for secondary education) but the development of educational systems that assist basic learning for all people (emphasizing functional literacy, numeracy, and vocational skills). However, before this interest can translate into significant new programs, answers to a host of basic questions must be found.

The question is not whether to support mass education, but mass education of what type(s)? By what means and with what approaches? Beginning at what age and for which age groups? For how many years?

Although such questions have not been resolved (many would argue that a different "package" must be designed by and for each country, and possibly for each subgroup within each country), it is now widely accepted that alternative approaches to the present primary school model must be considered and tried, including some that may bear little resemblance to primary schooling as we now know it.

In addition to the obvious necessity to provide relevant content, it is necessary to provide it in an appropriate form, through an appropriate vehicle and at times and locations that enable the individual to make use of his or her opportunity. As yet there is little experimentation with such large-scale alternate models.

None of the present institutional models seems capable of providing a basic education to all at a feasible cost. Any educational model in which the main cost is salaried teachers (up to 90 percent) will prove too expensive for mass application in many developing countries. With typical expenditures of $25 or less per child enrolled, even relatively wealthy developing countries, such as Nigeria, would require the entire government budget to provide six years of primary education to all school-age children, let alone to meet the educational demands of other citizens. The undertaking is even more infeasible for poorer countries such as Ethiopia, where some 95 percent are not now in school.

A partial response is the attack on unit costs and wastage. These are not two separate problems, but one. Unit costs can be looked at as the cost of keeping one student in school, or as the cost of producing one successful leaver. UNESCO has made important progress in quantifying the wastage problems, but as yet there has been little research identifying the causes and even less in studying the consequences and developing alternatives. Most research seems to have been done rather haphazardly by individual scholars only indirectly supported by assistance agencies and rarely as part of a concerted research program.[1]

There does not seem to be much room for improvement in unit costs; in fact, the pressures are to increase them. Student/teacher ratios are being reduced, auxiliary services, instructional media, better texts and facilities are being added, teacher salaries are increasing. While there is hope that these costs can be kept under some control, there is little prospect of reducing them. Nor, for that matter, is there much sense or justice in trying to reduce them. A consultant, completing his work in a West African country, makes a plea for realism:

> When I contemplate the primary school . . . the first
> thing that strikes me is not that it is a rote learning
> institution rather than a problem-solving activity-
> oriented one. No, the most obvious shortcomings are:
> (a) The building is falling down and the roof leaks;
> (b) The teacher is an untrained teacher and in any
> case has gone to market and his class is unattended;
> (c) Last time a supervisor visited the school on a
> professional visit was nine and a half months ago;

(d) There are three English books among 35 children and no arithmetic books;

(e) The teacher does not have a copy of the syllabus for the course;

(f) Six-year-old children in the first grade are learning in a language which is quite strange to them and comprehend little of what is being said.

The second cost, the cost of producing a successful leaver, offers more hope. These costs are so extreme in some countries that they can only improve; for example, in rural Guatemala, only 35 out of every 1,000 primary school entrants complete six years of primary school, even after repeating grades three and four times. It requires an investment of some 70 instructional years to produce one successful six-year leaver. Worse, over 90 percent of the dropouts leave before completing the third year, taking with them little if any educative benefit. This is an extreme case, but most other countries have patterns that offer substantial room for improvement.

Though there is as yet little progress in countering such extraordinary, near total, waste, it clearly results from something more serious than low instructional quality and inefficient management. Students are motivated to enroll and do not hold themselves back by choice but drop out when it is useless or difficult to continue. There must be severe rigidities, locational problems, intimidating injustices, and learning obstacles (particularly linguistic) that are almost impossible to overcome. Greater "efficiency," in the sense of reduced wastage, may require systematic reform.

It seems clear that "tinkering" with such a system is not going to solve the problem. The problem is that the school, as presently constituted, does not meet the needs of or lead to real opportunities for the mass of these rural people. The choices are either a very different type of school or a very different type of society, or both.

If the research emphasis were shifted from the attempt to explain why the learner doesn't fit the school (why the school is inefficient) to why the school doesn't serve the learner (why the school fails), research might then begin to suggest an education that is compatible with the learner and his or her reality. One of the more recommended emphases is for research on the consequences of success or failure (including dropouts) in school. Does it make any difference? To whom? How? Will more schooling provide similar benefits for others?

Some excerpts from the introductory essay by the authors of the International Bureau of Education (IBE) study "Antecedents and Consequences of Early School Leaving" seem pertinent:[2]

The importance of the early leaving problem and the nature of the concern it evokes are closely related to a country's educational purposes: where major emphasis is placed on education as a national instrument vital to political change or economic development, early leaving tends to be evaluated principally in terms of its impact on these collective goals. The efficiency of the education system looms as an important question especially where resources are short. . . . In these circumstances, the emphasis is on early leavers as an aggregate rather than as individuals and they are often dealt with in statistical terms. Early school leaving takes on a rather different meaning where education is considered above all as a basic right and social good to be distributed to as many members of the society as possible. Here concern is more with loss of individual rights and benefits. . . .

The great majority of studies on early leavers have treated the individual as the object of analysis and locus of the problem. . . . This attention is consistent with a usually implicit assumption that dropping out or early leaving is a voluntary act. This assumption is also reflected in the fact that remedial action is generally designed to change individuals, either directly or through modifications in their environment. Too little research has been done on structural characteristics of schools and even less on the active role of the school in discouraging children from continuing.

If dropouts do not differ in significant ways from those who went further, the schools have failed. . . . If a central goal of education is an improvement in the quality of productivity of individual lives, and hence national life, it is clear that an evaluation of education should include the relationship between schooling and life in society rather than just focusing on the pupil while he is in the closed environment of the school.

Analysis of the kind described above forces the schoolmen to consider what they are doing with their schools, and may provide answers to the attacks of critics like Illich and Freire. The former denies that schools accomplish anything except the sorting of persons on the basis of class characteristics, while the latter claims that schools do well, too well, at socializing

135

us into mindless acceptance of a passive role vis-a-vis
our environment. Together both urge that education be
seen as a truly developmental force, generating among
all men an awareness of their tremendous potentialities
as moulders of the world in which they live and giving
the insights and skills necessary to remake the world
according to their self-developed version of it. The
criticisms of Illich and Freire focus on the mass of
people denied access to schools and the larger numbers
who are systematically weeded out before having enough
exposure to begin to benefit from education. Other critics focus on the remaining few who may reap the economic rewards of educational certification, but are as
alienated from themselves and from truth as those who
never went to school, and perhaps more.

. . . Some of the research evidence clearly suggests
that it is the organization or climate of the school system
itself that discourages students and promotes early leaving. Hence the problem may be less a matter of the characteristics of the student and his family milieu, as is
commonly supposed, and more one of the discouraging
school that is inadequate to meet the demands and needs
of all children who enter it. Such questions require more
precise evaluation.

Little of this research and even less experimentation has been
done to date. Language problems are getting attention in several
countries, with assistance from the Ford Foundation (for example,
Yoruba primary schools in Nigeria) and UNESCO-UNICEF (for example, Quechua in Peru). However, these efforts have only begun to
suggest solutions to the problems of multilingual societies. IBRD,
UNESCO, USAID, FAC, and ODM are experimenting with media applications, but so far these efforts seem to have concentrated more
on delivery systems than on content or purposes. Apprenticeship
systems (such as INACAP in Chile and SENA in Colombia) are getting
attention from IBRD and others, mainly as promising ways around
the financial impasse. Most agencies support curriculum reform
(for example, the United Kingdom's CEDO), but most of this work
seems mainly refinement of the existing curriculum and improvement
of the materials and pedagogy. There is little research into what
the curriculum needs are, either nationally or comparatively. Experimentation has been mainly in vocational training, teacher training,
and literacy efforts.

The IBE study cited above suggests three reasons for the relative paucity of research on the consequences of early school leaving

and on the relation of education to the leaver's role in the world outside the school. Educators and educational systems generally consider
their responsibility to the student to end when he leaves school; few
educators have seen any purpose in testing for differences between
the more and less schooled, since it is almost universally assumed
that education does make a difference; and, a more cynical reason,
some systems may care who drops out but otherwise consider early
school leaving a desirable phenomenon, reducing pressure on limited
facilities at higher levels. It might also be argued that the paucity
results from a general lack of sustained support for research of any
type or purpose.

It seems fair to say that despite the general concern for the
efficiency and efficacy of primary or basic education, most assistance
to this level has supported expansion, managerial improvement, and
"tinkering" rather than research on basic educational needs or the
development of more appropriate delivery systems. Put another way,
most assistance to basic education (mainly primary schools) has tended
to foster development along conventional lines, strengthening the
modern sector and preparing students for more education but doing
little to support local change and to assist people with the problems
of living outside the modern sector.

Educational Research

Most problems eventually come down to a question—a why?
How? How much? How long? What? Most such questions lead to a
search for a model or an index—a tool with which to measure and
manage the system. The question of Why? is not usually answered,
except inferentially, by such tools.

Attention is beginning to turn to the demand side of the educational equation. This is partly because planners despair of controlling
the supply of educational places or of relating these places effectively
to manpower demands through the use of policy tools, in part because
the educational supply has already outstripped the capacity of the
economy to absorb its products and to sustain its expansion, but
mainly because of a growing awareness that the critical problems
of education are questions of value and motivation, rather than of
content or numbers.

Why is education so important? Why do parents send their
children to school and why do children desire to continue in school?
What do the clients of the education system expect it to do for them?
What do they expect to learn and how do they evaluate that learning?
What rewards and opportunities do they expect as a result of school-
ing?

137

Equally important: What are the sources of dissatisfaction? What skills are not being learned? What needs are not being met? Why do children drop out of school? Why do young people leave the rural areas, refuse certain employment, stop using their mother tongue, affect new social values and behaviors? Why do some parents resist education for their children?

The research that is going to be most valuable to educational reformers is that which provides insights into questions such as these, in forms intelligible to the users of education as well as to the planners and providers.

A new research emphasis such as this would be more than just additional research on a different range of questions. In important respects this research is conceptually different from the aggregative and evaluative/descriptive research presently available and would probably require a different relationship between researchers and research institutions and the researched.

Much more of this research must be done by local researchers and through local institutions than has been the case to date. This is suggested for three reasons: (1) much of this research involves sensitive issues that may be difficult for the "outsider," including unfamiliar national researchers, to grasp; (2) as research attempts to assess values and motivation, considerably more insight into local behavior and local perceptions will be necessary for interpretation of results; and (3) much, if not most, of the necessary information will not be accessible to the short-term researcher or "off-shore" scholar. Most data will not be available in published form, and the data centrally available in most systems (even where the data exist in some accessible form) will continue to be too numeric and aggregative to provide much insight; hence, much of the most important research can only be done by extensive field work (including follow-up and tracer studies) and close contact with local communities, families, and leaders.

This is not in any way to say that there is no longer a role for external expertise or research assistance; in fact, the need is greater and more urgent than ever. Rather, it is to say that the need is changing toward support for local institutions and locally controlled research, toward the development of local researchers rather than the provision of actual field researchers, toward technical assistance with the assessment of research and information dissemination rather than with the research itself, and toward assisting experimentation and pilot study of alternative educational efforts on the basis of the research implications.

This seems to be what is most needed as a research emphasis in the major developing countries. There is neither the time nor is it wise to spread resources to do a similar range of research in all countries. The commonality of some problems suggests efforts such as the following.

1. Attention should be directed to countries with similar problems, attempting to find answers useful to more than one country. This may mean regional groupings, associations, and institutions, with shared training and cooperative research efforts. However, it may also be useful to think of building links and shared efforts between countries with similar problems, regardless of location and proximity.

There is support from most agencies for a wide variety of regional associations and institutions serving more than one country within the region (SEAMEO, with its resource centers, seems one of the more promising), for efforts within the Commonwealth and AUDECAM matrices, and for agencies establishing their own regional and subregional offices with specialized advisory staff such as UNESCO's Regional Education Offices. There is almost no support for interregional activities except indirectly through headquarter-level policy and research bodies such as those of UNESCO or secretariats such as the Commonwealth secretariat, or through bringing officials into contact at headquarters through such mechanisms as the Economic Development Institute (EDI) seminars provided by IBRD.

2. There is little sense in continuing to duplicate experiments, repeat mistakes, and develop models independent of accumulated experience. Much can be done now in the way of sharing information and experience—through publication of case studies, sharing of key staff, international conferences, and consultative groups. This seems generally agreed, and one of the more promising recent developments is the apparent openness of agency and country files and the willingness to share information and experience.[3]

3. There are a number of examples of educational developments in a given country having significant demonstration effects for other countries. The ILO studies in Sri Lanka (Ceylon), Colombia, Kenya, and elsewhere are clearly leading planners to rethink priorities and tools. The Schools Television projects in the Ivory Coast, Samoa, Niger, and El Salvador are being looked to as models. It seems probable that the successful experience with the Sector Review in Ethiopia will lead to similar efforts elsewhere. Particularly interesting is the Tanzanian self-reliance experience, since it was not instigated by external assistance but is now a prominent example referred to in most discussions of educational innovation. Thus, what is experimentation in one country may be research evidence for another, and vice versa. More might be done to speed up the circulation of such experience between the developing countries themselves, possibly by means as simple as arranging for key educators to see for themselves what other developing countries are attempting.

4. There is a range of research effort that can only be done internationally. It is impossible to get much comparative information with which to evaluate relatively unitary and homogeneous national systems without contrasting across borders. One of the best examples is the six-subject study of educational achievement carried out by the International Association for the Evaluation of Educational Achievement during the 1960s, which is now providing precious comparative information on cross-national achievement and some of the factors that account for it. By definition, cross-national research requires multinational participation, if not sponsorship.

5. Another range of research is on the more purely technical aspects of education. Such research is often beyond the financial and technical resources of most developing countries and in any case will be used in many places irrespective of where it is developed. This might include the development of media and instructional technology, basic research into the nature of learning, data-processing systems, inquiry into alternatives to the copyright and patent laws, school-building design, research into the learning aspects of intermediate technology, and so on. IBRD, UNESCO, ODA, FAC, USAID, and the Ford Foundation are giving attention to such problems.

Local Leadership and Expertise

Resources are clearly necessary for implementing reform, but they are not a sufficient condition. In general, where there has been real commitment to reform, the necessary resources have been available (though perhaps not as easily as they should be), while, where there has not been, the infusion of more resources has had little effect.

Several countries have the resources to undertake reforms that they themselves know to be needed. However, the systems continue to expand more than they change. Educators know how to do, and they have the resources to do, more than they are now doing and to do it better, yet they don't. This suggests that part of the problem or shortage is one of understandings, priorities, effective leadership, and political capacity. It also suggests that at least one of the keys to the problem is in the developing countries themselves.

The point was made by one of the participants at Bellagio in 1972 that for assistance agencies to take the position that there are not enough experts in developing countries and that there is still a major need for imported expertise is to admit the failure of their own massive efforts to create indigenous leadership and expertise. There are systems and leaders in every country, often supported by the efforts of development assistance during the 1950s and 1960s, and for agencies to try to go counter to them is to undercut their own creation.

Attention must be paid to the leadership and decision-making capacity in the developing countries. This is not just the need for more and better research or ideas for projects—in fact, some would argue that there are already so many of these that it muddies the waters and allows any given research-based suggestion to be countered with another, leaving decision-makers confused and at the mercy of the theoreticians, with the result that they mainly act on nontechnical criteria, especially in response to pressure for more schooling.

Even where critical questions are being asked and alternatives are being suggested, they are often not acted upon, either because they are not known or understood by the key people or because those key people have their own opposition. A consultant working in East Africa wrote recently regarding research on education in rural areas.

> We would, of course, be a great deal happier if it were possible to make use of indigenous research on the matters at issue, but there is virtually none of it. It is possible that some of the insights necessary to stimulate research on such subjects as primary school examinations are not yet widely enough present among those in responsible positions: but it may also be that subjects of this kind represent political problems of such difficulty as to deter people from approaching them scientifically. What is, I think, clear is that there will not, in fact, be much research into these important issues until there is conviction in the countries concerned of the necessity for and possibility of such research.

Educational reform in developing countries cannot be approached as though the systems exist in a vacuum. There is an educational establishment in the developing countries just as there is in the developed countries. They now have large systems with their own stock of physical facilities that must be maintained and used, politicians who have built their careers on certain educational positions, economic plans that have adopted and reinforced certain conceptions of the relation of education and development, a wage-employment labor market that has been structured on formal qualifications, an accepted value of education that is deeply embedded in the people and that creates powerful pressure for more of the same education that gave power to the present generation in the modern sector, and most importantly, large numbers of teachers and educational civil servants—in some countries half or more of all those in wage employment—represented by increasingly powerful unions whose main imperative is to protect the status quo and ensure the continuance of emoluments, improved working conditions, valuation of prior training, and ever increasing wages.

There is little that can be done without the political will in the countries themselves to confront their own systems and to make the politically difficult decision that reform is necessary. External bodies cannot make this decision, but they may be able to facilitate it. Finances may be key in one country, research facility in another, and the availability of a feasible alternative in another. However, the leaders are already there and need to be assisted, not supplanted; the ideas need to be induced, not imported; and the most important resources to mobilize may be human and political, not financial.

It may be necessary to separate those countries that only have people and problems from those that also have resources. In the first countries, it may be true that finance is the key to making anything possible, whereas in the second it may be much more of a need for new ideas and the leadership to implement them. Quite different positions may have to be adopted regarding assistance to the 25 or so least developed countries than are adopted toward those more capable of financing whatever educational services they decide upon.

Having argued that at least some of the countries must accept more responsibility for their own problems and exert more forceful leadership in reforming their own systems, one is tempted to place the entire responsibility on them and view the role of international assistance to education as little more than a financial transfer. This would clearly be irresponsible and would facilitate neither expansion nor reform.

Expansion of assistance is clearly helpful and is expected to continue, but the effects it will have will depend on how and for what it is used, particularly whether it is used to support the attempts of local educators to bring about reform or merely to supplant them with imported expertise, materials, and financial underwriting of educational expansion.

Further, educational reform is not just "their" problem. Education is being questioned throughout the world, and the reform and reconceptualization of education in developing countries, though it may arrive at different conclusions, is not completely separable from similar efforts in the more developed countries. The problems are too complex and the tasks too urgent for educators to argue the right to err independently. There is a mutual interest in supporting reform and learning from the mistakes (and successes) of others.

The emphasis of the past decade on basic institution building and the filling of short-term skills needs seems to be ending. There seems to be a general deemphasis of the training of additional top educational leadership and a growing emphasis on the upgrading,

142

further training, and support for research by educators already at work. Several agencies have allocated funds for broadly determined areas of research and scholarship, to be allocated on a fellowship basis to local scholars, preferably in local institutions: for example, the Ford Foundation in Brazil, Thailand; ODM in Commonwealth Africa; USAID and IDB in Latin America; Rockefeller Foundation in Latin America and Asia. IDRC is explicitly charged with supporting research, wherever possible by local researchers. There is growing support for training educational researchers, administrators, and curriculum specialists in local institutes and in counterpart relationships rather than overseas. IBRD includes educational planning in seminars run by its Economic Development Institute, and UNESCO has similar courses associated with the Regional Education Offices. Both bilateral and multilateral agencies include counterpart training in their technical assistance, and it now seems more emphasized than is the technical assistance.

There is much more that can be done to strengthen local research and local educational leadership, particularly in strengthening local research institutions and local or regional professional organizations, but there seems to be a clear and growing pattern of support for such efforts. Perhaps the main criticisms are that despite the growing support for local efforts there are too few examples as yet of effective partnership or collaborative effort, Cooperation often means the assistance of expert teams ("expert" being nearly synonymous with "expatriate"), and assistance agencies themselves have been slow in making use of local expertise and research done in local institutions.

External Assistance and Educational Reform

One of the most difficult issues underlying the entire discussion of "education," "development," "assistance," and the social, economic, and political values inherent in the terms, is the question of how far external agencies can go in encouraging reform and restructuring of education systems.

While there is some tolerance for external agencies employing economic criteria as a condition for assistance, there is little tolerance for and much hostility toward any attempt to impose judgments of social values. In spite of the fact that it is generally acknowledged by both donors and recipients that the basic problems of education are problems of values and relevance, external assistance has relied mainly upon macroeconomic and quantitative tools for planning education and has not used equity criteria or shown much concern with social costs and relevance. In part, assistance agencies have not

143

been oriented toward such concerns, but they have also been effectively proscribed from being so.

Similarly, on the part of local educators, most concern has been with the expansion of education and the meeting of manpower needs, with only secondary attention to content problems and equity considerations. Even at the primary level, where many countries are committed to universal enrollment, content irrelevancies and social inequities are treated as problems mainly as they result in dropouts (inefficiency) or financing problems. Again, it is not that local educators are unaware of or unconcerned about such problems, but that they are faced with overriding political and economic imperatives, which leave little time or resources to work on other aspects, even were there a consensus on alternatives and the political will to act.

This situation results in a curious and often self-defeating adversary system, pitting external bodies, with their resources and agency mandates, against internal political and educational leadership, with its local imperatives and inadequate resources. "Cooperation" in such a context can often mean paternalistic intervention on the one hand and xenophobic defensiveness on the other.

One of the results of this has been that although there is considerable opinion that educational reform requires decentralized administration and decision-making, most assistance for research and planning has been channeled to central ministries and institutes attached either to the ministry or to one of the prominent universities.

To a considerable degree, as long as the developing countries are in competition with the developed countries (in whatever sphere), they are forced to organize and develop in similar fashion. In fact, since they are starting from an uncompetitive position, they must sometimes accelerate the process, even to the point of making some of the same mistakes more rapidly and more traumatically. There are distinct limits to the degree of relevance of education to traditional forms and values that can be achieved without limiting the ability to compete internationally. There are real questions of how much university-level education, for example, can be deemphasized without increasing the reliance on imported technology.

However, a basic impetus for development is the desire to get out of the impotent position of dependency, of being a recipient. Thus, the competitive nature of development is largely a drive for autonomy and self-sufficiency. It is logical to expect a measure of nationalism as part of the development process—in fact, it can be seen as a positive and necessary force. One of the primary tasks of external assistance is to respect this process in such a way that nationalism does not become xenophobia and insularity, with consequent self-mutilation, stoppage of growth, and blockage of communication.

The debate over the direction of educational reform may be less a debate between the appropriateness of a "Western" model and a locally derived one than it is a struggle for control and an insistence upon local decision-making.

Some countries (developing and developed) may feel that it is not possible or wise or necessary to develop fully autonomous relationships and encourage the development or retention of separate value systems. I do not deal with that question here, except to assert that it is unrealistic to expect much basic, structural educational reform as long as the developing countries are in subservient positions. It is more possible after countries have moved to a position of substantial autonomy, or at least to a relationship with the developed world that is of their own making and in which they have substantial control over their own affairs. Countries that do not feel this control will not likely have the self-confidence to assert their own values and to look inward to reform their institutions to meet their own needs.

The drive for independence, following from the drive for a competitive rather than a subservient position, also means a drive for equality. Inferior education, or education that is seen locally as being inferior, will be resisted. Countries are striving to gain control over their own societies and institutions, but this does not mean that they are willing to accept second best. In fact, it often means the opposite, sometimes to the point of taking pride in having "our elephant whiter than theirs." Universities must not only be as good as their European counterparts, they must look as good, with at least equally impressive buildings and landscaping.

Some cautions for educational reformers, particularly external bodies, seem to follow from this:

1. Though much of the movement for educational reform in developing countries is a move away from dependence on "Western" models, it remains true that models that are unacceptable for the more developed countries will not be readily accepted in the less developed countries. Reform that is part of a worldwide effort, including experimentation in the developed countries, will be more acceptable than that which is not. International research and experimentation should be a joint effort, working on common problems and looking for understandings and solutions with general application. A separate set of activities directed exclusively to developing countries, particularly when financed mainly by external sources, will be resisted as tending to foster a second-rate education for second-class world citizens, regardless of its objective feasibility, practicality, and relevance for developing countries.

2. If, as many argue, there remains a need for educational efforts in individual countries, which are radically different from "mainstream" efforts, such efforts must be initiated locally.

External bodies can assist local innovators and innovative centers and stand ready to support their efforts, but they cannot press alternatives upon countries. It may now be said that the surest way to ensure the failure of an innovation is for one of the external agencies to become its chief proponent. In the few instances where countries have adopted their own educational models—as with Tanzania and "Education for Self-Reliance"—a key element in the model's acceptance has been that the reform was proposed and supported by local leadership. There are few instances where enduring major reform has been successfully proposed or imposed from the outside, except during colonial rule, but there are many examples of attempted reforms that failed because local leaders had not had a sufficient shaping influence for these reforms to meet local needs adequately and for leaders to implement them under their own sponsorship.

3. Though much of the need for educational reform stems from the very real financial constraints and political, economic, and social problems of formal institutional education, the search for and presentation of alternatives should not be argued on such negative considerations, but rather on the more positive ones of how the alternative provides more relevant education, better opportunity, more equity, or otherwise provides an improvement in the ability of the system to meet the needs of the people whose choice it is to participate in and accept the system or not.

A few illustrations. If agricultural or rural education is presented as a response to the problem of urban drift and urban unemployment, it will likely be resisted by those who resent being kept "down on the farm" and who see their opportunity for advancement into the "modern" sector being blocked and foreclosed. A rather different response can be expected if this education is part of a focus on agriculture and rural development as a primary growth sector and thus such education is made part of an effort to improve the lot and opportunities of the farmers and others living in rural areas. The difference is more than a shell game to convince the farmers to accept what must be done anyway. The perceptual distinction results in a different set of goals and criteria and can thus allow quite a different type of education to evolve.

Similarly in urban areas, if renewed attention to apprenticeship or on-the-job training is presented as a response to the impossibility of building enough craft shcools and polytechnics, the applicants are justified in seeing their education as inferior and a second-choice entry to the technical training institution. However, where it can be shown that such education is a surer and quicker means to employment, or that it enables training that can't be accomplished in the schools, or that it provides opportunity at a more convenient place and time or at a cost the applicant can afford, a more positive response can be expected.

146

Such distinctions seem critical to the debate between formal and nonformal educational approaches. There seems to be general agreement that there should only be one education system, that there cannot be a main system reserving the more desirable and efficacious opportunities for a preferred group, with the remainder relegated to a secondary or alternative system with second-choice means and opportunities.

On the other hand, there is agreement that alternate means of stimulating learning and providing opportunity can be found, some of which may be as or more efficacious than the extant system. The task of reformers is thus not the development of an alternate system, but the demonopolization of the present one, making it more flexible and open, able to incorporate a sufficient variety of means and to offer a curriculum broad enough to serve the educational needs of a diverse clientele.

The same distinction should be made in distinguishing between the education systems in developed countries and the systems in developing countries. Though clearly circumstances are very different in the most and the least developed countries, it is not acceptable to argue for a different type of education because of the difference in capacity. The distinction must be made in terms of needs. Clearly a very poor country cannot sustain an education system on the European or American pattern. However, more important (and certainly more politic) than the argument that such a country can't afford the education system of an industrialized nation is the understanding that it needs a very different system, with its own scale, priorities, and content.

Political and cultural autonomy may be more readily achieved than economic—where sustained growth at a reasonable level and self-sufficiency in basic commodities are reasonable goals, but full autonomy is essentially impossible and undesired. The politically influential people in most countries themselves benefit from economic dependence, and reform that threatens their economic position can be expected to be stubbornly resisted. In any case, political and cultural independence seems more important than economic autonomy for purposes of obtaining movement toward reform of educational means and content.

Although educational systems may come to be more carefully tailored to local financial realities and more sensitive to local traditions, values, and social realities, they will still be expected to produce the mixture of middle- and high-level skills the economy requires. Basic reform of the size, shape, and composition of the post-primary (or postbasic) educational output will remain closely tied to the economic system and its priorities, with the opportunity for educational flexibility closely tied to the skill needs of the economy and the degree of flexibility obtained in the labor market.

147

Educational reform can't ignore the motivation of individuals. In fact, it must start with the motivation of individuals, provide them with the information and opportunity for decision-making, and then trust them to act in their best interest. The line of action necessary for longterm change is to work directly on the "signals" and reward structures, including the social values and prestige that determine the demand structure of the system. Evaluation of such demand structures presupposes that the country has reached some consensus on its long-term goals.

Cultural factors are closely related to personal and group identity (hence motivation) yet are a largely neglected area of development activity, both in the application of external assistance and in the use of local resources. Much of such activity as has occurred has been in the nature of cultural exchanges, which are only indirectly supportive of local artistic and cultural efforts. Curriculum efforts have concentrated on adapting content and forms rather than adopting locally derived materials and practices.

The themes of "reassertion of local values," "relevance to local society and traditions," and mutual respect for the diverse peoples of a pluralistic world recur over and over again in current discussion of education and development. Yet little has been done, and most movement has been toward the values and structures of the industrialized social and economic model.

Though the specifics of what might be done are not yet apparent, there is substantial agreement that one of the first steps toward educational reform is the strengthening of local social science research. As well as strengthening the capacity for such research, it must be given a stronger and more legitimate place in policy-making.

There are strong recommendations (most prominently from the economists and social scientists themselves) that social science research must not only be done by and/or in close cooperation with local researchers and research institutions but must deal with local problems. It must get beyond (below) the macro-issues of the econometricians, demographers, and political scientists and provide more basic information and insight on local values, needs, motivational factors, and concerns. It must help planners to plan rather than just project; explain the labor market rather than just count the workers; explain the motives rather than just describe the phenomena; and provide a voice for the people's needs rather than just a description of what government is providing and its consequences.

In the long run, the development of better data bases and research traced and checked over time is essential, even though it may not, in the short run, provide the answers necessary for decision-making.

Nevertheless, much more is felt to be known than is now being utilized, and one of the first priorities should be a serious effort to

148

pull together, evaluate, and disseminate existing knowledge. This can be done for modest amounts of money. Further, if directed through the local academic communities and institutions (rather than done by imported researchers or done "offshore"), it may be one of the most direct ways of involving institutions of higher education in the real problems of their societies.

This seems the point to which the discussion of how to proceed in bringing education into some sensitive relationship with the values and needs of local societies keeps returning. The only way to do this without being interventionist or paternalistic on the one hand or xenophobic and defensive of the status quo on the other is to develop the local capacity to undertake open and academically excellent research on the problems facing local decision-makers. Such capacity and achievement is felt to be the key to the self-awareness and self-confidence needed to effect local reform.

If external assistance can contribute to this process, it can play a role in educational reform. If it cannot, it cannot do much more than continue to assist the further expansion of education systems that are the counterparts of the systems of the industrialized world.

Notes

1. Some useful summaries of existing research and emerging needs: "Antecedents and Consequences of Early School Leaving," Educational Documentation and Information Bulletin No. 182, UNESCO: IBE, 1st Quarter, 1972; "Social Background of Students and Their Chance of Success at School" [as above], No. 179, 2d Quarter, 1971; Roland G. Paulston, "Non-Formal Educational Alternatives for Ethnic and Disadvantaged Groups," University of Pittsburgh, 1972 (mimeo); William J. Platt, "Research for Educational Planning: Notes on Emergent Needs," UNESCO: IIEP, Paris, 1970.

2. Prepared for the IBE by Russell Beirn, David C. Kinsey, and Noel F. McGinn of the Center for Studies in Education and Development, Harvard University, 1972, pp. 12-27.

3. As examples, one might point to the cooperation afforded Coombs's ICED team in the IBRD-UNICEF study on nonformal education for rural development, and the James Sheffield-Victor Diejemaoh study of nonformal education in Africa (USAID-supported) and to the IEA multinational studies of achievement; to the open publication of the ILO country studies on education and employment; to the availability of candid policy papers, sector reviews, and monographs from most of the agencies; to the flow of conference papers, and specialized papers from the UNESCO bodies and other secretariats; and, not incidentally, to the openness of information and opinion encountered in the Bellagio meetings.

VECTOR PLANNING FOR THE DEVELOPMENT
OF EDUCATION
William J. Platt

In their report Learning to Be (Faure et al., 1972)* the members
of the International Commission for the Development of Education
brought together a world picture of the movement of education in new
directions. The movement, although of great variety, is not aimless.
It is a search for a learning society. The search requires a commitment to accelerating innovation as a process—innovations that explore
on a large-scale basis the changes that hold promise of major improvements in equality of opportunity, in relevance to individual and
societal development needs, and in greater effectiveness per unit of
cost. Under this challenge, educational planning must become largely
the planning and management of the process of innovation.

Much of educational planning in the 1960s could be characterized
as target planning—that is, the programing of educational activities
and flows to meet quantitative levels at specified times in the future
within projected resource constraints. Target planning, while still
necessary in guiding the allocation of scarce resources in education,
may need to be subordinated to what I shall call vector planning. By
this term I mean the designing, programing, and diffusing of educational innovations, giving particular attention to the direction of movement likely to result and making provision for the use of feedback for
self-correction.

Perhaps a useful analogy to help explain vector planning is the
art of aerial navigation. In a flight plan, one knows the general orientation—the vector—for his destination but will depend upon subsequent
positional fixes and the changing conditions of wind and weather aloft
and en route air traffic in order to correct his progress along the
way. So too in education we need vectors for getting started in the
right direction and en route feedback for making course corrections.
But this analogy is too simple in that the educational navigator must
simultaneously give attention to many vectors at once to make sure,
for example, that progress toward diversifying educational offerings
doesn't bring with it an unfavorable effect upon student mobility, or
upon unit cost. And the analogy is too simple also in that ultimate
destinations of educational progress are less known than the general
direction in which we want to move.

The concept of vector planning may be useful because it puts

The views expressed herein are those of the author and do not
necessarily reflect the views of UNESCO.

*Bibliographical information on references cited is in Biblio-
graphy at end of this section.

primary emphasis on the direction of change, without presuming yet to specify absolute target levels to be achieved at destination. This is also realistic in view of the uncertainties of predicting specific educational outcomes for particular learners through the employment of particular educational resources. Education is not that much of a science. But it is a quest.

A job of planning, then, is to select from among the repertoire of possible arrangements and experimental evidence those programs that prima facie, offer reasonable prospect of helping to transform education in desirable directions.

As a means of illustrating vector planning, some of the frequently observed orientations of educational reforms consistent with the recommendations of the Report of the International Commission and with the emerging development objectives and ethics are listed below. It should be cautioned that the vectors to be selected in a particular case would need to be uniquely tailored to the values and objectives being sought in a society and to a diagnosis of how existing and possible learning arrangements contribute to or impede the achievement of such values and objectives. The following listing, of necessity, is expressed in highly condensed language.

Vector	Planning Implications
1. Toward lifelong education	redefine education's system boundaries in time and space, ultimately to include the learning society
2. Toward diversification of learning opportunities	revise admission arrangements to encourage multiple entry and re-entry into educational activities
	provide plural offerings in school and out of school to serve a variety of learning wants and styles
3. Toward mobility of learners from one educational experience to others	design ladders, bridges, linkages from nonformal education to formal, across disciplines, among courses, from one level to another, interregion and inter-country
4. Toward education as an integral part of other development efforts	identify education and training dimensions of development programs and projects in other sectors

151

Vector	Planning Implications
	plan mutual adjustments so that education and other efforts reinforce each other
	stress through education the preparation for performance in the world outside the classroom, not just preparation for more schooling
5. Toward equality of educational opportunity	prepare school maps with view to equalizing spatially the access to relevant education
	organize "second chance" arrangements to serve drop-outs and push-outs
	remove obstacles to full participation in education by girls and women
	identify causes of educational inequality
6. Toward relating the world of work to education	organize work-study programs, school-connected apprenticeships, simulations that introduce world-of-work problems and materials into the curricula
	coopt employing establishments, farming cooperatives, and so on to offer education and training activities
7. Toward enhancement of the quality of life, artistic expression, and cultural development	include indigenous creative arts in school and community activities— music, drama, artistic expression
	encourage students to find and record traditional indigenous folklore and art, as was done in preparing Foxfire (1972)

Vector	Planning Implications
8. Toward a scientific point of view	include simple do-it-yourself science experiments in primary and secondary school curricula
	teach powers of observation
	foster drawing of inferences from observations
	use local environment to understand ecological balance
9. Toward solving educational problems by harnessing new technologies and the findings of behavioral sciences	establish cooperation between education and communication media of TV, radio, newspapers
	examine possibilities of self-service education centers in libraries and community centers
	apply the concept of "education as liberation" (see International Commission Report)
10. Toward mobilizing resources not now employed in education	inventory skills and facilities in the community having learning potential
	enlist volunteers as aides, animateurs
	institute systems of student fees and loans so that beneficiary shares in the cost of his education
11. Toward serving the remarkable learning capacity that characterizes the early childhood years	undertake research and development to find feasible combinations of parent education and community efforts
	harness informal education potentials such as TV and radio

Vector	Planning Inplications
	recognize the intimate connection between early childhood education and the further liberation of women
12. Toward democracy in educational content and learning processes	suppress hierarchical distinctions among teachers, between teacher and student
	foster participation in educational governance by representatives of education's major stakeholders
	make school attendance voluntary
13. Toward teaching by inquiry and problem-solving methods	train teachers in inquiry processes such as the use of convergent and divergent questioning
	encourage student-to-student inter-action as distinguished from only student-to-teacher interaction (see Postman and Weingartner, 1969)
14. Toward higher edu-cation's responsi-bility for leadership in national and com-munity development (see Leys, 1971)	involve universities in solving de-velopment problems
	explore national service arrange-ments by which university students can reimburse the state for part of their educational benefits.
	link universities with the reform of other levels of education and of nonformal education
15. Toward education for international under-standing	apply materials developed in UNESCO's network of associated schools
	convene multination committees to examine curriculum materials for fairness and tolerance

Vector	Planning Implications
	simulate international problem-solving in classroom
	encourage international exchanges of students and teachers
16. Toward international cooperation in solving educational problems	draw on multilateral agencies for advice and documentation regarding experience in educational innovations
	join networks that share information and risks in particular types of educational innovations
	participate in regional and international seminars and conferences on education

A number of principles can help guide the application of vector planning in the necessary restructuring of educational efforts. A first one is to take a good deal of care in selecting points of entry—those points in the formal and nonformal education system that offer interesting potential for experimentation, where there is a climate of readiness to take risks along one or more desired vectors of change, and where there may be leverage for propagating and diffusing more widely the benefits realized in the innovation.

Since points of entry are specific to a given situation, it is hazardous to give illustrations. In one case it may be the widespread perception of a need for in-service updating and reorientation of teachers. In another it may be the beginning of reform of an obsolescent examination system. Again it may be a pioneering effort in adult education well adapted to certain felt needs. Alternatively it might be experimentation with shorter cycles by which learners can acquire mastery of a set of needed understandings or proficiencies. The point of entry might well be even external to the formal education system—for example, a staff development program in an employing establishment—but at the same time have the potential to be usefully linked in a work-study arrangement to some level of formal schooling.

In looking for points of entry, special attention should be given to indigenous micro-innovations. These are the too often neglected local departures from conventional educational practice in which a pioneering teacher, principal, district supervisor, or even group of students is using an approach that offers progress along one or more desirable vectors. Indigenous innovations with learning potential may have developed outside the formal education system, in an employing establishment, in a club or association such as a cooperative.

While in nearly all indigenous innovations, there is an important ingredient of personal and sometimes charismatic leadership, there are generally other essential elements that can be combined to favor more systematic experimentation and can facilitate propagation of successful results. The trick is in first having sufficient sensitivity to identify such spontaneous innovations. After identification, there is a need to see in what way the mobilization of additional resources would help movement toward desired vectors. The resources to be mobilized are not only those of finances and expertise but also the organizational resources for the experiment itself and for the subsequent propagation. It is psychologically important for future adopters elsewhere to become involved early in the experiment so as to build a sense of commitment and to start thinking of the modifications that might be required for transfer.

Mr. Philip Coombs, in assessing experiments in nonformal education for rural development, says that too often there existed no "contingency plan for success." By this he means that countless educational innovations, even though locally useful, have remained small-scale pilot projects. No one bothered to ask, "What if we win? What if the scheme really works?" Propagation elsewhere in the district, region, nation, or beyond seldom happens automatically. While there does not need to be a large-scale master plan at an early stage, at least there should be contingency planning for the next stage of diffusion.

In planning for propagation of successful innovations, careful attention must be given to possible scale changes. These are the discontinuities that might occur in going from pilot operations to substantially larger implementation. If, for example, the pilot operation depends on the free time of people otherwise employed (say community health or agricultural agents), one has to ask about the availability of these resources under larger-scale conditions. The same must apply to the joint use of facilities. Often such harnessing of underemployed resources can be arranged for under larger-scale operations, but only by means of significantly different political arrangements. These need to be anticipated so that cooptation can evolve naturally to aid the propagation and diffusion process.

Included in my definition of vector planning was the provision for feedback. This is in conformity with the cybernetic concept that decision-makers and planners can learn experientially when feedback loops have been designed into an operation and when provision has been made for iterative corrections in the light of such feedback.

And it must be appreciated that corrections can apply not only to activities themselves but also to the goal structures that gave rise to the experiment in the first place. In short, vector planning is itself a learning process.

In many cases where the vector selected is designed for a long-term benefit—say, improved international understanding and tolerance—one will have to settle for short-run proxies to measure feedback in the attainment of the longer-term objective. Thus in the example cited, one might measure pre- and post-attitudes reflecting tolerance and intolerance toward members of another local group, and then, with some reason, extrapolate these findings to the longer-term vector of international understanding.

A purpose of all planning is to get as far as possible within the area of maneuver defined by resource constraints and knowledge constraints, and to explore means of widening this area of maneuver. Fortunately, the boundaries of both kinds of constraints in education change with time. Therefore part of the feedback design should be that of learning from probes into the boundaries of resources and of existing knowledge. In the case of resources this might be illustrated by an educational financing arrangement that instituted user fees and scholarships covering part of education previously state-supplied, to see whether in so doing truly additional resources might be harnessed, while still moving toward equity. With respect to probes of the boundary of knowledge, presumably the innovation itself is plowing new ground locally, if not for some other locations; responses and outcomes from such probes should be monitored in the feedback system. But in addition every experiment should try to incorporate probes that would increase the area of maneuver for this and other experiments.

A final principle to be observed in applying vector planning is to watch for indirect and side effects of a program undertaken for selected vectors upon other desired vectors. Trade-offs and opportunity costs are perhaps the very essence of planning. An excessive preoccupation with goal interdependencies could of course stifle decision-making. But it would be hoped that programs and innovations can be found that offer positive benefits for several desired vectors. A reform of the examination system, for example, might at the same time aid in democratizing education and increasing its environmental relevance, provide incentives for inquiry learning, and so on.

Planning as Process

Up to this point I have dealt primarily with the substance of helping orient the directions of the quest for a fundamental restructuring of learning arrangements. But the substance cannot stand alone; equally important is the process of planning. As Ralph Waldo Emerson said, "What you do speaks so loudly, I cannot hear what you say." Educational planners must be aware of the silent language of their practice. If their style of planning is participatory and openly responsive to learners' wants and concerns as well as to overall constraints, planning can reinforce educational vectors toward democracy and equality of opportunity. If the style is technocratic and hierarchical, that silent message will drown out whatever effort is intended toward favorable vectors.

The inquiry into planning as process in education is greatly aided by the work of Huberman (1973). He identifies three models illustrating how changes take place: the "theory-into-practice" model, which is the rational sequence from discovery through implementation; the "social interaction" model, which emphasizes person-to-person awareness and adoption; and the "problem-solving" model, in which the user diagnoses his need and collaborates with others in trials and adoption. All three processes are at work to some degree in any innovation, but one model may need to dominate in fitting local administrative style. It seems likely, however, that the direction of educational reform and of development ethics mentioned earlier will require increasing reliance on the problem-solving model.

In The Politics of Expertise (1972), Benveniste has contributed importantly to our understanding of the relationship between planning on the one hand and policy-making and implementation on the other. He disposes of any false innocence the planner may have harbored by demonstrating throughout his book that "the planning process is both politics and technique and the role of the planner involves both dimensions" (p. 17).

Benveniste shows how the process of planning can affect the substance of policy by virtue of the expert's altering the expectations of decision-makers. He shows that for planning that can make a difference—what he calls "intentional planning" to distinguish it from "trivial planning" or "utopian planning"—planners must work with decision-makers in forming working coalitions of clients, implementers, and beneficiaries. This is a start into the broader territory, much of it unknown, of participatory planning.

There is not space here to elaborate adequately on this critically important aspect of educational planning after the turning point. The following two suggestions on participation must, however, be mentioned. The first is derived from a small book of lectures Margaret Mead delivered on the generation gap. In Culture and Commitment (1970) she sees mankind arriving as pioneer-immigrants on the shores of an era made new by the pace of technological advance and by the recent awareness of the finiteness of earth's resources. But curiously, the young among these pioneers are more familiar with these new shores and with the language used there than the adults, since the young, unlike their parents, have been reared only in a finite and interdependent world of instantaneous communication. Miss Mead's insight that children's prevision is in some respect superior to that of adults reared to values less appropriate to the new era suggests that educational planners, dealing as they do with helping to design the future, must find a way to involve representatives of the young as well as all of those who have a stake in the educational enterprise.

Second, the technique of simulation and gaming would seem to offer potential for both enriching the quality of vector planning and for broadening participation in the process. Simulation is the modeling of a real activity or system, in which one or more players act as independent decision-makers seeking to achieve their objectives in some limiting context. The principles of developing games or simulations and applying them to education and decision-making are well described in Clark Abt's Serious Games (1970). While some game structures are complex and need computers to show the consequences of successive rounds of play, what I have in mind are much simpler "manual" games such as were developed in the Ecuador* project.

The features that would appear to recommend the gaming technique to participative vector planning include the following:

(1) It is a way of experimenting with alternative educational innovations and alternative points of entry under conditions of a

---

*An interesting application of simulation in education in a developing country is to be found in the cooperation between the Ministry of Education in Ecuador and the University of Massachusetts Center for International Education. The project is funded under the auspices of the United States Agency for International Development (Evans and Hoxeng, 1973).

The Ecuador project was undertaken to explore some of the potential of nonformal education in Ecuador. It was found that nonformal educational materials in the form of games that could be developed by Ecuadorians drew considerable interest and seemed to be effective in increasing participants' understanding of the social and physical environment and how they might exercise some influence over their own development.

An interesting application of simulation techniques in training for cross-cultural work is described by M. Schnapper in "Culture Simulation as a Training Tool" in Focus, International Development Review, no. 1, 1973, p. 3-5.

FIGURE 1

Vector Planning

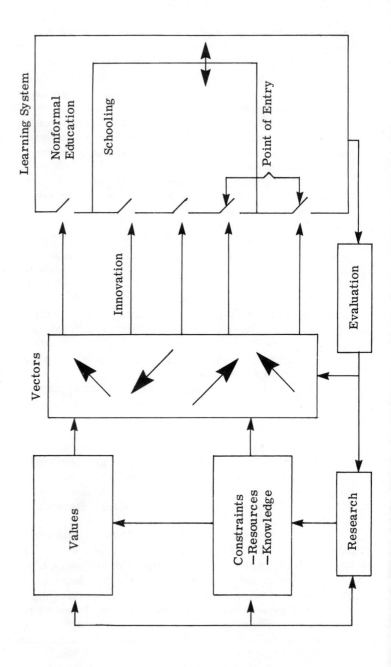

changing environment and under various degrees of uncertainty (the latter can be introduced into the game simply by the throw of dice or by spinning a pointer).

(2) The experimentation can be undertaken by either representatives of those involved in educational innovations, or by the real actors themselves, but without the risk of irreversible and costly consequences of real operations.

(3) Simulation relaxes the constraint of real time, permitting the playing out of several years of interaction during a few hours of simulation.

(4) As suggested by Benveniste above, the planning job must include the formation of working coalitions of clients, implementers, and beneficiaries, many of whom have both common and competitive interests in relation to vectors and to particular proposed educational innovations.

For the foregoing reasons, it would appear useful to employ simulation and gaming as a means of developing consensus on desirable vectors of educational change, as a means of identifying interesting options among innovations, as a means of exploring points of entry, and as a means of learning about propagation and implementation of successful local innovations. Because games are participative and have been found to be motivating, they could be a way of involving those on whom successful educational innovation will ultimately depend.

Summary

Vector planning is diagramed in Figure 1. One selects various vectors of reform or reorientation, the selection being conditioned by societal values and taking account of constraints in resources and knowledge. One identifies promising innovations found in theory or practice likely to promote movement in the vector direction, and chooses those points of entry for innovations in the formal or non-formal system where readiness for change and potential for propagation are favorable. One designs in a continuing evaluation to help the process to become self-correcting and to generate results for guiding other experimentation in the future. Where possible, such evaluation should apply the principle of comparing experimental and control situations, with pre- and post-observations of outcomes.

Bibliography

C. C. Abt. Serious Games. New York: Viking Press, 1970.

G. Benveniste. The Politics of Expertise. Berkeley, Calif.: Glendessary Press, 1972.

P. H. Coombs. The World Educational Crisis: A Systems Analysis. New York: Oxford University Press, 1968.

Ethiopia Education Sector Review. Education: Challenge to the Nation. Addis Ababa: Ministry of Education, August 1972.

D. Evans and J. Hoxeng. Ecuador Project, vol. 1. University of Massachusetts, Center for International Education, 1972.

E. Faure et al. Learning to Be. UNESCO-Harrap, 1972.

Foxfire Book, ed. by Eliot Wigginton. New York: Doubleday, 1972.

M. Huberman. Understanding Change in Education: An Introduction. UNESCO IBE, 1973.

International Labour Office. Employment Policy in the Second Development Decade: A United Nations Family Approach. Geneva, 1973.

C. Leys. "The Role of the University in an Underdeveloped Country." Fifth Commonwealth Education Conference Report. Canberra, 1971.

R. Maheu, "An Aid to Reflection for Necessary Renovations." Prospects (UNESCO) 3, 1 (1973).

M. Mead. Culture and Commitment: A Study of the Generation Gap. London: Granada Publishing, 1972.

Neil Postman and Charles Weingartner. Teaching as a Subversive Activity. New York: Dell Publishing, 1969.

PRIORITIES OF INTERNATIONAL RESEARCH IN EDUCATION
Torsten Husén

In the following I shall try to outline briefly three problem areas that seem to me to be of highest priority all over the world, both in the economically developed and the developing countries. Major emphasis will, however, be put on the latter.

Adequacy of Institutionalized Education

Universal elementary schooling was introduced in Western Europe in the middle of the 19th century, when the family could no longer serve as a training ground and when parents had long working hours. A certain level of literacy was needed among industrial workers. In many countries the compulsory elementary school was often resisted by the peasant class, partly because it was felt to be an intrusion upon their prerogatives to train their own children and partly because this function was fulfilled by letting the children begin work with their parents at an early age. The developing nations have, to a large extent, either inherited or tried to emulate the institutionalized school practices of the developed countries. Their secondary school system is, in many ways, a replication of that of their former colonial masters. The elementary schools have, by and large, been developed according to the model of formal education that emerged in Europe or the United States.

In recent years the lack of institutional adequacy as well as the formidable costs of running a conventional school system have resulted in various suggestions of introducing formal or out-of-school alternatives to formal school education. Considering the type of economy and cost development in the developing areas, it has become increasingly obvious that in the foreseeable future, it is difficult to envisage the implementation of the Western type of elementary schooling of full-time instruction for all children over a period of five to seven years. The institutional patterns of wealthier nations are not applicable in most of the developing ones.

Under the heading of adequacy of institutionalized education a series of problems can be subsumed that have to do with the explicit or implicit relevance of the objectives of the educational systems.

The educational objectives need to be clarified much more effectively. It is striking that in adopting educational strategies for developing countries, certain objectives are contradictory. One cannot, for instance, promote economic growth and equality of educational opportunity without letting these two clash occasionally. Just an expansion of educational facilities is not a sufficient condition for economic growth.

The school as an institution emerged with the task of promoting primarily cognitive development in children, that is, imparting certain knowledge and skills. In the developed countries, the scope was later widened to include some socializing functions—the inculcation of values and preparation for adult working life. The goals of the school in the Western world could be divided schematically into (1) imparting knowledge and skills, (2) providing custodial care, (3) contributing to socialization, and (4) inculcating certain values. The emphasis on these four goals would have to be quite different in developed and developing countries, but the emulated formal school model implies, by and large, that the pattern would be the same in both types of countries. Analyses based on empirical survey data derived from appropriate population samples in developing countries are badly needed in order to arrive at a proper set of concrete goals that will adequately serve both the individual and society.

The high wastage rate in terms of dropouts and repeating is a convincing indication that the educational systems in many developing countries are not in harmony with the sociocultural system, the family, the economy, and the value system, that is, of which they are supposed to be integral parts. One of the main shortcomings, pointed out by many observers, is the lack of integration between schooling and working life. The elementary school lacks a profile of its own in the sense that it does not equip its pupils with a repertoire of skills and knowledge that makes them better workers or farmers. Instead, it implicitly strives to prepare them for the next stage in the educational hierachy, which in its turn tends to prepare them for the next one. Many of the activities (one is tempted to say rituals) of the school serve mainly to perpetuate the system itself by self-feeding selection procedures.

The preoccupation of the wealthier countries with one single academic track has been strongly criticized. The same tendency is even more prevalent in many developing countries. The verbal-abstract-recitation atmosphere tends to alienate the students from the world of work.

Massive attempts ought to be launched by means of surveys conducted in three or four countries representative of their respective areas, in order to assess more specifically what needs could be served by a formalized educational system. Such studies should be linked to the attempts that have been initiated by means of international seminars in curriculum development and evaluation to provide guidelines for curriculum improvement. Furthermore, they should be tied to the comprehensive evaluation of entire educational systems (including four developing countries) that have been carried out by the International Association for the Evaluation of Educational Achievement (IEA). Thus, for instance, science curriculum and outcomes of science education have been related to the various social, economic, and pedagogical factors that are supposed to affect learning in school. It is thereby possible to identify certain key indicators that can be manipulated through the school system by policy and planning (for example, through the curriculum).

In some developing countries the highly competitive and/or selective practices that have particularly characterized the secondary school systems of the former big colonial countries have not only been copied (or earlier imposed), but in some cases even become more pronounced. Schooling above a certain minimum is regarded mainly as a means of social promotion and an avenue to enhanced social status. This has resulted in a strong emphasis on examinations, diplomas, and certificates, which serve the purpose more often of social selection than of certifying that the student has acquired a relevant amount of competence. Such a system also tends to reinforce the atmosphere of abstraction and verbalism. This has tended to disparage vocational or trade education, which would have to be reconceptualized in terms of the relevance of the examination and diploma requirements.

The relevance of the curriculum is, of course, reflected in student motivation. The mere fact that about half of the elementary school students have dropped out before the end of the third school year could be interpreted as an indication of lack not only of motivation but also of relevance. But motivation is not only related to the teaching-learning strategies employed. It has already been pointed out that the institutionalized patterns of schooling that were once developed in Europe are to a large extent inadequate and inappropriate in the third world. It is important to identify the proper setting for the school as an institution and to realize its limitations in an underdeveloped agrarian society where the family or the local community has to be the major agent of education and where teaching has to tie in with the daily problems the children encounter and has to be conducted linguistically on the same wavelength as the "clients" use, be they children or adults. Considering the demographic structure the developing countries are going to have for the foreseeable future and the teacher-salary structure that prevails, it is even entirely unrealistic to conceive of a system of universal full-time schooling covering some six or seven years. Therefore, alternative strategies should be developed, such as community schools that serve the family as a unit and where teaching is limited. In order to overcome the cost problem, it does not suffice to have "paraprofessionals." One would have to consider a system whereby everybody, by virtue of some experience and competence, can contribute to teaching those who have less experience and competence. Problems of this type ought to be tackled by a task force that should also be charged with the development of manuals spelling out the strategies identified (through research) as appropriate.

Within the framework of experiences gained in conducting international seminars on curriculum development and evaluation, regional seminars should be organized with participation from groups of countries with similar curricular problems. During such seminars the participants should learn the techniques of developing and evaluating learning units.

Qualitative Evaluation of Educational Systems in Order to Identify Indicators Which Can Be Manipulated and the Assessment of Educational Productivity

Formal education often tends to be regarded as a homogeneous quality that can be measured mainly in terms of the number of years of schooling. For instance, it is taken for granted that what is achieved in one elementary school in a given country is equivalent to what is achieved in another elementary school. As has been shown in the IEA between-school analysis, the range of average performance (even when social background is accounted for) can be considerable with any one given country. The assumption of equivalency of outcomes of the same amount of formal schooling becomes grotesque when cross-national comparisons are made. The IEA Science and Reading surveys indicate that the average level of performance attained in highly industrialized countries after about seven years of schooling is roughly two standard deviations above that of some developing countries. University entrants tend to perform two or three school years below the level of their coevals in Europe or the United States.

The overriding purpose of comprehensive, qualitative evaluation of educational systems is to obtain a basis for policy action. In order to take appropriate action one needs to know what factors are accounting for the outcomes and to what extent the resources that have gone into the system have contributed to achieve the goals set and at what price. So far the state of affairs in respect of obtaining such a knowledge base has been very unsatisfactory. Technical assistance in education in the developing countries has been provided on the basis of conventional wisdom, in most cases without any real evaluation— that is, without any attempt to relate outcomes to resources provided. In order to obtain answers to the following types of questions, certain studies, or in some cases massive surveys, should be launched.

1. What indicators should be used in order to assess the qualitative outcomes of an educational system? To what extent are these indicators applicable cross-nationally? There is evidently a strongly felt need to know which ones, which are manipulable in terms of

policy action, account for differences between schools. But we also need to know if and to what extent these indicators are valid from one national system to another. In case they are valid cross-nationally, one can thereby obtain a mechanism that more easily lends itself to routine evaluation of such systems than do comprehensive surveys.

The overriding purpose of the present "six-subject survey" of IEA is to identify from among some 500 "input" factors in the economic, social, and school domain those that are of greatest importance and from among them to identify those that can be manipulated by policy action. Twenty-three countries, four of them developing countries, have participated in the survey.

2. Closely related to the problem indicated under (1) is that of how the "productivity" of an educational system should be assessed. Obviously it is far from satisfactory to use, as has been the case among some researchers, either the number of students enrolled at a certain level of the system or the percentage of them graduating from a certain educational stage as criteria of productivity. The "output" cannot primarily be defined by a number of individuals at a certain stage, but rather by the amount of competence that has been imparted to these individuals. As was indicated above, a given amount of schooling (number of school years or a certain certificate) can by no means be regarded as comparable quantities from one system to another. Furthermore, it is not satisfactory to limit oneself to the end products of a system when evaluating its power to take care of the pupils that enter into it. Since attrition, particularly in terms of dropouts, is in many countries very high, one important question that needs to be answered when attempts are made to evaluate the productivity of the system is, How many students are brought how far?

The more elitist a system is, the higher the costs tend to be for the end products. It is therefore important to try to weigh the quality of the end products against the total resources that have gone into the system. This is of particular significance in developing countries where the costs of formal education are far more taxing on public resources than in the wealthier nations.

3. During the last two decades much has been said in favor of achieving so-called functional literacy among the masses in the developing countries. But we have not yet been able to define functional literacy in such a way that it could be translated into operational programs. Many who have been involved in technical assistance in education have taken more or less for granted that the model of universal elementary school education, once developed in Western Europe, could readily be applied in developing countries. Such a model is based upon the assumption that children should enter elementary school at the age of say 5 to 7 and remain there full-time until the

age of 12 to 14. Furthermore, it is assumed that there is a linear relationship between amount of exposure to instruction and outcomes in terms of retained knowledge and skills. These assumptions do not seem to be valid even for the developing countries. Some evidence has been advanced in favor of having children enter school earlier, in that now they can learn to read and write successfully before what was previously regarded as the self-evident school-entering age. The IEA mathematics study seemed to indicate that the number of years of instruction or the number of periods of instruction during these years was not closely related to retained competence in mathematics. Similar studies in both developed and developing countries are now under way in the IEA six-subject survey, where, among other things, science and reading achievements are related to a host of instructional factors.

In order to be able to investigate to what extent the resources going into technical assistance in education have been invested properly, we ought to make the following problems the subject of massive field studies: (1) At what age would it be most convenient, in a family-dominated, subsistence economy, to introduce formal reading instruction and how should the teaching of reading be related to the out-of-school experience that the child is obtaining both during school age and later? One ought to conduct studies in which formal reading instruction (considering the differences in the printed representations of various languages) is given to children and adults together and where the age of starting such instruction can be varied considerably (compare the Iranian Primary Reading Project). A considerable number of those who drop out from elementary education seem to lose the rudimentary reading skills they have obtained. This could partly be due to the poor grounding they have received, but it could also be attributed to the lack of reinforcements in their everyday life after they have left school. Our knowledge about these processes is amazingly scarce and the gap could only be filled by means of surveys conducted in different types of developing countries. The IEA survey of the level of reading skills among representative groups of 10- and 14-year-old school children is the first evaluation study in such countries ever carried out. (2) How many years of formal instruction in reading could achieve a retention of reading skills that could last for life, provided that during a person's life a minimum amount of application of these skills is called for?

Increased Equality of Educational Opportunity
between Sexes and between Socioeconomic and Ethnic Groups

Inter alia a vast amount of survey research has been conducted in the developed world in order to elucidate factors that impede the democratization of, in particular, secondary and higher education. Formal education has in the industrialized countries tended to be perhaps the most influential factor in upward social mobility, giving access to elite roles, though the expansion of educational facilities does by no means automatically lead to a more equal representation of the various socioeconomic groups in advanced education. Those whose starting point in life is favorable tend to take better advantage of increased opportunities than those who are not so well off. There are indications that the role played by education in social mobility is even more powerful in developing nations. Since in the foreseeable future the economies in developing countries cannot absorb more than a small fraction of an age group having received upper secondary or university education, the elite promotion role of education there can be expected to become even more pronounced.

We know, however, comparatively little about the patterns of recruitment into selective secondary schools and universities in developing areas. It is desirable, therefore, to conduct field studies that could provide answers to questions such as these:

How is the expansion of educational facilities related to the equalization of educational opportunity?

What factors (economic, social, cultural) restrict the achievement of equality of opportunity?

When drawing up plans for the development of an educational system, one should not overlook the conflict that can arise between the economic growth motive and the equalization motive. Particularly in nations where resources are very scarce and where hard priorities face the planners, aspirations for economic growth would sometimes have to take precedence over egalitarian objectives, especially when the political pattern is conducive to such decisions.

Summary

I have suggested three major types of activity that should be considered and that would cover, among other things, the following:

Research

I have suggested that research would be useful for the following areas:

1. The identification of the needs of certain societies and the assessment of the adequacy of existing school systems to fulfill those needs.

2. The identification of teaching-learning situations and strategies in which all people in the community would be involved and that would enhance motivation and reduce wastage.

3. The conducting of small-scale surveys to provide educational systems with base-line data; to identify relative strengths and weaknesses, and various cognitive and noncognitive outputs at various points in the system; to identify the relative importance and manipulability of inputs to the system and processes within the system; to provide data on the total educational "productivity" of the system.

4. Within the realm of functional literacy, to undertake research concerning appropriate ages for beginning reading and also to identify those factors conducive to relevance and retention of reading skills.

5. The conducting of research to examine the degree of equality of access to and progress through the system of education.

Training

The provision of training through workshops, seminars, internships, and so on, for the study of curriculum development and evaluation, educational planning and organization, and training in research techniques applicable to problems in developing nations.

Task Forces

The setting up of special task forces, on which both field experience and technical competence would be represented, for the reconceptualization of the school as an institution, with particular reference to the individual needs of the various societies. Special attention would thereby be given to the needs of agrarian societies.

FOSTERING EDUCATIONAL RESEARCH IN
THE THIRD WORLD
C. Arnold Anderson

The first part of this section focuses on some strategies of research for, or in, the developing countries. It then takes up some ways of strengthening the capability of developing-country specialists or citizens to make decisions about education and raises some questions about procedures used by assistance agencies. The paper concludes with an exposition of two ways to look at the improvement of educational systems: in terms of the productivity of schools, and how schools emancipate individuals from the constraints of family background.

First, in the main part, a few strategies of investment in educational "research and development" activities within and for the developing countries are evaluated.[1] Inasmuch as the range of topics for educational investigation extends from the most esoteric scholarship to the most grubby on-the-job learning, with each type having several levels, only a few principles of strategy can be exemplified.* Mainly the position of the aid-assistance agency is taken, but the range of examples will go beyond the passive relationships that so often characterize development assistance. Developing countries need to learn not only how to solve problems at home or in similar societies but also how to take up development problems that perplex even the most advanced countries.

Second, the prime goal of this kind of assistance to developing countries is that they shall become proficient in making educational policy decisions over an increasingly wide and diverse span of situations and issues (including capabilities for perceiving new sorts of options).

Third, some judgments must be made about the procedures being used in assistance, mainly by the multilateral agencies. The tasks of bilateral agencies are in principle simpler, irrespective of either the range of countries covered or the size of funds involved. If the goal of enhancing the developing countries' capability for decision has high priority, discussion of some questions about both productiveness of assistance and its probity becomes inescapable. In the process, the distinction between fashionable, if threadbare, clichés about education and a sounder understanding of how education becomes enmeshed into social change leads to some profound

---

*Interspersed throughout the text are references to a list of illustrative projects (items) on education, especially suitable for the developing countries, found in the Appendix.

counterpoints of policy that transcend the present utopian and formula thinking.

Strategies for Investment in Educational Research and Development

Though we are concerned mainly with assistance in establishing effective R and D programs, projects, and capabilities in the developing countries, these strategies must be subjected to judgments of cost-effectiveness and/or benefit/cost ratios whenever possible. (Item V.) Even the most affluent countries can find resources for no more than a fraction of the basic projects, even considering only those aimed at domestic problems. A large part of the most serious literature about education deals with disputes about which topics most deserve investigation. If my conclusion that "the educational process" is one that will not experience a major technological breakthrough is sound, choice of the most promising topics for research becomes even more critical. Despite the labor-intensive character of education, I anticipate no dramatic discoveries of new potentials for educational television, teaching machines, or monitorial systems. When one turns, however, to examining such topics as the potentialities for "out-of-school" training or of new linkages between it and the conventional formalized schooling, the scope for research or development that will pay off widens.[2] The line between rather elementary fact-finding and research, however, is always difficult to keep clear. (Item VII.) Even if the pay-off from R and D in education remains slight for any given case, a steady flow of tiny improvements can compound into impressive alterations of even the most complex systems within a short period.

Clearing Away Unwarranted Notions

A major assurance of high yields from R and D investments is to avoid frittering resources of money, time, and personnel upon sterile operations. Put another way, R and D policy should concentrate upon those educational operations that promise the most pay-off, not excluding long-shot experiments that would prove highly effective in the successful instances. (Obviously, criteria need not be solely economic.)

There is little that any outside agency can do to make sure that the schools in a given country (or research designed to improve them) will have local roots. (Item II.) (I pass over the use of local history, geography, or folktales as examples not needing elaboration for readers of this discussion.) Local color is given to a school

172

system not through expensive curricular reforms (that must almost inevitably be outside sponsored) but by helping to train local personnel in ways to scrutinize and assess their own school system in terms of activities that relate to "development" and to other definite aims. (Item VII.2.) Even after restraining developing countries from rushing down illusory dead-end paths seeking a school system that is supposed both to support "our own way of life" and to facilitate economic and technological development, aid-assistance agencies can do little more (and not much less) in fostering the social sciences than they can do in building new programs in chemistry. (Item VIII.)

It is quite feasible to help local people learn that lagging economic growth is not due to some "inappropriate mix in the outputs" of schools. (Item VII.1.) The closer adjustment between educational systems and their milieus is mainly an outcome of complementary activities by producing agencies (especially the innumerable small firms), advanced R and D agencies, and "common schooling," whether within spic-and-span new schools or in back-street apprentice shops.[3] All educational systems are imported (in at least some of their main features), and local personnel need to learn how to search for features of those imported systems that are indisputably malfunctional. But it is perhaps more important to learn how to identify which features of training are of basic importance despite the fact that in only minor respects (for instance, teaching the 3-Rs) will one easily find parallels to the schools about which one studied in foreign graduate school.

Policy-makers must learn that usually it is not the schools that are divorced from what people call "reality" but rather the aims governments set for schools or the policies chosen for other sectors of society. It is, then, wasteful to use the time of scarce educational researchers to diagnose the local milieu (or to copy that diagnosis from the proceedings of some international conference) in the belief that one can make a good "fit" between schools and local life.[4] Indeed, a really tight fit between schools and local life would misadapt schools for their task of preparing youth to perform capably in a future way of life that is as yet perceived in only dim outline and that will change substantially through time. In truth, even in what one might call a "simple" society, the environment within which education or training must operate is highly diversified. Not even in societies with the largest stock of diligent social scientists can researchers as yet tell us how most productively to adapt schools to their settings.

Nondevelopment in a developing country, to give a last illustration for this section, cannot be attributed to either the defects of existing educational arrangements and goals or to overexpansion of the wrong kinds of schools or courses. The debate as to whether a rise in schooling leads or follows a rise in GNP will not soon be resolved, since there are interactions with varying leads and lags from one time and place to another. But we do, I contend, have a sound basis for concentrating our R and D efforts relating to schooling upon observable existing practices, including apprenticeship and similar nonformal programs, that can be flexibly expanded on the basis of both home-grown and foreign models. (Item X.) Countries with a drive for development are more likely to be alert to possible improvements in or adaptations of an already effective training system.[5]

R and D Policies for Slow-Growing Technologies

Though medicine launched upon its revolution in discovery and application over a century ago, the seemingly predestined aims and structures for that area of "people-serving" activity are just beginning to emerge: (1) improvement of health through direct clinical treatment of patients (rather than indirectly through altering their environments), (2) sufficient proliferation of paramedical personnel to allow the master physician to concentrate upon therapy, and (3) a delicate tension between research by therapists and by research specialists who command no patients. One moral of this perhaps forced parallel is an injunction to be patient about changes in schools. That patience should be reinforced by a realization that most of the indexes used to measure achievement by pupils ignore what the pupils have learned in common beyond what their grandparents got from their schools; most criterion tests have a mean of 100 and a norm of dispersion.

If we tentatively agree that education will experience no technological breakthroughs, the proportion of D in the total R and D investment presumably will be relatively large for the field of education. (Item III.) It follows also that a clever educational investigator in a developing country's system will have distinctively large responsibilities as compared to his colleague in chemistry or meteorology. I would infer also that all aid agencies must expect to spend relatively more for sending developing-nation personnel to advanced-country centers of research in the field of education than in most other fields because learning to make adjustments in a less technological field has more the quality of apprenticeship. Moreover, despite my contention that a "good fit" of schools to society is not feasible and that adjustment to the "local culture" is a misleading goal, intensive interchange of R and D discoveries among the developing countries has a distinctive importance despite preponderant training of R and D personnel in societies with the more complex kinds of school system.

No one knows how capable developing-country personnel have to be at research in education or in any other specialty in order to be good borrowers of new research to schoolroom operations in their own society.[6] (Item VIII.) Present estimates of the pay-off

174

from research plus dissemination in agriculture (once locally suitable plants and practices have been produced) are high, but as yet we have only guesses as to the importance of the dissemination compared to the research component in this hybrid yield to development.[7] Seemingly, R and D training in education has hitherto trained individuals lopsidedly for adaptive research, but such activity also surely requires top-flight men. They need to be well-trained if only to be able to discard the fads and to winnow the mountainous sheaves of advice poured by the advice agencies upon the developing country's ministries.

Perhaps one of the least debatable recommendations for developing countries and their counselors is to accelerate the education for girls. No solution for the undersupply of teachers can be found until a country possesses a large stock of schooled young women. (Item VII.2.) But it is likely also that the encouragement to educational aspirations and to various other modernizing aspirations among youth will flourish only in countries that do not inhibit schooling among girls. In perhaps no other sphere of culture related to education are local traditions and predilections so salient. And, once school-going by girls becomes conventional, "wastage" will perhaps wane more rapidly than in systems enrolling mainly boys.

If my hunch proves correct—that adaptive research will be particularly important in the field of education—there will be an especial need to continue programs for out-of-country training of superior persons from various segments of educational systems in developing countries. (Item III.) And the associated policy of domesticating R and D agencies in the developing countries within which such individuals can work will need to be continued—indeed to be expanded given the worldwide fiscal crisis of schools that must be dealt with. In many realms the educational systems of developing countries must continue to make small adjustments that entail coordinated changes among and between teachers and pupils: decisions about curricula, new forms of training or upgrading teachers, shifting the balance from instruction toward learning, encouragement of nonformal training, and so on. (Item XII.) The effective improvements will not be dramatic reforms such as "new mathematics" but more modest changes on the order of introducing real chalkboards in place of painted wood. (Item XI.) The criteria of decision-making in adopting and adapting these modest novelties must be learned by local ministry and R and D people so that they can learn sooner how to make the changes that are suitable for their conditions rather than having to allow aid-agency technicians to foist ill-founded advice upon them. Pay-offs from these "old-fashioned" practices can be very large.

175

Training Educators from the Developing Countries for Decision-Making

The previous section was composed of mainly a few general cautions and a rather pedestrian list of illustrative, and certainly unrepresentative, projects suitable for educational assistance. But when one turns to the key task of assistance—to train people in the developing countries to make their own educational decisions-logical difficulties become greater.

Some Things Not Worth Doing

It may again be useful to clear away some underbrush by discarding a few topics that are favorites in at least some aid agencies on educational matters, because the advice is misleading and usually wasteful to educational R and D resources. To begin with, proposals that countries be subsidized to learn how to write textbooks or to propose trying to identify qualified and effective authors in advance display little knowledge of how effective books are produced. Such a proposal is also the acme of intrusiveness into local affairs.

Second, I am unenthusiastic about investing money in subsidizing "guidance" systems. (Item XII. 1.) There is little evidence that guidance supplied to pupils is effective or valid under even the comparatively optimal circumstances of affluent societies in which children grow up amidst abundant supplies of occupational information. It is utopian to believe that the "fit" between educational systems and putative "manpower requirements" can be improved through guidance of pupils. Even in comparatively prosperous countries few educators are knowledgeable about their economy, especially not about the out-of-school schemes that provide most of the technical skills used in the economy. Not incidentally, any serious effort at guidance would absorb large numbers of the best-trained teachers and most promising headmasters in any educational system. A flow of occupational information, on the other hand—and here educational television would be especially suitable—has much to recommend it, though few of the lowest-income countries will be able to adopt this practice.

One hears often that evaluation of projects in education is peculiarly difficult because of mixed and ambiguous aims, but I suspect that the criteria of effectiveness are little more precise for projects in transport, irrigation, child (though not infant) health, or training for the higher civil service. (Item VII. 1.) One difference (as will be elaborated below when discussing indicators) is that convention accepts the measures of "yield" outside of education with fewer reservations and that "hard-headed" project men accept the supposed "externalities" for transport more readily than for schools.

And as we come seriously to training persons to decide educational questions by complex analytical criteria, we will discover that collection of appropriate data about both costs and benefits of education will increasingly become respectable charges against funds for pre-project surveys. My point, of course, is not a "'tis-t'ain't" argument about relative productivity of sectors but to emphasize the need to train developing country specialists to use the best available criteria in making their informed judgments about the relative merits of different projects for their own society.

I am skeptical also about our soon coming into possession of viable and tidy mathematical ways of testing the congruence of educational with other sorts of plans; attempts to force a neat congruence would rigidify education in the image of the model, thereby reducing its functional utility. (Item X.4.) Indeed, there is a need to undermine the widespread confidence in global planning generally—a point I have discussed at length elsewhere. Some writers even assert that without educational planning there cannot be clear aims or steady policy. On the contrary, as I see it, controlled adaptation of education (even when broadly conceived) to the goals and schedules of noneducational planning is rarely possible in practice—and may be an intrinsically undesirable aim. Sound quantitative educational planning at this level can rarely go in definiteness beyond a few routine mathematical exercises.[8] Where elaborate specifications for educational planning are incorporated in system models, appropriate consideration of the merits of nonformal sorts of training will tend to be shirked. We should not encourage specialists from developing countries to believe that one can survey and assess the operations and effects of an educational system as a whole.

It is to be hoped that we can avoid encouraging the idea that rigorous "decision analysis" must be suspended when discussion begins to deal with factors of "tradition": local languages, nonforeign elements of a culture, and so on. Speaking only about the subuniversity sectors of educational systems, I become uneasy about proposals to encourage development of multiple vernaculars as teaching media. I remain unconvinced that the populace of many countries would choose that or many other elements of tradition if they have experience with the new things and ideas that modernization can bring to them. Of course many actual or pseudo-leaders will claim a following for such looking backward. Only an insensitive man would deny that tradition is worth saving in many forms, but analysis of educational policies should not have to cease or take refuge in obscurantism when these kinds of topics arise. (Item I.) It is possible for people to learn to make decisions in the most "sensitive" situations and by use of the most subtle methodologies of social sciences or humanities. To take a cautious (as distinct from a sensitive) position on such topics is to expose policy discussions to subversion by demagogues whenever political feathers are ruffled.

Again, while agreeing about the importance of preparing developing country specialists to be prudent and alert decision-makers, I dissent from the rather frequent recommendations that new techniques for educational management (or even new sorts of managers) must be developed to deal with the fiscal impasse in developing country educational systems. One hears the same recommendation for our own schools these days. But administrators of elite universities are in just as much hot water—as are hospital administrators, heads of the most renowned corporations, and the civil service—in every country where public opinion is expressed freely. Looking at Britain, on the other hand, there is much evidence that their informal creation of headmasters would be worthy of adoption anywhere—provided the size of individual schools is kept modest.

Pulling some of these suggestions together, I would envisage training in the exercise of decision-making on a scale that obviates calls for big bureaucracies and big development funds. Shifting major responsibility for "technical assistance" to assistance agencies would be tacitly to denigrate management on the local scale. If management is envisaged as normally entailing large funds and extensive personnel, it will take most countries generations to acquire a stock of decision-makers in their schools. (Item IV.3.) Before suggestions on the content of training for decision are followed, I urge that precautions be taken against portraying decision-making as an esoteric art that comes to fruition only in advanced societies.[9] To encourage such conceptions of scale would be one of the most offensive sorts of intrusiveness, dependence, and paternalism; by comparison, recommendation that English be retained as the medium of instruction from the first grade is a modest and diplomatic hint.

The Basic Format for Decision

The prime task of policy-makers who deal with "mass institutions" such as education or training is to inaugurate systems of motivation or of incentives that will induce individuals and families to make the most appropriate choices among opportunities for education. (For the most part, I assume explicitly, wiser selections among opportunities will be made by informed and concerned persons than by official "gate-keepers.")[10] Ultimately no effective strategy can be envisioned that does not presuppose a system of incentives appropriate to the growth situation of the given society. The aim should be to institute a system of (mainly economic) signals so that those who wish to sell (offer) or to buy (even if only with one's time) this or that kind of instruction or learning can make a productive bargain.

(Item X.) It is of the utmost importance to grasp that this situation does not require advance knowledge by planners (public or private) of what the variety of supplies and demands of training will be. The problem is to ensure that a signal system can operate and that it not be subverted by subventions (which usually are concealed) or by pretentions that "out-of-school" training ought to be coordinated and integrated with the more formal sorts of education in scornful disregard of the capability for shrewd adaptive behavior by the many smaller decision-makers. Indeed, centrally coordinated informal education is a contradiction in terms; efforts to attain such integration would subvert the very freshness and adaptive qualities that are the strength of nonformal training.[11]

Crucial for this model of an educational scheme is the fact that progressively larger proportions of the citizenry are brought into the process of making decisions that to them are utterly realistic. The few crucial decisions that are left to the bureaucrats, being few, are more likely to receive adequately serious attention. I am of course assuming that individuals or families will use home-made benefit/cost ways of making their choices. (Item VIII.) Obviously also, as I see it, claimed externalities for various sorts of training will be more thoroughly scrutinized if the people who are going to gain or lose are fully part of the decision process. Already two impressive dissertations (by authors from developing countries) have bolstered the foregoing point of view in challenging claims for formalized vocational education; each author displays confidence in the canniness of those who will choose a useful kind of training if given an opportunity to do so. (Item X.)

Plans to Foster Decision-Making

The foregoing rather abstract scheme can be made more definite. We can institutionalize the opportunity for "little men" to make pertinent decisions about education. A mounting literature is vindicating the ability of peasants to make sager judgments than their ministers within the field of farming. I see no reason why there should not be a similarly satisfactory outcome from an extended autonomy within the complex field of education. Clearly it has become desirable to undertake a wholesale reorientation of the literature on educational planning in order to embrace the characteristics of decentralized decision-making. This puts the central emphasis on plans to foster decision-making as against direct planning of the content of the decisions that will be made.

Writers on these topics almost uniformly have emphasized that educational systems should be "adapted," "flexible," "integrated," and congruent with the basic features of other "national plans."[12]

Whoever the decision-makers for education, their wisdom must be judged in the light of what resources were available for them to shift among uses. And of course, the more a system is constrained by fiscal or political factors, the more carefully must resources be balanced among uses.

Informed readers will have discerned that I prefer to maximize the shares of educational costs that are on private account and on local rather than on central budgets. Apart from philosophical assumptions, my preference stems from the conclusion that only by such procedures can societies cope with what is so often described as "runaway expansion" of educational systems. No firm specifications for "needed" numbers and sorts of trained individuals can be set down for any society. At the same time, the "social demand" for education is pushing enrollments steadily higher—which should surprise no one since this sort of demand specifies only how much schooling people will accept if its cost to them remains relatively cheap or approaches zero. The convention of "socialized" financing—which incidentally gives an unfair advantage over nonformal kinds of training and undercuts virtually every present study of nonformal types of training—makes the choice for at least the brightest youngsters between staying in school or going to work one they are not called upon to make until relatively late in their youth. In effect, various sets of officials make the choices for individuals without any adequate basis for setting the pace at which various sorts or levels of school will be expanded. Moreover, since individuals or families (under the foregoing circumstances) need to make few educational choices, educational officials lack feedbacks of responses in relation to the real costs of educational programs. (Item VII.3.) Cast adrift, officials and their expatriate or international advisers lack a basis for deciding whether, for example, the acceptable ratio of university to elementary school costs per pupil annually is 5:1, 50:1, or 300:1.

Solution of the fiscal crisis resulting from ballooning school systems lies not in locating new sources of revenue but in relating decisions about continuing in school (of course, with a means test) to decisions about which kind of education to pay for and to use. Almost certainly the correspondence between who gets the schooling and who pays its cost has become more tenuous and obscured in recent generations. Needless to say, opportunities for experiments and research with different arrangements for eliciting and evaluating choices among educational programs and among fiscal schemes can take up any idle hours aid-assistance staff members might have at their disposal.

The Importance of Microeducational Decisions

The availability of large grants or loans encourages the making of educational decisions on a far too aggregative basis. But big decisions can entail big and nonreversible errors before feedback corrections can come into play. Moreover, diffusion of responsibilities to make genuine small decisions provides a setting for informal learning-by-doing that could be an important sort of "education for development" in itself. The large decisions often foreclose such opportunities.

The inauguration of (or pressures to inaugurate) a large system of formal vocational training is an example. (Item I.) Such arguments will always seem more impressive when backed by an international agency and couched in terms of "needs." But both adaptive behavior and confidence in the soundness of micro-decisions in choice of training are more likely to accumulate if there is a continuous testing and feedback from "tracer studies" that show how different components of the labor force are actually being utilized. (Item VII.1.d.) And this is more likely also to direct attention to how labor-market institutions facilitate or impede effective allocations of human resources. In fact, serious analysts of the linkages between schools and society have for more than a decade been affirming that (with some special exceptions) formalized middle or secondary vocational schools rarely could match on-the-job training in turning out the kinds and numbers of skills that enterprises are ready to buy.

Not only are many decisions about education policy made "in large chunks" before the supposed beneficiaries are aware that decisions are being made; many decisions about education are made covertly when setting policy for other sectors. Funds for marketing boards are viewed as soft taxes, and then farmers disconcertingly respond to low prices by decreasing production of the crops that earn foreign exchange. (Item VIII.) Similarly, expensive international commissions drowsily decide to "ruralize" village curricula in order to reduce the pressure of new entrants upon urban labor markets, but migration to towns is not due to ignorance about farming, and the migration would go on in those rural areas that are changing most or have most contact with cities whatever the content of school lessons.

Far too many decisions about education stem mainly from education clichés that circulate at worldwide meetings. Surely a school system that does not seriously try to supply textbooks for all pupils has little capability for managing any sort of new project or for setting priorities among possible improvements in local schools. (Item XI.) For officials to spend much of their work year at international conferences on educational planning, or being lectured on how to introduce "new math," is to ensure that decisions will continue to be largely

ill-considered and irresponsible. Rarely will decisions come down
to the micro-situations that are the heart of schools as distinguished
from "educational systems." Under the ceaseless bombardment of
abstract plans by officials in supranational agencies, private or public,
developing country educators have few opportunities to make those
small decisions that change a poor into a cumulatively better system
of schools. More important, the officials sluggishly refuse to believe
that they have the capability to make adequate and cogently supported
proposals. Growth or development really is not made up of aggre-
gates; it is alteration in the mix of a nation's life that comes through
small changes in many very local agencies and institutions. It is
practice in making the relevant decisions that marks the modernizing
man.

Social Indicators as a Basis for Policy Decisions[13]

A major shortcoming in the upgrading of officials concerned
with educational decisions in the developing countries is failure to
ensure that they learn how to devise and use educational indicators
diagnostically. (Item IX.) Indicators can refer to the nation as a
whole, but such aggregate indexes have little utility apart from international compendia. Indexes for less aggregate categories (districts
or provinces, school districts, classrooms, pupils) can be made into
crucial evaluative devices applicable to any given situation.

The variety of indicators is almost endless. One can find out
what percentage of pupils have textbooks; in at least one developing
country this apparently is one of the best predictors of pupil performance. Apart from comparing one local set of schools with another
or one datum with another, it is possible to examine also the pace
at which a new practice is spreading and how far it has penetrated
into different subpopulations. One may also measure the skewness
of distribution among local units. Usually when new practices are
spreading, one first will observe localities to become more unlike
as leaders emerge; then others follow until eventually the skewness
is reversed and a few lagging districts form a lower tail on the distribution. We often forget that data about school pupils were among
the historically first indexes of individual performance within mass
institutions.

One can also make use of system development scales, as Farrell
has done for Latin America;[14] clues for major institutional programs
can be deduced from such ordered scales. One can compare now
developing systems with early stages of the now advanced societies.
One can measure the spread of educational innovations either in terms
of growth curves for separate areas or by means of chronologically
arranged maps.

It is striking that all the classic social differentials (as in wages) are reappearing in education for the developing countries: urban above rural, educated or skilled excelling the uneducated or unskilled, large firms higher than small firms, towns on major communication routes leading those in more isolated districts, and so on. (Item I.) One can measure the spread of education among subpopulations in order to identify the districts most in need of "administrative therapy." One can contrast the degree of social inequality in recruitment to secondary schools or universities of Latin America with the imparities to be observed in Africa, European countries, or the Far East. Availability of education for disadvantaged groups can be compared with that for the more fortunate.[15]

Most of the foregoing examples call for ingenuity and thoughtfulness more than for statistical erudition, and zeal for working out these kinds of graphic indexes marks the man who has a realistic concern for what is happening in the schoolrooms of his society. With any of these or more complex techniques, one can set up norms suitable for comparing different societies. Each index can be correlated with economic or political features of the same social units in an effort to identify what the network of causation in development is like. Enthusiasm for using such indexes marks out the specialist who is more eager to test his hunches (or even learned theories) about development than ritualistically to apply folk wisdom or the dicta of international conferences. (Item VII.2.) Thus one can compare the degree of divergence among districts with that between ethnic groups or age or sex categories. These devices encourage officials and leaders from the developing countries to look at their educational systems objectively. The qualified individual can also move on to proficiency in more intricate and sensitive techniques for measuring change, testing hypotheses, and so on.[16]

Gradually it is becoming possible to move onto a much superior level of analysis by making use of data about educational performance of individual pupils, aggregated appropriately by classrooms, family background, type of community, and so on. Gradually one can then move to more refined regression analyses that will begin to identify the aspects of local education where definite changes of policy can be expected to have measurable impact—or, alternatively, to prove sterile.

Appendix: Illustrative Projects

As I remarked in the text, I am considering here mainly projects suitable for assistance from a donor country or agency and have not tried to list projects most suitably "home grown," let alone

classify them by development stage of the recipient country. The
implications for priority-setting (discussed in the World Bank's
sector document) have been worked out only in very broad terms.
I have also had to omit all discussion of an important area of reflection: What went wrong in the projects that did not work?

The vital topic discussed by Light and Smith—"Accumulating
Evidence: Procedures for Resolving Contradictions among Different
Research Studies" (Harvard Educational Review November 1971)—
has been almost entirely ignored. References to some of the following
items are noted in the chapter to which this section is an annex. No
claim is made that the items are either comprehensive or most logi-
cally arranged.

I. Questions relating to equity:

1. Basic to all decisions about "people-serving programs" is
the balancing of the equity criterion with that of efficiency and that
of freedom of choice. Training in the implications of these conflicts
is crucial if developing country personnel are to make cogent decisions.

2. Techniques for measurement of inequity are vital parts of
training programs.

3. It is important that programs and programing recognize
the extreme internal diversity in all countries among individual schools
on any measure of imparity.

4. It is important to realize the tension between pedagogic
improvements and their equity implications. If it be upheld (as is
argued in a paper by W. Rohwer, Jr., "Prime Time for Education,"
Harvard Education Review 41, 1972, pp. 316-42) that pupils could
begin school at age 10 and know as much at 18 after four years as
if they had started at 7 and had four years, it is important that countries learn how to work out the equity implications of such a policy;
private schools and urban schools would immediately arise to give
the more fortunate an early start in school. Many pedagogic practices
have the same mode of effect upon equity, and ability to perceive and
to dissect such sorts of situations calls for diverse projects.

II. Coping with local traditions:

1. The whole gamut of research that we call "ethnic studies"
presents a range of research that is treacherous but tempting.

2. Closely related is the set of projects revolving around the
interrelationships between old and new intellectuals, for assistance
always affects both.

3. A major area within which social science guidance can be
useful concerns ascertaining whether lagging development reflects
traditional cultural restraints or rather the sluggish diffusion of new
incentives for new ways.

III. National interchange of high-level personnel:

1. Almost certainly the main contribution of foundations and bilateral agencies is the provision of opportunities for one- or two-way exchange of specialists, particularly for training. Investigations of how those people function upon return warrants much more investigation than it has received; Robert Myers is studying this problem in Peru.

2. A project that I regard as of special promise would be to investigate the scholarly productivity in later years of individuals who received foreign area fellowships, compared with unsuccessful applicants and with matched nonapplicants.

IV. Networks of research centers:

1. However long discussed, we have little information on the extent to which capability for borrowing innovations depends upon capability in making innovations. The linkage to the problem of "premature displacement" of expatriate specialists is obvious. (See unpublished paper by Richard Nelson, "Less Developed Countries, Technology Transfer and Adaptation, and the Role of the National Science Community.") Effective combination of human with physical capital turns on our ability to think this problem through.

2. The respective merits of country research networks resting mainly on connections between persons (versus networks mainly comprised of projects) remains unexplored.

3. If we may speak of countries as being at different places on the "ladder of R and D work," presumably there are optimal combinations of countries that are at about the same level of capability for some kinds of problems, while for other kinds of problems combinations of quite disparate countries will yield more output of R and D. The problem of establishing regional centers is part of this issue.

4. Judging by some recent work by Robert Evenson, research centers below a certain critical mass of personnel will produce little. Taking into account the local politics of higher education, this conclusion would suggest that aid agencies face major problems of strategy in assisting countries to improve research capabilities.

5. Though it sounds rather low-grade in contrast to no. 4, a major contribution in diffusion of knowledge (about, say, pedagogy) can be made by disseminating large quantities of simple pamphlets dealing with various items of professional life; on a much higher level, contributions can be made also by dissemination (again in many languages) of key papers about basic educational problems (such as are discussed at length in the report).

V. Stimulation of research on fiscal topics:

1. Information about how to analyze costs, with special reference to opportunity costs, is desperately needed by specialists or officials in most countries.
2. Closely related are techniques for improving the effectiveness of tax systems.
3. Analyses of the data collected by international agencies about levels of cost for given sorts of school in different situations are vital to any program designed to train people for decision-making.

VI. Adult literacy versus child schooling:

1. Despite the long years of debate and the constantly modified trial projects, the merits of adult concentrated schooling as against the more conventional schooling during youth remains undecided. The recent work of Rohwer (already cited, on age for best learning) raises the whole problem in a new form. Whether there are general answers, at least for countries in which children have a stimulating milieu, is not settled. The lapse from literacy and the low correlation between literacy or schooling and job level among employees (reported by Simmons from Tunisia, for example) forces us to design some appropriate projects. A recent report by Dr. John Smyth and Dr. K. Izadi, respectively of UNESCO and of the Institute of Social Studies at the University of Teheran, attempts to make a cost-effectiveness assessment of the literacy experiments there.
2. A parallel but much more difficult set of projects would deal with the yield of civic alertness, wiser judgment on education questions, and so on, of schooled (or literate) versus the unschooled residents of different types of society. Without taking space to elaborate the argument, topics such as these provide abundant opportunities for insinuating good social science methodology into the research centers of developing countries.

VII. Data for decisions:

1. A whole series of R and D projects will have to be carried out and replicated for various countries, the purpose of which is to test and expound the respective merits of different techniques for decision-making:
(a) For what topics can manpower projections be useful?
(b) Distinction between "social demand" and weighed choices between education and other employments.
(c) Utility of rate-of-return techniques (for example, Daniel Rogers, "Student Loan Programs and the Returns to Investment in

Higher Levels of Education in Kenya," <u>Economic Development and Cultural Change</u> 20, 2 [1972]: 243-59).

(d) Utilization of manpower of various qualifications; also called "tracer studies." This is the most cogent information, especially when related to pay structures and trends toward hypertrophy of the civil services, for evaluating what education is contributing to a society.

2. Simple indicators of relative performance (among districts, countries, and so on) deserve major emphasis, partly because they stimulate the establishment of data-collection procedures for diagnostic items (as possession of textbooks or comparability of the "school certificate" examination in developing country systems descended from the same imperial prototype). These sorts of data can also be scaled (as in the cited article of Farrell), and where combined with suggestions of Appendixes below can yield meaningful country profiles of educational systems.

3. In one or two developing countries today (but in several tomorrow), it will be possible not only to find out which countries are getting the most learning into pupils but also to identify the major determinants of the national contrasts, as in the international mathematics inquiry.

VIII. Studies of agriculture and of migration from the village:

1. The recent studies by Heijnen for Tanzania and of Brownstein for Kenya (and the earlier study by the writer and its follow-up by Olson in Kenya) are showing some of the ways that "tracer studies," inquiries about migration, and data useful for the formulation of employment policy can be linked together.

2. It is possible not only to relate migrants to the features of the communities they leave or enter but also to inquire whether modernization exacts a high price in personal tension and what effects cities have outside the economic sphere.

3. As mentioned earlier, we greatly need to separate the effect of extension services and other communication from the effect of research that is useful to farmers; this bundle of problems includes the question as to what proportion of trained farmers are needed in an area to provide the "critical mass" that facilitates farmers' coming into contact with new practices that will pay.

IX. Studies of "wastage":

1. Strictly, this discussion belongs under VII, but it is related to assessments of migration and its causes. Clearly we need more studies that try to identify causes of dropping out (as Levy,

"Determinants of Primary School Dropouts in Developing Countries,"
Comparative Education Review 15, 1 [1971]: 41-58). Inquiries that
place this problem in the context of diffusion of educational aspirations
particularly are needed.

2. Closely related is the family of inquiries about "relevance,"
"standards," examination procedures, and estimates of what percentage of children need to attend a given level of school to allow an adequate pool from which to recruit candidates for the next level. Obviously, these inquiries cannot start with the assumption that steadily
rising ratios of enrollment is the normal expectation; studies of utilization are more basic.

X. Choosing between formal and nonformal sorts of training:

1. The basic opener for this family of projects is to focus on
identifying and locating the pools of skills in the society; occupations
are not the appropriate rubrics.

2. One then is faced with following up the work of Callaway
and Peil on apprentices in order to make solid inventories of the
types of training from which the needed skills are (or are not) coming.
In short, production coefficients for skills are needed.

3. When to formalize the inculcation of vocational skills is
subject to cogent analysis, though almost never done by planners;
this topic also links up with analysis of the major determinants of
the kinds of skill-training that a given society generates.

4. Clearly massive projects are going to be needed for estimating the demand and supply curves for specific kinds of training
or schooling and (as said earlier) of the criteria by which the appropriateness of different training systems can be evaluated.

5. A major uninvestigated topic in this broad area relates to
the scarcity of extension programs for businessmen, particularly
with reference to the much-discussed programs for job creation.

XI. Problems relating to curricula:

1. I classify content as follows for convenience
                                      Universal Parochial

Cognitive
   Technical-manipulative
   Verbal-mathematical
Affective
   Technical-manipulative
   Verbal-mathematical

One can also further subdivide each type according to whether we are dealing with the overt or the covert curriculum.

2. It is possible to make inquiries about the time spent on different materials, about the spread of innovations in material or mode of presentation, or about the transferability potential of given material as between societies.

XII. Topics relating to teachers:

1. Most topics in this area are very familiar, and the task is mainly to design studies on the familiar topics for a given society. One question is: which supplementary personnel besides classroom teachers bring the greatest benefit: guidance, inspectors, in-service trainees, educational planners?

2. A major topic relates to the utility of textbooks and library books in large quantities irrespective of the "quality" of particular books. Related is the question as to how feasible it is to use booklets as forms of programed instruction.

3. Is it more practicable to improve the qualifications of teachers or to substitute tightly controlled syllabi?

4. The constraints upon teachers arising from overall scarcity, tribe, level or grade, language, attrition from the cadre, and so on open up projects everywhere.

Notes

1. This discussion relates to assisted research about developing-country schools; a list of useful projects without explicit relationship to sponsorship or assistance would be different. The mutations in "motives" for assistance to developing countries are reviewed and assessed by Robert Asher ("Development Assistance in DD II," International Organization 25, 1 [1971]: 97-119). But also one should examine "The 'Crisis of Aid' and the Pearson Report," a lecture by Harry Johnson at the University of Edinburgh in 1970 as well as his paper on "Some Economic Aspects of Science" (Minerva 10, 1 [1972]: 10-18).

2. See the Teachers College dissertation of H. W. Lee, "A Multivariate Analysis of Education and Unemployment," 1971, and O. Iziren, "Education in Nigeria's Small Enterprises" (Dissertation, Toronto University, 1971).

3. See the many papers about apprenticeships in Nigeria by Archibald Callaway; for example, his "Training Young People within Indigenous Small-Scale Enterprises: The Nigerian Example"

(prepared for a December 1971 conference at IIEP). His inferences in various papers that migration to towns is caused mainly by too much or the wrong kind of rural schooling seem to me to be largely spurious. Rather, on that point I would depend upon the analyses of Carl Eicher et al. ("Employment Generation in African Agriculture," Michigan State University Institute of International Agriculture, Research Report no. 9, 1970), Michael Todaro ("Income Expectations, Rural-Urban Migration and Employment in Africa," International Labour Review 104, 5 [1971]: 387-413), and Charles R. Frank, Jr. ("The Problem of Urban Unemployment in Africa," unpublished, 1970).

4. Many papers on this aspect of ecucation, and on schooling for rural people generally, can be found in the proceedings of the World Conference on Agricultural Education and Training that was held in Copenhagen in the summer of 1970 under sponsorship of several multilateral agencies.

5. Though relating mainly to the role of communication in diffusion on new technology, because of its abundance of detail, the recent mimeograph report by Everett Rogers and associates ("Diffusion of Innovations in Brazil, Nigeria, and India," 1970) exemplifies the circumstances that in more abstract form colleagues and I have used to argue against the "adaptation" concept of LDC education. The many papers from the Chicago Center are presumably familiar; we think their argument is cogent.

6. This very general problem is examined in recent work by the International Council of Scientific Unions; see the unpublished proceedings of their 1970 conference on "The Role of Science and Technology in Developing Countries." See also the unpublished paper by A. Copsarow with the same title of the conference and prepared for it.

7. See various papers by T. W. Schultz, and more directly on the point just raised, see the forthcoming papers by Robert Evenson and Finis Welch from a University of Minnesota conference on agricultural research.

8. The importance of humdrum "back of the envelope" calculations was shown in the report I turned in to the mission of the World Bank to Kenya in 1961; it was shown that a ministry has to make a hard choice between large rises in demands for teachers due to reducing pupils per class or a large rise in demands due to expansion of girls' attendance—or the enormous saving by resisting both changes. An equally dramatic but more up-to-date example of this kind of simple numerical scrutiny of policy is to be found in John Hanson and John Henderson's "Report on the Supply of Secondary Level Teachers in English-Speaking Africa: Uganda " (Michigan State University, mimeo, 1969) and in a somewhat different manner in Philip H. Coombs' The World Education Crisis (1968, Appendix 21).

9. Gustav Papanek, "The Development of Entrepreneurship," American Economic Review 52, 2 (1962): 46-58.

10. Particular commendation is due to OECD for its acknowledged skepticism about manpower forecasting as a direct result of its own exploration of the problem.

11. See my "Reflections upon the Planning of 'Out-of-School' Education," prepared for the same meeting cited in note 3 and my earlier papers on the same topic.

12. "But from the point of view of the nation as a whole, the agrarian school [of mid-19th country in the United States] was doing a very significant job and doing that job effectively. For in preparing people to literally and figuratively escape from the agrarian way of life, it performed its vital function in the larger context of the changing American society." Solon Kimball and James McClellan, Education and the New American (1962), p. 96; see also pp. 90-95.

13. Social Information for Developing Countries, The Annals (v. 393, January ,1971).

14. Joseph Farrell, "The Structural Differentiation of Developing Educational Systems: a Latin American Comparison," Comparative Education Review 13, 3 (1969): 294-311.

15. As has been shown in earlier papers, and in subsequent studies by other writers, one can use familiar techniques for inequality, such as Lorenz distributions or Gini coefficients; for the United States it turns out that education is a distinctively evenly distributed good. One can also weight school years by cost, quality, or other attributes; the Lorenz distributions will be altered according to the assumptions made.

16. A host of comparatively new and sophisticated techniques (such as linear and nonlinear programing, and new regression methods) are being applied to educational analyses; see, for example, the reports by Martin Carnoy on Venezuela. The desirability of encouraging advanced-country centers to work out suitable training programs for developing country specialists and for the latter to pioneer new applications needs no elaboration here.

HIGHER EDUCATION AND NATIONAL DEVELOPMENT:
ONE MODEL FOR TECHNICAL ASSISTANCE
Kenneth W. Thompson and Colleagues

Beginning in the early 1960s, the Rockefeller Foundation under-took to provide technical assistance for overall university development to a few selected institutions in the developing countries. The program had a definable rationale, involved institutions selected in accordance with explicit criteria, proceeded according to a design or plan through various stages of development, and undertook to assist the building of institutional capacity for grappling with problems of national development. In describing this approach to university development, these four topics will provide a focus.

Institution-building is at the heart of the Foundation's tradition. The rationale of university development was rooted in this tradition plus the belief that, for the developing countries the missing factor was educated people or trained leadership. The remedy lies not with outsiders; to meet these human deficits, indigenous institutions are needed to prepare the missing leaders.

A second part of the rationale underlying institution-building is that a concentrated attack on a single urgent problem, while necessary, is insufficient. Often the only thing worse than failure may be success. It is imperative to identify pressing human needs, but no less to grasp their interrelationships. The earlier triumphs of public health in re-ducing mortality have had some part in ushering in the population explosion. The "green revolution" of our time will ultimately prove successful only if its relationship with employment, internal migration, and political structures is recognized and dealt with.

Developing universities provide a framework within which problems of this order can be considered as part of an integrated effort. One of the dividends of a technical assistance staff working together on an across-the-board basis within an institutional framework is the possibility of interdisciplinary cooperation. University development has brought staff and resources together to join in the task of building educational institutions. A university can be a prime mover in the transition from traditional to modern ways of life, but this requires many different kinds of trained people. It must build professional competence in key disciplines and furnish a scientific and scholarly base for relevant problem-solving. The provision of human and material capital, of people and things, is directed toward this purpose.

Criteria of Selection

Once the Rockefeller Foundation decided in the 1950s to shift program emphasis from Europe and the United States to the developing countries, it was faced with critical problems of choice. It had to measure unlimited human need against severely limited resources. There was concern that, even with income being augmented through expenditure of capital, the comparatively small sums available could readily be frittered away, leaving hardly a trace over the vast reaches of Asia and Africa.

This led the trustees and officers to evoke once again the principle of concentration. In the same way that the decision had been made to work with one Ministry of Health or Ministry of Agriculture in a chosen country, it was decided to work with one university. The choice of the right university was a difficult one. The Foundation was determined to work only with institutions that had the potential of serving national or regional needs. As the program unfolded, a set of criteria evolved for the selection of University Development Program (UDP) centers. The first was the existence of a genuine request for help formally and informally communicated. Review teams comprised of representatives of all sectors of program at the Foundation visited each prospective center to determine whether help was desired and to what extent conditions for indigenous growth in a given discipline were present. They "put down the scientists' rod" to test the depth and potential of resources in fields in which the Foundation could be helpful. They looked for determination to move ahead, for academic and administrative leadership committed to change and for the prospect of increasing support from other sources.

In the same way that not every nation has made the hard decisions prerequisite to benefiting from foreign assistance, not every institution has prepared itself for genuine organic growth. It may have failed to come forward with a practical design for upgrading its faculty, neglected research opportunities, overlooked salary problems, or forgotten about community support. It may have lacked a nucleus of devoted and responsible leaders willing and able to foster institutional growth, if necessary at the expense of their own professional advancement and prestige. There are certain matters that institutions, no less than individuals or nations, cannot leave to chance. What is to be their role in a wider geographic region? How are they to weigh numerical growth against the pursuit of excellence? How much or how little should they undertake in a specific field? Is their mission to train the teachers, public servants, engineers, and doctors to serve the nation and other social and educational institutions? Or is their role conceived in more parochial, if worthy, terms of building a civic culture for their immediate constituents? Finally, has the leadership made a fresh and self-critical review of strengths and weaknesses and laid down the broad guidelines for responding to institutional needs? Recognizing that its resources are always more restricted than its needs, how far has it gone in establishing priorities for determining points of emphasis next year, three or five years hence?

Partners in institution-building, who can at best assist only a few institutions, cannot escape the obligation to assess the many factors essential to growth. Perhaps what is needed is an institutional equivalent of the pilot's check list before clearing the aircraft for flight. But in the end, when the many factors essential to growth have been considered, partners must consider the institution as a whole. For whether the aim is developing a university or building a strong and vital research institute, the organization is somehow more than the sum of its parts. Those who assess in order to help must acquire the knack of measuring the potential and strength of institutions in the process of evolving. Universities in some parts of the world are little more than loose collections of faculties. If it is the university that invites development, this fact may lead to their exclusion, or it may require a new approach to institution-building. If outside donor organizations concentrate their resources at a few developing institutions, the corollary of their assistance is single-minded concentration by indigenous leadership on the central problems of institution-building.

Perhaps the most crucial criterion is the estimate those who assist must make of the prospects of partnership. Full and frank exchange of ideas is the result, not the forerunner, of mutual commitment. Yet intimate, unguarded, and self-critical discussion is vital if assistance is to make a difference. To mold a partnership in institution-building is to build a framework within which consultation goes on and mutually acceptable, far-reaching decisions are made. By contrast, casual involvement in institutional development results in hit-or-miss direction of those actions that shape the future. Whether the subject is selection of a fellow or reworking the syllabus or planning a new curriculum, the partners are engaged in what is ultimately the institution's most serious business. Whether they succeed or fail depends on whether these topics are considered casually en route to the airport or through the solemn and deliberate processes of ongoing institutional life.

If the Foundation could call on universities to have a plan, it was obligated to have one too. The great issue was whether its staff could match up resources and capacities with urgent needs at selected institutions. Objectives had to be formulated in terms of definable tasks. It was vital there be a timetable; the plan required a beginning, a middle, and an end. In operational language, the Foundation had "to get in and get out." In 1961, President J. George Harrar, in presenting the program, spoke of a possible 12-15 year effort, which might cost up to $100 million. The trustees accepted the proposal without blinking. In fact, expenditures over the first eight years totaled about $40 million.

Broadly speaking, the plan envisaged at least four distinct phases varying as between the several UDP models described below.

Phase I involves the giving of assistance in speeding the transition
from a colonial to a national university. Toward this end, the Foundation made available, on long-term assignments, a few members of
its professional staff. The prior question involved identifying and
defining discrete and manageable areas of assistance. This need is
an outgrowth of the essential nature of technical assistance. Outside
help, even public and international-agency help, is inevitably marginal
help. At the peak of the Marshall Plan, the flow of aid never exceeded
4 percent of Europe's capital needs. Private foundations particularly
must come to a judicious determination of the focus of their aid.
Policies follow questions that go to the heart of cooperative efforts.
What are the recipient country's most urgent and pressing needs and
what is it doing about them? What is it doing for itself and what does
it seek from others? Viewed realistically, what capacity does the
donor agency possess, or can it acquire, for assistance in those areas
where it can make a genuine difference? Whether the choice is agriculture or virus research or improving an economics faculty, there
are dividends in defining and identifying areas of need and matching
them against available outside resources.

Once the major thrust has been determined, the selection of
visitors and professionals skilled in the complexities of institution-
building follows. Here a career service of men engaged in assistance
to developing institutions is essential. If Henry Wriston is right when
he states that first-class problems attract first-class minds, the
rallying of qualified personnel should not be impossible. The Rockefeller Foundation, in its University Development Program, has been
encouraged by the interest of first-rate scholars in serving abroad
as visiting professors, heads of departments or research institutes,
and even as deans. Some have been recruited as regular Foundation
staff, others as temporary personnel, and others as scholars on leave
from their own universities. A career service for university development must be flexible enough to provide for commitments ranging
across a sliding scale of interest. Some will be engaged more or less
permanently, others for a year or two. It is obvious that any plan
for a career service that would attract the best minds must allow
for both service and research—the continuation of a scholar's most
deeply cherished interests. Essential will be the presence, in any
organized effort at a university development center, of at least a few
top-flight leaders devoting themselves full time to academic administration and teaching. Their presence at the heart of the development
enterprise leaves room for researchers who teach by carrying forward their inquiries.

The Rockefeller Foundation, in this spirit, has made approximately 25 university grants to institutions in Britain, France, Canada,
Switzerland, and the United States. First, the universities concerned

extend assistance to developing institutions through visiting professors and cooperating junior colleagues in specific disciplines. For example, the Yale Growth Center, the Williams College Institute of Economic Development, and Northwestern University give help in economics. Princeton, Notre Dame, Cornell, Duke, Michigan, Wisconsin, and Minnesota Universities send visitors in the social sciences, as do Toronto, Sussex, and McGill Universities. Second, the developing universities themselves play a determining role in the selection of cooperating Western universities and the choice of individual professors. Third, a schedule is worked out of visitors for successive academic years so that both the developing and developed universities can plan for the years ahead. Fourth, the professionals concerned, including career service personnel at the developing universities, play an active role, not only in selecting visiting professors but also in defining their role and working out the most meaningful assignments before they arrive. It would be impossible to exaggerate the pivotal role of the senior foundation representative in planning, consulting, and paving the way for the visitors and assuring they have a serious piece of work to do without wasted time and effort. Fifth, the watchword is flexibility. A Western university principally engaged in strengthening university X is not precluded from assisting university Y. Equally, university X can receive help from more than one source, if appropriate. Sixth, the role of visitors is part of a total university development plan, and their contributions are made to mesh with the overall design.

The machinery for assisting developing universities is of course less important than its purpose. Once an institution has entered into a cooperative program with the Foundation, the first step for those who come to help is to make themselves expendable. Through fellowships and scholarships—for study both locally and abroad—the training of national educational leaders is facilitated; counterpart relationships between visitors and emerging national leaders are integral to the process. The Foundation's 54-year fellowship program under which over 10,000 fellowships have been awarded has proven an indispensable factor in this aspect of the UDP. As scholars return, key academic departments come under local leadership, and there is a magic moment of change to which visitors must be sensitive and alert. There is a time for visitors to leave or move to the background —but when is it? Is it when three Ph.D.'s have returned to a department, when one is serving as departmental chairman, or when two-thirds of the departments are under local leadership?

The tests for the ending of Phase I are at best rough and ready, and the developmental phase, even for disciplines with initially favorable prospects, may vary from a period of 5 to 10 years. But at some point, cooperating institutions must assume the first chapter is complete. It is time to change the form and substance of cooperation. Phase II signals the emergence of national leadership. However tempting it may be to protest that the transfer of responsibility is premature, the issue at this point is not negotiable. No one should expect that the new leadership will be carbon copies of the old. The type of person sent abroad to assist in Phase II should be more an adviser than an institution-builder, patient and responsive rather than aggressive, and willing to work through others while remaining in the background. His aim should be less to initiate, more to plant ideas in the minds of others. If Phase I requires a critical mass of outside institution-builders, Phase II calls for a very few, low-profile advisers. The time required for Phase II may be anywhere from one to three years.

Phase III is a period of consolidation, of putting new capacities and institutions to work. It involves planning for graduate programs, serving the community, and turning emergent human resources toward the solution of national and regional problems. Phase III is a period of reaping the harvest of earlier developmental efforts. The application of trained intelligence to problem-solving is for the first time fully possible. Not by accident each of the International Agriculture Institutes is located next to a university development center. Equally, an attack on unemployment problems profits from economics, engineering, and agricultural resources in university centers.

Phase IV is a time for giving back by those who have received. It involves first-generation university development centers helping second-generation centers. Thus, leadership in the newest UDP center at the University of Bahia is being provided by men such as Gabriel Velazquez of Universidad del Valle; at the University of Zaire by leaders from the University of East Africa; or by Philippine economists such as Dr. José Encarnacion teaching and directing research in Thailand and Indonesia.

To be effective a plan must be flexible, taking its cue from the strengths and weaknesses within each institution and adapting its timetable to changing needs. Because institutions differ, forms of assistance vary. The university centers that have been assisted fall into at least four broad categories or models (the Foundation during the 1960s gave some form of assistance to approximately 10 institutions or complexes of universities, but major support was concentrated in five centers).

Model I is university development in which the Foundation has been virtually a coequal partner over a sustained period, sharing a major part of costs and manpower needs. The Universidad del Valle is a provincial university in Cali, Colombia, with a student body of 5,000 and a new concept of a university for a developing country. Its goal has been to keep the university close to the community addressing itself to urgent social needs. It has been a leader in medical education for all of Latin America, directing the interests of students toward rural peoples through mandatory clinical residency in the Candelaria Rural Health Center, and teaching preventive medicine, child care, and family planning. In the early 1960s, the Medical School, which had enjoyed assistance throughout the 1950s, towered over the rest of the university, but a concerted effort was made to help raise the level of engineering, economics, and agricultural economics university administration, the humanities, and the basic sciences.

Model II finds the Foundation as in East Africa playing the role of catalytic agent helping initiate change or, in Raymond Fosdick's graphic phrase, providing the "extra engine put on to help . . . over a stiff grade." The Foundation's contribution has always been minor, first to the three independent national colleges, then to the federated University of East Africa, and most recently to the three national universities bound together by numerous functional ties and a common Inter-University Committee. However, 66 percent of all East African faculty have been Rockefeller Foundation scholars or holders of Special Lectureships established with Rockefeller Foundation funding for returning national scholars for whom an established post was not yet available. If the sample is limited to East Africans who are full professors and deans, 80 percent have had assistance. The Agricultural Faculty at Makerere College in Uganda reoriented its curriculum with greater emphasis on crop production during the leadership of Dean John Nickel, Rockefeller Foundation staff menber. The Institute of Development Studies in Nairobi reached maturity in the years of Dr. James S. Coleman's directorship. For a far-flung multinational university in these countries, help at crucial points can affect the entire university even though the total resources provided from outside may be small relative to the overall educational budget.

Model III involves help to more fully developed universities to complete or round out institutional development, or some aspect thereof. At the University of the Philippines, the application of this approach is illustrated in a dual sense. When General Carlos P. Romulo became president in 1963, he declared he would seek help for fields other than agriculture, engineering, and medicine, which had been strengthened through outside assistance over the years. Unless other areas including the social sciences and humanities could be developed, Romulo was convinced the university would not be worthy of the name. At the same time, the university pressed ahead to bring the graduate program in economics to the Ph.D. level and to establish the agriculture faculty as a regional center for graduate studies. In both instances, the Foundation provided supplementary fellowship funds and visiting professors to fill gaps until local faculty returned from study abroad.

Model IV involves help to strong points in a complex of universities within a city or region or to independent but cooperating universities. Institution-building in agriculture, the biomedical sciences, and economics has been fostered in three separate universities: Kasetsart, Mahidol, and Thammasat respectively, in Bangkok, Thailand; the strategy has been one of building on existing strength at the three centers. The goal for each has been the building of institutional strength capable of serving a wider geographical region (nine young Indonesian scientists are currently engaged in Ph.D. study at Mahidol University). While ideally university development should go on within the walls of a single institution, practically differing forms of institutional cooperation are possible with aggregate effects similar to the strengthening of one university. Once again, imagination and flexibility are of the essence.

Universities and National Development

The two lessons of greatest moment that derive from a decade's experience with the RF-UDP model are (1) the need for scientists and educators working abroad to operate within a framework reflecting the interrelatedness of human problems and knowledge; and (2) the need for continuity within a broad strategy or design having definable stages of development and looking toward points of completion.

With regard to the first, the very successes of foreign assistance can create new challenges and problems, some more exacting and perplexing than the failures. The work of development too often has been a "catch-up" operation. It is probably unfair to say that the success of the International Health Division created the population explosion, but surely it was a contributing factor. Improved health, lower mortality rates, and longer lifespans thereby add to a nation's problems. We see now some of the hazards in pursuing health or agricultural programs in isolation. The unique opportunity that university development presents is that advances on one front can be coordinated with determined and concentrated efforts along other fronts. Programs in improved health delivery systems can go on simultaneously with population control. Efforts to increase food production can be accompanied by inquiries into the economic and social consequences of the "green revolution." Instead of "catching up," the developing countries can be assisted in preparing for the problems that lie ahead 3, 5, or 10 years down the road.

On the second lesson, there is a striking difference between the approach of the International Health Division or the cooperative agricultural programs and many undertakings in international cooperation. It is sometimes noted that foreign assistance often involves the struggle to meet 20-year needs with a three-year program, two-year personnel, and one-year appropriations. By contrast, the Rockefeller Foundation's Mexican Agricultural Program was inaugurated in 1943. It has evolved from a limited exploratory effort, through a national program carefully housed in the Office of Special Studies within the Ministry of Agriculture, to the current International Maize and Wheat Improvement Center. Almost 30 years later, a handful of the original team of Rockefeller Foundation agricultural scientists continue to serve as participant-advisers in a fully Mexican international agricultural program, aiming to share with others the accumulated knowledge developed over the past three decades. There is a time to give assistance and a time to withhold it or bring it to an end. The University of the Philippines, under the vital and dynamic leadership of General Carlos P. Romulo, reached the stage, particularly in the arts and sciences, where strategically placed assistance could enable it to move to a new level of excellence. How short-sighted it would have been for agencies that had faithfully provided fellowship help in other periods in its history to have terminated aid at that point. Now, with the growing nationalization of the university, the possibilities and need for aid become more restricted and more sharply defined. But continuity of effort is essential if enduring institutions are to be developed.

The ultimate goal of institution-building is of course national development—to widen the range of choice open to the general population, improve the quality of life, and serve the most urgent needs of the people. As nations undertake this complex and many-sided task, they must rely to a large degree upon the strengths and involvement of their universities, with their necessary concentrations of talent. The universities, to be effectively involved, must understand the nation's needs and how best to meet them; this requires that universities participate with other agencies in the planning and execution of national programs. In this way, the university faculty and students can contribute to national progress as they teach and learn. Course offerings should become increasingly relevant, as new information related to national need is developed. University graduates should be much better equipped with both the knowledge and skills required for participation in accelerated national development. Faculty must increasingly teach from a basis of understanding derived both from a study of efforts of others (past and present) and from experience gained through involvement in meeting real needs of the region and people served by the university. Nor should the study of the humanities and social values be ignored, for these are determinants of the ways knowledge and skills will be used.

As universities demonstrate their usefulness not only as centers of scholarly effort but as institutions capable of joining scholarship with effective action, appreciation of them and support for them can be expected to follow.

EDUCATION FOR NATIONAL DEVELOPMENT:
THE UNIVERSITY
Michael P. Todaro and Colleagues

The University in a developing society must put the emphasis of its work on subjects of immediate moment to
the nation in which it exists, and it must be committed to
the people of that nation and their humanistic goals. . . .
We in poor societies can only justify expenditure on a
University—of any type—if it promotes real development
of our people. . . . The role of a University in a developing nation is to contribute; to give ideas, manpower, and
service for the furtherance of human equality, human
dignity and human development.[1]—President Julius Nyerere
of Tanzania and Chancellor of the University of East
Africa

University Development and National Development

Higher education (3rd level) in developing countries is a very
much smaller world than that of the 1st and 2nd levels. The proportion of enrolled students in the 3rd level was less than 3 percent
compared to over 97 percent in the 1st and 2nd levels in 1968. The
proportion of the number of teachers in the 3rd level was less than
8 percent compared to over 92 percent in the 1st and 2nd levels in
1968. Variation in the proportions for developing countries by major
regions in 1968 was as follows:

Regions	Percent of Enrolled Students in			Percent of Number of Teachers in		
	3d level	2d level	1st level	3d level	2d level	1st level
Asia	2.9	19.8	77.3	6.2	28.9	64.9
Africa	1.1	13.7	85.2	3.2	21.8	75.0
Latin America	2.5	17.4	80.1	7.2	31.1	61.7
North America (for comparison)	12.9	33.4	53.7	19.0	36.5	44.5

Source: Leo Goldstone, "A Summary Statistical Review of
Education in the World," (Paris: UNESCO, June 1971), Tables 3 and 8.

While there is a considerable variety of institutions in higher education—for example, colleges and professional schools—the university is generally identified as the most important and apex institution. It is important to realize that universities in the developing countries now have and will continue to have a very real monopoly of the training of the national intelligentsia, and that the great majority of those who will be in positions to influence the future course of education in these countries in 10 or 15 years are in their universities today. Yet universities in the developing countries have been found by practically all informed observers to be as dysfunctional and disoriented as educational institutions in lower levels. Many of the problems basic to primary and secondary education recur in more or less aggravated form in universities: annual increases in the order of 10 percent in student enrollment, rising costs, declining pupil-teacher ratios, deficient facilities, inappropriate curricula, administrative inertia, and ever more serious problems of unemployment or malemployment for university graduates.

The basic causes of university defects have been examined in what is now a substantial literature and are generally agreed upon. Practically all universities in the developing countries have been modeled in structure and function after the older institutions in the industrialized societies. In the 1950s and 1960s, most international programs for university development have resulted in (even where it was not the primary intention) patterning university additions and changes in the developing countries to resemble university organization and practices established in the United States, Great Britain, and other more developed countries. By long and powerful tradition the universities of the Western world are structured by disciplines or professions, as they have been since the medieval period. This structure, departments (disciplines), and their grouping (faculty) was exported on a large scale to universities in the developing countries, with little thought or effort given to questions of how this mode of academic organization would fit or serve existing conditions. "Excellence" continued to be measured in terms of international academic standards rather than contributions to national development.

In recent years, however, increasing attention has been devoted to the functions and structure of universities in the developing countries that directly relate to goals and needs of national development.

The Rockefeller Foundation University Development Program

In its own efforts, and these have been substantial, the Rockefeller Foundation has concentrated exclusively on universities. This

UDP has been highly selective both in the choice of universities and in providing the kind of support deemed appropriate for different stages of university development. These stages inevitably vary among the particular universities selected, and over time in any one university. Distinctive aims and features of this program have been set forth in the preceding essay.

During the 1960s, however, the distinction between university development as an end in itself and university development as a means toward national development has been blurred. Accordingly, the time has come to clarify and define our higher education goals in the broader context of national development and to delineate the operating mechanism for achieving these objectives. University development must be seen and must function not as an end in itself but as a fundamental and essential means toward the realization of defined national development objectives. The term "university development" is itself a misnomer since it can easily and often has given a misleading notion of our ultimate objectives. A more apt phrase might be "Education for National Development." Furthermore, success should not be measured in terms of the number of departmental faculty trained or the international reputation of a particular scholar or cluster of scholars. Rather, success or failure should be measured in terms of the degree to which the university community has participated in and contributed toward the solution of national development problems. Finally, while the focus is on education, it should be pointed out that the same concept should apply to all other programs and efforts in the field of national development.

What We Mean by "National Development"

What are these national development problems? And are they sufficiently general to serve as a common operational set of objectives with appropriate measures of success or failure in programs of support of higher education in Africa, Asia, and Latin America? While recognizing that priorities and needs differ from country to country, the fundamentals of national development can indeed be delineated and their ubiquity is sufficient to justify a common methodological approach.

One starting point in determining what we mean by national development is to ask the central question raised by Gandhi's life and thought, "what are the necessary conditions for a universally acceptable aim, the realization of the potential of human personality?" And how can this potential be crystallized at the national and regional level? We believe that national development efforts, to be really meaningful, should focus on the appropriate production and more

206

equitable distribution of the following three basic elements: food, income, and quality social services, including education and health. Moreover, it is important that a fourth basic element be included, namely, cultural values and national identity.

In view of the above factors, the relevant questions to ask about a country's development are the following:

1. What has been happening to the production and distribution of food and to nutrition?

2. What has been happening to unemployment and the distribution of income?

3. What has been happening to the distribution of social services and such indices as rates of mortality, morbidity, and literacy?

4. What has been happening to the awareness and directions of cultural values and national identity?

If all four of these have been improved, then clearly there has been a period that we could confidently call one of "national development." If two or three of these central problems have been growing worse, especially if all four have deteriorated, it would be strange to call the result "development," even if per capita incomes, aggregate food production, and educational enrollments have grown.[2]

The fundamental question, therefore, to ask with regard to any assessment of the impact of support for higher education and training in agriculture, medicine, humanities, and the social sciences is "how and in what way is this support assisting the university in its effort to contribute to the solution of the basic problems of undernourishment, poverty, inequality, and values?" In many instances the university's impact will be difficult to measure, but this should be no excuse for a failure to undertake such an assessment. It is clearly preferable to a system of minimal assessment with no meaningful success criteria. Counting the number of Ph.D.'s is clearly insufficient.

The fundamental question just posed, however, involves others: What is the nature and cause(s) of underdevelopment, or backwardness? Once alternatives are worked out, what solutions are to be adopted? What kind of society should development create? How sound are development policies and priorities now in force? The study and resolution of these and related problems can and should be a primary, if not the controlling, function of a university in its established activities of teaching, research, and service with regard to factors such as food (agriculture), income (economics and business), health and other social services, and culture.

Some Thoughts on a Model for a "University for National Development"

Recognizing that universities in developing countries have rarely in fact been organized to further national development, nor have they often contributed directly to it, the question arises, "What would a university addressed to national development in a developing country be like?"[3] How might it be structured more effectively? This question must be examined in some detail for the four development goals, or problem areas, already named—food, income, health and other social services, and culture.

At the center of university work toward national development are the tasks of identifying and resolving developmental problems. To be effective, these problem-solving functions require the appropriate structuring of academic activities and resources in education and training, research, and services. The major divisions of a university for national development should accordingly be directed to and organized around major national development problem areas. For example, in terms of the problem areas identified, the relationship might be as follows:

Problem Area	University Division
Agricultural Production and Distribution (Food, Nutrition, and so on)	Division of Agricultural Production and Supply
Economic and Social Affairs (Poverty, Social Justice Distribution of Income, and so on)	Division of Economic and Social Affairs
Social Services: Health / Education	Division of Health / Division of Education
Cultural Development and Identity	Division for Cultural Affairs

Besides these four development goals or problems, it is important to note that there are others such as industrial production, housing, power and water supply, transport, fuels, and communication facilities. Their treatment within a university could be along lines of similar divisions organized by major problem areas with needed disciplinary inputs.

Each division might have at its top, or be immediately related to, a center or institute (for example, the Center for Rural Development, the Center for Educational Reform, and so on) engaged in strictly problem-identifying or problem-solving activities. It would then be important for these several centers to work closely together so as to ensure integrated approaches wherever possible to problems of national development. Each division would be composed of departments that would focus their research, teaching, and services on identified problem areas, as shown, for example, in the following chart:

University Division	Constituent Departments
Agricultural Production and Supply	Production (by product type and condition)
	Policy (resource use, prices, wages, finance, mechanization, and so on)
	Supply (storage, processing, distribution, marketing, and so on)
	Education (teacher education; formal curricula and institution; nonformal systems)
Economic and Social Affairs	Population Problems
	Poverty and Unemployment
	Social Justice: Institutions
	Rural and Urban Development
	Education for Development
	Social and Economic Policy
Division of Health	Medicine
	Nursing
	Medical Assistant and/or Nurse Practitioners
	Auxilliary
Cultural Affairs	Languages
	Cultural Studies
	Arts

When the orientation to development problems is pushed one step further, the major units within each department would also be problem focused. Two examples are as follows: the Department of

Medicine (Division of Health) would be made up of these four main units: communicable diseases, nutrition, population, and individual medicine. In the Division of Agricultural Production and Supply, the Policy Problem Department would have units for resource control and use; price, wages, taxation, stabilization; agricultural finance; exports and imports, technology, and mechanization; and special programs. Departments would not be unidisciplinary as in conventional universities. Rather, they would consist of those disciplines relevant to the particular problem unit.* A notable feature throughout is that disciplines are subordinated to problem-oriented functions, not the more familiar other way around. Moreover, each of the various divisions is envisaged as part of an integrated network designed to focus on problems of national development from a multidisciplinary perspective. Students would be primarily associated with a specific division and their training would have a necessary degree of disciplinary concentration. However, a graduate, say in economics or agriculture, would be quite different from his typical counterpart in conventional developing country universities. He would embody training in a variety of relevant disciplines essential to the goal of understanding and solving identified and real national development objectives.

All departments would have teaching responsibilities that would stress problem identification, diagnosis, and solution. An important instructional requirement is that each division, though not necessarily each department, provides training for all levels of activity within respective problem areas (such as health services) from the least to the more sophisticated and complex. This is essential to achieve two purposes. One is that development work in any field, such as agriculture, requires a team or concerted approach, the interrelated effort of many skills and techniques; a person engaged in development work should therefore be acquainted with all the various skills and techniques pertinent to his particular lines of endeavor, which are bound to change over time. This might be epitomized in the rule "Don't ask others to do things of which you are ignorant."

The second purpose has far-reaching consequences for education. It is to foster practical attention and adaptive performance in the university to virtually all levels of education and training in development areas (even though the number of students trained at any level be small, even nominal). The university is thereby informed of and

---

*More detailed description and discussion of this problem-oriented university organization is available on request from the Rockefeller Foundation.

equipped in the conditions, problems, and processes of all levels of education, formal and nonformal, primary and secondary.

This second purpose leads to brief comments (worth fuller exposition elsewhere) on ways the university can—and should—contribute to primary and secondary education as institutional means to further national development. For reasons hard to explain and still harder to justify, universities have generally chosen to ignore or taken for granted (often with considerable disdain) education outside their own level and immediate commitments. The obvious exception is a university unit (institute, faculty, department, college, and so on) in education, which, whatever its work and effect, is agreeably not typically recognized by other dominant parts of the university. When it exists, the education unit usually trains secondary, even primary, teachers and prepares curricula and teaching materials at those levels, but it proceeds without a problem-oriented and serious interest and input by other major divisions of the university. In other words, except for their education units (often the weakest part) universities have not taken the world of primary and secondary education as a significant object for attention, study, and appropriate action. Individually, university staff members may worry about this when their children are in schools: Then they face up transitorily to the realities of the pre-university education.

Given the huge number of persons relative to university enrollment in primary and secondary education, problem-oriented departments can and should attend to "lower" levels of education as important and neglected avenues toward national development in their respective spheres of concern. What is urgently needed are detailed studies and well-conceived experiments undertaken primarily by indigenous universities and governmental agencies working together with the partial assistance of outside donor agencies to answer such questions—among many—as the following: [4]

1. At what age should a child, who is going to have only a few years of primary education, enter school?

2. Should primary education in a rural community in a developing country be full or part time?

3. Given some type of formal education for children, do literacy and numeracy constitute the highest-priority area of instruction for those destined to spend the rest of their lives in a rural zone?

4. How can the primary school curriculum be restructured to provide the majority of students who are likely to live and work in rural areas with the knowledge, skills, and new ideas necessary to function effectively in their rural environment?

Most of the pupils in the developing countries live in rural areas where the bulk of the population, land area, and potential resources are concentrated. The development of these rural areas is a sine qua non of national development; and rural development goals and problems center on those four national development objectives summarized earlier. University work on rural development is even more urgent and important than in primary and secondary education, though the two are obviously related. This work is of such overriding significance for national development that support for universities in developing countries should be focused in the first instance on those countries where there is a rural integrated program. This would make possible concerted cooperation and support of both a rural integrated program and a university for national development in the same country committed to working with and serving that program. Thus the balance and integration of efforts urged on the one hand for university work geared to national development, and on the other for rural development, would be applied to both spheres.

Any university oriented toward national development and structured along the unconventional lines suggested above should ensure that its staff members and students have appropriate recognition, primarily in the national but also, to a lesser extent, in the international community, as bona fide scholars and scientists. Insofar as this continues to be viewed in terms of the attainment of accepted international professional standards, it may encourage keen interest in and attraction toward the international scene, even professional careers in foreign countries, to the disadvantage of national development in the country where the university is located. To minimize risks of emigration, the university, in cooperation with the public and private sectors, must be able to manipulate prestige factors purposefully through financial and nonfinancial incentives. Some of these factors or incentives lie within the scales of cultural values within the country in question, recognizing that cultural values and how they are rated vary greatly from one country to another. (A serious problem for either an international or national point of view is excessive self-interest, where the person puts his own enhancement before anything else.) In the 1950s certain institutions and groups deliberately promoted the Ph.D. degree as a symbol of achievement and qualification, making it virtually a union card for academic advancement. Today other standards need to be devised and fortified, standards that elevate and reward work for national development.

Notes

1. From his opening speech, "The University's Role in the Development of New Countries," World University Service Assembly, Dar es Salaam, Tanzania, June 27, 1966.

2. For a more complete statement of this approach to defining development, see D. Seers, "The Meaning of Development," Agricultural Development Council, September 1970.

3. A timely discussion of this issue is contained in C. Leys, "The Role of the University in an Underdeveloped Country" in Education News, Department of Education and Science, Canberra, Australia, April 1971, pp. 6-14.

4. Nicholas Bennett, "Primary Education in Rural Communities: An Investment in Ignorance," mimeo., 1972, pp. 5-6.

HIGHER EDUCATION IN ETHIOPIA IN THE 1970s AND BEYOND: A SURVEY OF SOME ISSUES AND RESPONSES
Aklilu Habte

This section reviews the development of "modern" higher education in Ethiopia, analyzes some problems likely to arise in the future, and suggests ways and means to meet them. While the paper speaks of Ethiopia, I believe it could have a broader interest because it treats issues of common concern to many developing countries and to those providing them with assistance.

It is now fashionable in some literature on educational planning to question the value of universities to the world's poorer countries. I sympathize with some of the concerns that generate these questions but not with the negative conclusions sometimes expressed. Using Ethiopia as an illustration and by concrete examples, I will try to show that universities can play a dynamic role in helping to meet some of the crises of the 1970s and beyond.

The First Decade

Haile Sellassie I University (HSIU) was founded in 1961. Its charter consolidated existing, autonomous colleges for agriculture, public health, technology, arts, and science. In the following three years, steps were taken to organize new faculties of education, business, law, medicine, and social work as well as to develop a broad extension program.

Unlike many universities in sub-Sahara Africa, ours was not modeled on any particular foreign counterpart, nor was there any original "master plan" or clear conception for its development. The various professional schools differed from each other in terms of academic traditions followed and international background of staff. Each enjoyed considerable flexibility and autonomy in formulating its aim and devising its programs. Despite and because of this diversity, and the initial shortage of Ethiopian staff, we were able to mold these divergent patterns and be eclectic in choice of policies for institutional development. The basic principle has been as follows: This is an Ethiopian university; it must, perforce, be sui generis. This theme underscored a truth often overlooked, that while the term "university" may have some universal meaning, one should not assume any particular model in developing countries to denote the character of an institution administering higher education.

Haile Sellassie I University's growth from 1961-62 to 1972-73 is sketched in the following table:

	1961-62	1972-73
Number of regular day students	948	3,941
Number of evening extension students	1,026	3,293
Inservice teacher education	192	1,908
Graduates: (totals 1961-72)	—	—
Certificates 1,033	—	—
Diploma 4,779	—	—
Degree 3,695	—	—
Proportion of Ethiopian staff (percent)	34	56.5
University service participants	129	543

I wish now to recapitulate several underlying ideas that characterized development over the first decade and affect our approach toward the second.

Meeting the Manpower Needs of the Country

First, there has been a pragmatic concern about the variegated character of the requirements for high-level manpower and the kinds of higher education needed in Ethiopia, Accordingly, the university has been deliberately developed as a multipurpose system of postsecondary education rather than a homogeneous, monolithic institution with uniform standards governing academic programs, admissions, faculty recruitment, and the like. At the outset, a series of important decisions legitimized and stressed various kinds of programs as integral functions of various faculties and of the extension division. Consequently, professional schools have undertaken part-time or subdegree or other special programs concerned with the education of, for example, rural sanitarians and community nurses, school principals, secretaries, surveyors, community development officers, police officers, judges, and members of parliament and many other groups. Evening programs have enabled many hard-working people, including some high officials, to win degrees or diplomas in law, business, public administration, and other fields. At any given point, in recent years, more than 50 percent of our students have been enrolled in part-time subdegree programs; thus, when one thinks of "the students," the programs, and the objectives of HSIU, the range of vision must be broad if it is to be accurate.

Rural Orientation of the University's Programs

Second, for a long time, there has been concern about the relation of higher education to the diverse rural sectors of the country where over 95 percent of the people live. Two university campuses are located in rural areas. Much of the university's enrollment will shift to them so that eventually they will provide the basis for systems of regional higher education that put stress on rural and regional development. From the beginning, the Public Health College has sent teams of students to local health stations where, under supervision, they live and work for extended periods as part of their regular training. A year after its effective formation, the Faculty Council (Senate) of the university borrowed the idea from the Public Health College and launched the Ethiopian University Service (EUS) program. Each full-time regular student is now required to spend a year in the countryside, working in a service capacity related to his field of study, while paid only a modest living allowance by the employing agency. Many EUS students have taught in rural schools, and nearly 40 percent each year have worked in other fields—for example, local administration, courts or tax offices, community development, construction projects, provincial banks, or other jobs related to their professional studies. While "service" is one function of EUS, the primary rationale is educational: to create greater appreciation of the diverse regions of the country, the way in which most Ethiopians live, the problems of rural development, and the value of practical experience in that setting. The faculty is directly involved through selection of service projects for students, staffing of EUS orientation courses, assigning individual research projects, and maintaining liaison and seminars in the field with students. While much needs to be done to develop the academic potential of EUS, it provides the basis for participation of teachers and students in rural development.

University Planning and Development

Third, the university has long struggled with the problems of how to develop priorities, fix enrollments, and inspire critical self-study and innovation. Various devices have been used to make planning a pervasive, continuing task. A special 50-member Presidential Commission worked through the academic year 1967/68 to identify longer-range goals, evaluate the costs of various university operations, and recommend "phase-outs" and "consolidations" of lesser priority or duplicatory programs. Thereafter, a permanent university planning office was established and a five-year plan produced, which set out various manpower policies and projected the shifting of much instruction to the rural Alemaya and Gondar campuses. This plan was then presented to the board and to the government, and its main themes have been incorporated in Ethiopia's third five-year plan (1968-73) and, more recently, in the government's Education Sector Review of 1972.

Again, on a macro-level, a distinguished multinational Chancellor's Advisory Committee has twice reviewed the university's planning and progress, reporting directly to the emperor in his capacity as chancellor.

From the beginning, the Faculty Council fixed quotas governing the flow of students into various professional schools. Almost 60 percent of all students have been enrolled in the fields of agriculture, scientific, and technological studies, and about 30 percent of the total in the education programs—obligating themselves for service to the nation's schools.

Other efforts have been directed toward the stimulation of critical, realistic planning in each major professional sector of the university. Meetings have been convened, often lasting several days, to bring together academic persons, civil servants, business people, and other professionals to evaluate educational and research needs and develop a more effective procedure of "feedback." Recently, many university staff played significant roles in the work of the Education Sector Review undertaken by the government. Many university staff are now members of the government's Sectoral Planning Task Forces and other working committees and commissions. Thus, slowly, we have developed indispensable linkages with the government and the public and have capitalized on this experience for future planning. However, as I shall indicate below, much remains to be learned and to be done.

Challenges of the 1970s

Following guidelines laid down at the UNESCO Conferences in Addis Ababa (1961) and Tananarive (1962), during the 1960s Ethiopia put great stress on secondary and higher education. In my view, this was right for the times: The nation desperately needed all kinds of high-level and middle-level manpower in every professional sector, notably in education. Virtually none of our graduates have gone unemployed, and urgent need for talent in many sectors will long continue. Indeed, without the university's growth in the 1960s, it is hard to envision how we could move to confront problems of the "second development decade."

Yet, quite different kinds of human resources problems face us now. While data are lacking (a problem itself), it seems safe to enumerate them as follows: (1) a growing amount of unemployment, among secondary-school-leavers and school "dropouts," particularly in urban areas; (2) diminishing employment opportunity for university graduates generally trained in the arts and sciences; (3) a continuing increasing public demand for education at all levels; (4) limited resources to expand the present educational system in its present form; (5) a need to develop rural communities and create new opportunities for local rural-centered employment; (6) a need for planned development of the various regions of the nation; and (7) a need for a "new breed" of diverse human resources to engage in the work of rural development. All these point to an overall need to restructure the educational system in order to respond to new conditions and new objectives.

Within the university, among other things, we have faced the persisting problem of student unrest and more political protest activities, financial uncertainty, and the need for a new kind of university teacher and for new methods of perceiving and developing the role of university teachers. We need to build a profound, pervasive, new philosophy that will characterize the underlying values and purposes of the university as a vehicle for national progress. I assume many of these challenges might be common to many other countries. Outlined below are some steps being taken to meet them.

The University and National Human Resources: Priorities: New Tasks for Higher Education—An Overview

I have sketched a somewhat familiar profile of human resource needs and employment problems confronting Ethiopia. The Report of the Education Sector Review (1972) projected, among other things, the following policies and programs:

1. A basic redesign of and new priority on efforts to develop rural communities, including a new system of Awraja (district) administration (discussed below) and the new systems to deliver, in tandem, educational, health, agricultural, and related technical services to Awraja communities.

2. A significant shift of resources within the educational system to expand "first-level" rural schooling and extension and nonformal education in Awrajas, and a redesign of these programs to provide "minimum formation education" and other forms of training relevant to local human resources objectives.

3. A redesign of secondary education to limit its growth, make schools more "comprehensive," and emphasize "terminal" programs; to develop more schools as centers for "apprentice" and "on-the-job" vocational training and for continuing education programs (both formal and nonformal).

4. Initiation of a National Service Program, which will enlist secondary-school-leavers and others into rural public works cadres, provide them a subsistence allowance, teach them job skills, and accord service "veterans" a priority in terms of university admission.

218

5. Shifting much of the burden of costs of higher education to those who receive it through a system of tuition and loans.

6. Initiation, throughout the educational system, of methods to achieve a more sensitive monitoring and study of manpower trends and needs.

7. Other reforms and innovations supportive of the above policies and generally designed to emphasize such goals as rural development and development administration.

The implications of these decisions for the university are exciting. Contrary to the speculation of some international experts, I believe higher education must supply indispensable leadership if policies of this kind are to be realized. Illustrative of new task confronting us are the following:

1. Redesign of many programs within the Faculty of Education and participation in the development of new methods, curricula and teaching materials for both rural elementary and secondary education;

2. Participation, probably through the university service programs and a system of University Rural Centers (described below), in the development of the National Service Program;

3. A panoply of new university extension and nonformal programs to provide teachers and training projects for farmers, rural teachers, community development officers, Awraja government personnel, and others;

4. A new emphasis in various professional schools on the administration and the delegation of new powers of self-government to the Awrajas;

5. Creation, in cooperation with the government, of new institutions for development-centered research;

6. Development of a system of tuition charges and loans for full-time students (described below) and expansion of part-time education; and

7. Development of our system of university planning in accord with these guidelines.

The Education Sector Review Report recommends continued enrollment growth of the university at a rate of over 5 percent per year to the end of the century. In accordance with guidelines established by our own planning (notably the Presidential Commission of 1967/68), this expansion, in the immediate future, will largely occur on the rural campuses of Alemaya and Gondar. Through a general system of quotas, it will stream most students into training programs for education and teacher training technology, agriculture, community development, and medical and health services. Much of the cost of this increase, if it is to occur, will have to be shifted to those who will enjoy the benefits of university education. Of course, our growth must be controlled if available employment opportunities and manpower

needs and finance harden. But we must also think of the long haul.
In an increasingly complex world, it is hard to think of national capacity for social and technological change without a bigger stock of well-educated people. Our estimated current population is over 24 million people. An enrollment of about 20,000 regular students by 1990 seems a modest prediction for a population that will exceed 40 million around 1999.

The Development of University Institutions for Planning, Governance, and Accountability

Our charter, following Anglo-American conventions, created the university as a rather autonomous, "inner-directed" corporation. In a legal sense, it was linked and accountable to government only at the top, primarily through its Board of Governors and chancellor. Major powers to shape the institution were given to its faculty, looked upon in the traditional way as an independent body of scholars. While I deeply value academic freedom, scholarship, and faculty autonomy, it is clear that these concepts must be analyzed in a new context and balanced with other interests.

The university must be a participant in development, not simply a detached body of critics. It must be seen as an integral part of the total system of education. Its various goals must be the result of a very complex process of collaborative planning with many different government counterpart and other public bodies. The value of programs must be tested by measuring performance in terms of very concrete, albeit changing, goals. Our system of governance and accountability must stress these concepts and find new ways to institutionalize them. Unless such steps will be taken, it will be difficult to respond to other challenges.

Our successful experience in helping to shape the Education Sector Review teaches that the university must participate in national development planning in the same way as other major government agencies. The participation can be pervasive, since so many of our activities are identified with one or another sector of development— for example, education, agriculture, health, public administration, and legal and institutional development.

Internally, the university must redesign its planning machinery, including five-year plans correspondent with national plans. The central planning machinery must be linked to "sectoral" university planning bodies within each major professional area (for example, agriculture, health, law, and administration). These in turn must be linked both to correspondent government bodies and to the traditional decision-making centers within the university—academic (faculty) commissions, the university-wide Faculty Council, and the Board of Governors.

220

The university must develop other systems for accountability, which will also force more attention to the concerns of planning. Evaluation of academic programs should include (1) academic experts capable of measuring programs against generally understood international standards, as well as (2) Ethiopian external assessors drawn from the professions; these will evaluate both the preparedness of various professional graduates to assume functional roles and the relevance of much of our curricula and teaching materials to local phenomena.

In collaboration with other agencies, the university will develop a human resources research unit that will make continued studies of changing manpower needs, follow-up studies of graduates in various sectors, cost-benefit analyses, and other means for constant monitoring and "feedback" on manpower problems.

Some of these steps will require painful new orientation and external assistance, and this is, I think, a fertile field for future international cooperation.

The Problem of Costs—and Equalizing Opportunity

We need no reminder that higher education is a terribly expensive undertaking in our presently poor country. The financing of it has been a source of great frustration. Budget limitations have forced a decline in per student recurrent expenditure from U.S. $2,900 in 1961 to about $1,500. The Presidential Commission of 1967/68 engaged in the agonizing process of reviewing priorities, recommending "phase-outs" and "consolidations." Our students do not live in luxury, and our staff has little logistical support. Most teaching loads are excessive to the detriment of research and other creative work. Creativity and innovation require time, reflection, application, some institutionalization, and adequate support.

The Presidential Commission strongly urged a tuition-loan system to shift part of the costs of higher education to those who directly benefit from it. The university, in collaboration with the government, will gradually move to introduce a system of student fees and financial aid. While part of the cost might be paid in cash, the other part could be paid through long-term low-interest loans (with some remission of the debt for those who serve in critical hardship jobs in rural areas). Scholarships could be set aside for particular cases of proven need.

Obviously, it will be difficult to implement this decision. The critical task is to project it as part of a basic philosophy of sacrifice that must characterize participation in the work of the university at every level. Tuition must be justified on civic and educational grounds as well as public financial need. The private decision to attend the university will not be an easy one when the public pays so much of the investment in the individual's future. The individual himself must be prepared to commit more of his own future resources to his career; thus, his education will perforce become more valuable to him.

A second way will be through continuous review of our costs through more sophisticated budget and audit procedures. This requires a build-up, now under way, of an administrative capacity previously lacking.

Our studies have shown that the majority of university entrants come from Addis Ababa, Asmara, and the few other large towns of the nation. A disproportionate number are probably from the more economically advantaged families. I believe such conditions are common the world over, but, as with other countries, in Ethiopia we must correct them and broaden opportunity for access to education.

Historically, the university has experimented with special admissions streams for full-time degree study—for example, by recruiting students from diverse parts of the country for admission to the faculty of education through our own "experimental" senior secondary school and by opening streams of admission for students from several agricultural and technical schools and streams for provincial school teachers, for military officers, civil servants, and other "mature age" entrants.

Consistent with the government's new emphasis on rural development, the university might have to allocate deliberately a quota of seats within future entering classes to applicants from remoter regions who qualify under particular admissions criteria. Of course this must go hand in hand with a program for improving these schools and must be a temporary measure. If necessary, remedial teaching will be provided to educationally disadvantaged entrants, particularly in language skills. This may not be an easy undertaking. Hopefully, it will be better appreciated in the context of the university's broader new commitment to rural development.

The University and Rural Development

As noted, the government in Ethiopia will hopefully initiate major changes, including, I believe, these steps:

1. Delegation of powers to Awraja governments to tax and spend locally, to plan community development, to build and maintain schools, health clinics, roads, markets, and other facilities;

2. Reorganization of the structures of Awraja governments, including creation of an elective council;

3. Encouragement of micro-development planning at the Awraja level, and the "packaging" of services and projects noted below;

4. The redesigning and strengthening of agricultural extension services within Awrajas;

5. Development of nonformal, rural educational programs in literacy, home economics, health, and so on, and special training for local officials, police, and court personnel;

6. Redesign of rural schooling (as previously described);

7. Institution, where appropriate, of land reform schemes;

8. Provision of new human resources for Awraja administration to supply technical competence—for example, in law, accounting, taxation, and rural engineering;

9. Formation of cooperatives and other institutions to develop commerical agriculture and encouragement of particularly suitable agro-industries; and

10. Mass civic training about these activities.

The planning for mobilization and coordinated, effective use of diverse resources to engage in this work, initially on a pilot basis in a few selected areas, poses very difficult challenges. We will need a new breed of manpower, continued study of experience and, above all, a team approach—recognizing that Awraja development calls for a combination of high level skills working together. The implications to the university are exciting. In recent years, we have sought ways to use the university service as a more effective vehicle for "clinical" and multidisciplinary teaching, for more sophisticated work and research by teams of students and staff on the problems of Awraja development. Given appropriate assistance we will, in cooperation with other agencies, establish University Rural Centers in a number of selected cooperating Awrajas where teams of university service (and perhaps national service) students and teachers drawn from different disciplines will work together. The base of operations may be a school, a community center, or a church. It is our hope that, through its Rural Centers, substantial numbers of people from the university community can periodically be transplanted to rural areas, that these centers will open extraordinary new opportunities for clinical and cooperative education, research, service, and a sense of participation in the most critical work of the nation.

The development of the University Rural Centers can give impetus to other changes such as the redesign of teaching materials for rural schools; expansion of extension and "nonformal" training programs organized collaboratively with the schools of Education, Agriculture, Law, Social Work, and many others; a new emphasis on rural development within various professional curricula; and a new impetus for research and publication.

The high-level manpower implications of rural development need to be studied at the earliest opportunity. The university is now engaging in this work through participation in the sector reviews of the third plan and the preparation of the fourth and studies that will be undertaken by its new Institute of Development Research, which is more fully described below.

It is difficult for me to see how the fundamental plans for Ethiopian rural development can go forward effectively without deep university involvement. It is equally difficult to envision a university in my country that is not fundamentally engaged through almost all of its units, in this work.

The University and Research

Research has been limited because, among other things, teaching loads, in most units, have been heavy and funds for logistical support scarce, and capacity has been low and turnover (among expatriate staff) high. With Ethiopianization of our staff and the development of more systematic planning, we must develop new research policies and program budgeting to fulfill the following goals:

1. The continuous development of teaching material—notably Ethiopian-centered material—in the social and administrative sciences, law, history, and geography.

2. Applied research on important aspects of agriculture, education, public health, population, and biological phenomena—often in cooperation with other public agencies.

3. Development of school and extension educational materials (including audiovisual) and new teaching methods in cooperation with other public agencies.

4. Identification and preservation of Ethiopian archives, art, music, and historical artifacts—the build-up of resources to study our own culture.

5. Development of better testing devices to determine aptitudes and abilities of applicants to and students within the university; development of more efficient, objective testing methods to be used in various courses throughout the university.

6. Continuous study of high-level manpower problems (a topic discussed above).

7. Development of a multidisciplinary university agency that will work in direct, continuous cooperation with government on problems of formulating development policy and evaluation of programs and laws concerned with development, notably rural.

8. Selected institutions for pan-African research that will work with the UN and Organization of African Universities and other

agencies and, at the same time, contribute intellectual leadership to some important field of comparative studies. (The newly established Center for African Legal Development is an example.)

9. The build-up of infrastructure for research, notably for training in methodology, data processing and statistical analysis, and the formation of a university press service capable of producing and circulating a wide variety of materials.

A number of institutes within the university have been already created, as noted in the Appendix. The newest, and most exciting, endeavor is the Institute of Development Research (IDR), created to encourage university staff to work with Ethiopian public agencies and, sometimes, with cooperating foreign experts in applied research. Projects are selected in accordance with rigorous criteria, and contribute directly to the formation, implementation, and evaluation of development goals. IDR is a service agency with a governing board drawn not only from university disciplines but also from government and parastatal agencies. The goals are to build IDR's research capacity, to have a sufficient "critical mass" of core staff, to attract funds to produce results, and to quicken the interest of university teachers and public agencies. IDR's priority area will be rural development. The dearth of knowledge about our rural communities is appalling. IDR should serve as a major catalyst to define problems of rural development more critically. Ultimately, IDR will become a training agency to give young staff and advanced students a competence in research methods and data processing. This also should be a fertile field for international cooperation.

The University and Social and Cultural Development

Much of the currently fashionable literature on educational planning and "development" puts stress on instrumental, economic goals, paying scant attention to others. In my view, the civic and cultural development of our people is indispensable to other forms of development. Precisely because these problems receive so little systematic attention in the emergent discipline(s) of educational planning, it is difficult to treat them while avoiding flabby clichés.

In Ethiopia, there is a pressing need for basic civic education. We must foster a more rational, scientific outlook toward life. We must understand our true history, our environment—natural and social. We must appreciate the value and dynamics of a plural society. We must confront age-old discriminations against certain groups in our society—including women. The dignity and value of manual work must be stressed; service and sacrifice in behalf of social goals must be emphasized. Civic education must encourage understanding of democratic institutions and citizenship. The meaning of institutions for participation in the fundamental decisions affecting the community, local and national, and the nature of institutions such as Parliament and (in the future) the elected councils of local government, must be made clear. Civic education must also deal with the evils, economic as well as moral, of corruption. Justice and law as a means to vindicate the oppressed is a valued part of our tradition. However, the mass of people know little and may distrust the very new legal paraphernalia of law administration. We must find ways to educate people about our modern law's fundamental concerns and find ways to instill more confidence in new forms of legal processes.

The university can help to provide leadership to meet these needs. (A "comprehensive plan" to address them can be developed just as we plan for other sectors.) Basic books on history, government, goegraphy, and social studies could be written in the national language of our country. Extension, using expertise drawn from law, community development, government, and many other fields can use mass media to carry learning about modern institutions to our people. The law school will hopefully establish a "clinic" oriented toward legal problems of the poor, which I see as a vehicle to expose information now lacking about the problem of delivering justice and to generate wider concern about needed reforms. Similar "clinics" concerned with other professional services can be developed from this model so that more students know the concerns of the urban and rural poor. University and other agencies' centers can be a vehicle for civic education for all levels of the population.

In Ethiopia, we must be concerned with cultural education. We are importing indiscriminately, and our educated youth reject so much of our own tradition, that we may soon face serious difficulties of identity and purpose. We must find ways of discovering and sustaining the unique, core values of our own culture and subcultures. The mass of our people are deeply religious. They believe in the importance of family, in the virtue of true courage, in civility, in the dignity of individuality, in the wisdom of age and experience. Our historic music, poetry, and painting are similarly unique. But the arts of the nation and many other traditions, mostly oral, will soon be lost if they are not recaptured in more enduring forms.

Once again the field may call for more systematic planning. University people can help to provide schoolchildren as well as the general public with adequate books and other materials to enable them to know the whole country, to see its art and diverse geography and peoples and to hear its music. The hope of our Theological College is that it will carry a new spirit and administrative vigor to the church, which, for centuries, has been carrier of culture and builder of identity. Through the Institute of Ethiopian Studies and Creative

226

Arts Center, the university can encourage a wider appreciation of traditional art as well as the work of modern artists, and with audio-visual methods, performances can be brought to masses of people. Again, extension can be used creatively and systematically. Our linguists could be solicited to work on the pedagogic and linguistic development of Amharic to cope with new and technological concepts.

The University and Politicized Student Discontent

The problems here are in part understandable, in part intractable. In our present historical situation, some degree of "confrontation" is bound to arise when students perceive the gap between taught theories and possibilities for the betterment of the human condition and what exists; between announced official goals and apparent performance. Students have indeed found viable issues to protest and publicize, and they will find more in the future. But the causes of unrest include other complex factors, such as the strangeness of a university environment; naiveté about realities in life due to limitations of background; uncertainty about career motivation and the future and, for some, often gifted, the threat of failure and unemployment; lack of effective outlets to make tangible, recognized contributions to society; the frustrations of generation and cultural gaps and problems of identity; the agitation of age-old regional loyalties and intergroup suspicions, compounded by allegations or fears of discrimination; and so on.

The problem is to make sure that the work of the university should not be paralyzed by inevitable frustrations, unrest, and protest. I know of no panacea and can only suggest possible cures, which include the following:

1. The thrusting of more challenges and demands upon students—for example, through challenging service and clinical programs and engagement in the work of extension education;

2. The making of instruction, particularly in the social sciences, more relevant (and more directly centered on rigorous analysis of the practical problems of implementing development theory in our context);

3. Shortening the length of some academic programs and increasing their intensity and shortening the hiatus period when one lives, exclusively, the "role" of student;

4. Initiating the tuition loan system so that students will have a deeper personal stake and more motivation in their education;

5. Institutionalizing more joint student-alumni-faculty university meetings in various professional schools to develop a common identity;

227

6. Opening better channels between students and government including Parliament, where perhaps the university should enjoy representation;

7. Initiating projects, like national service, so that more "freshman" students may come to us after the maturing experience of periods of rural work;

8. Preservation of full freedom to speak and assemble peacefully;

9. Absolute fairness in applying reasoned law to speech and protest activities;

10. Improved testing and guidance services;

11. Dropping students who choose the activity of extended boycotting of the universities as their means of pressing grievances so that the place may be given to others more deserving; and

12. Creation of a clear, practiced philosophy of work and sacrifice in the university—reflected by the life-style of higher officers of the university and by the faculty, so that we all practice what must be pervasively preached.

During recent years, the university has experienced many crises arising from student protests. Both the university and government have learned something from this experience. Over the long haul, the more we can demonstrate our total commitment, involvement, and indeed leadership in development processes, the easier it may be to ride out these storms.

The Development of Human Resources to Staff and Lead the University

The university's staff is rapidly becoming Ethiopianized. It is crucial that we rethink the role of university teachers in Ethiopia, for we cannot borrow indiscriminately from a "model" that perceives a teacher simply as a detached, tenured, scholarly critic of society. Particularly in the social sciences and applied professions, we need to analyze criteria for selection, preparation, advancement, and career tracks of teachers. More emphasis must be placed among other things on the following:

1. The value of practical experience—the need for teachers capable of applying theory concretely to Ethiopia, the need to develop problem-centered methods of teaching, and the value of "clinical" instruction;

2. The value of public service as part of a teacher's career—so that more staff will be directly engaged in public projects that enhance their expertise, so that the university can maintain links and feedbacks to and from government sectors;

228

3. The importance of work in rural areas as a part of formative experience and as a university human resource need;

4. The importance of developing multidisciplinary perspectives in graduate training, particularly for those who teach in the broad area of development administration;

5. The importance of research that contributes directly to the formation or motivation of concrete development policies and programs;

6. The importance of a flexible career track that allows teachers to move in and out of public service assignments without jeopardizing advancement;

7. The value of dedicated, experienced part-time teachers and, in many areas, a broader use of them; and

8. The elements of a basic philosophy that should characterize university teachers: work and sacrifice.

While we need to do more thinking about this crucial subject, the development of human resources to staff and lead the university will imply, among other things, redefinition of policies governing recruitment, promotion, leaves, and so on. We must abandon the nine-month "academic" contract. We must take leadership in insisting that public salaries be less disproportionate to average income and urge a stricter government income policy. We must redesign programs concerned with foreign graduate study, reevaluate the significance of a foreign Ph.D. as a "credential," and work with cooperating foreign graduate schools to devise programs that will enable more advanced study, and particularly required research, to be done here. Projects could then be more relevant both to the creation of individual expertise and to Ethiopian research needs generally.

The university must place a higher value on relevant research and provide more logistical support. Through planning, each unit must identify the kinds of human resources it lacks and needs, and the kind of formal training and research required to develop those resources so that staff development programs are built more around institutional needs and less around individual inclinations. Again, staff development must envision and create flexible policies with the public service that enable mobility and part-time teaching and part-time public service.

I do not suggest all of these as rigid policies but as guidelines to be used imaginatively. Clearly, too, the reform of staff development programs is a fertile field for international cooperation, perhaps a matter too long neglected.

Longer-Range Planning: Thinking about the
1980s and beyond

Hard as it is to envisage Ethiopia in the 1980s and beyond, I have tried here simply to identify a few concerns about that future that have implications for ongoing university planning.

I have not touched upon the subjects of population, environment, and urbanization, but it is clear that, increasingly, we will share these problems with the "developed" world. We now lack a "critical mass" of experts and imaginative activity in each of these related subjects; our plan must take into account this topic, and it is, perhaps, a fertile area for international collaboration.

The technology of communication in Ethiopia needs to be studied. I believe it may soon be possible to provide television signals from a central broadcasting point that will bring this medium to most of the country. International broadcasting may also become more significant in our lives; perhaps it has great potentiality as a new service for international cooperation in education. The prospects and implications of the use of mass media in our future development need to be studied with care, and we must now consider formation of a university center for the study of this field.

The transformation of rural areas will produce a new politicization of many communities, and more strident articulation of local interests. Unquestionably, the demand for education will be pressed harder. Expansion is inevitable, and, I believe, the university must soon commit itself to fostering innovative new institutions of higher education in many provinces. In our planning, we have looked upon the university as a vehicle to develop and implement a new concept of rural community colleges—institutions that may combine formal and nonformal training and serve a wide variety of functions as civic and cultural centers. The development of media technology—if we are alert to it—may bring about new kinds of links to the central university and the delivery of many more programs. In long-range planning for higher education, we should think imaginatively about developing an open external university (drawing on the exciting innovations under way in Britain) that will use new technologies to make radio, TV, and correspondence instruction more widely available and challenging. All of these—and similar concerns—will call for the continuing education, or reeducation, of many of our staff, again a fertile field for international cooperation.

The transformation of rural areas will generate many other demands, such as the regulation of farm prices to prevent exploitation of producers, the creation of new forms of cooperative and business organizations and rapid introduction of a vast new body of law in tradition-oriented communities. The human resources aspects of these kinds of problems must be studied.

In the future we must worry more about the use of leisure and the pursuit of recreation in Ethiopia. There are few public parks, recreational centers, and recreational programs in the country. Sports and cultural activities are largely available only to selected people. Our lake shores should not be left purely for private exploitation. Physical, cultural, and civic planning must fill these gaps, for in the world of tomorrow the value of leisure must be perceived as a most important goal of "development."

In conclusion, most of my paper may appear to stress a number of pragmatic responses to various challenges of development. It is important to stress again, however, that the university is not simply an instrument of development, a mere training institute; it must also continue to explore and articulate the ideals and philosophy that make "development" a meaningful quest, worthy of sacrifice, tensions, and effort. We must find these ideals within our own culture and within the hopefully growing world consensus of the core meanings of "progress." The improvement of incomes, productivity, health, education, and management of development institutions are obviously only means toward realization of other values: more equality, more recognition of human dignity, more shared participation in the benefits of economic growth and the ordering of our society. The most basic challenge, to a university, is to keep these ideals alive and vital, particularly in times of crisis, anger, or cynicism.

International Cooperation

The university will continue to need external aid of the traditional kind in developing its basic infrastructure: physical plant (particularly its rural campuses), teachers (in certain areas), books and equipment, and technical assistance to develop particular operations.

I hope we can engineer new forms of international cooperation to remove some of the difficulties that sometimes reduce the effectiveness of traditional forms of external assistance—for example, to reduce some of the frustrating lags in the timing and delivery of aid efforts; to reduce some of the heavy burdens of paperwork; to share, coordinate, and avoid duplication of reporting and evaluation among external donors; to avoid the attempted imposition of externally conceived projects or foreign experts and consultants where locally qualified talent is available; and to develop more multilateral, cooperative efforts rather than allowing the proliferation of discrete projects of bilateral aid.

As we turn from more familiar aid projects to our problems and to those of the developed countries, I hope we can think of new forms of international cooperation, and I suggest some models:

First, I propose the radical, but I hope rational, idea that interested external assisters join with possible donors in Ethiopia to create a special fund (in the nature of a foundation) to finance, on a small scale, various kinds of development initiatives, notably of a research character. The foundation could be controlled by a multinational board selected carefully from private citizens, both foreign and Ethiopian, who already know the university well and who are prepared to spend continuous time on its problems in the future. The foundation would provide a more efficient vehicle to help develop institutional research, human resource planning, staff development, and new multidisciplinary teaching projects; it would have the great advantage of flexibility, continuity, private, and considerable local control. The time lag between mature conception of projects within the university and the provision of initial funding to start them could be reduced, for, all too often, crucial momentum is lost when such lags exist. In addition, I suspect that this private, multinational fund would cost far less, by way of overhead, than official projects, and it would be a notable experiment in international collaboration.

Second, I think we can develop new strategies of international cooperation for continuing, systematic study of the problems of ongoing development of discrete areas of the university—for example, education, agriculture, law, and administration, and to maintain our connections with experts and ideas from other parts of the world. Accordingly, I suggest creation of several small, multinational consortia of foreign and Ethiopian experts (both academic and others) to engage in this work on a continuing basis. The non-Ethiopian members would be persons familiar, by dint of previous work, with Ethiopia, who share an ongoing interest in it and are able to spend time on its problems. For example, a consortium in education might meet regularly (sometimes in Ethiopia, sometimes outside) to discuss relevant theoretical advances in the field, concrete research or experimental projects, new strategies for developing university staff, and other related problems of institutional and professional development. The various consortia would be funded through and accountable to the university, would be asked to provide a continuing source of new ideas to us and through us to international donors, and would be judged by their utility in this respect.

Third, in part through the strategies suggested above and other new initiatives, I hope we can create new ad hoc institutional arrangements concerned with staff development. We need to explore advanced-level joint degree programs with other universities that might have both a local and a foreign situs and that provide more relevance and more efficiency in the process of granting a Ph.D. or similar qualification. Given a "foundation" concerned with university development and links provided by the consortia, I think we can engineer such programs.

Fourth, there must be a shift in general policy formulation from the international "experts" to the "local experts." Policies on Africa can and should be made in Africa. Such a shift of donors to rely more on local expertise tangibly manifested in their policies, procedures, and administration of grants, loans, and so on, is likely to bridge the "credence gap" and to lead to a truly representative partnership among equals.

The proposals I have outlined are meant to be suggestive and illustrative of new principles of aid and cooperation: They stress allocation of more discretion to the university; achievement of greater flexibility and continuity, greater use of Ethiopian and of already engaged private foreign experts to develop policies and projects; greater efforts to deal more systematically over periods of time with discrete professional sectors of development. While we have much to learn, I think we can, through these processes of international cooperation, manage more of our development with fewer visible, official foreign programs.

Appendix

I. Research Center of the Faculty of Education

1. The Research Center is responsible for approving and coordinating all research activities going on in the Faculty of Education that require financial assistance from the university.

2. The Research Center will solicit from all Faculty of Education staff members their interest in research activities and will announce early in the academic year the research activities to be undertaken by staff members with the expected date of completion.

3. The Research Center will be responsible for assisting in the publication and dissemination of research results it has sponsored.

4. The Research Center will sponsor the publication of the Ethiopian Journal of Education.

5. The Research Center will take the responsibility for organizing educational conferences, workshops, and seminars.

6. The Research Center, in addition to sponsoring basic research, will stimulate the production of teaching materials based on this research for the Faculty of Education and the Ministry of Education.

7. The Center will run a research library in close collaboration with the central library and will be engaged in the documentation of worthwhile materials (published or unpublished) in the area of Ethiopian education.

II. Institute of Ethiopian Studies

1. The Institute of Ethiopian Studies has the following objectives:

(i) To conduct, promote, and coordinate research and publication on Ethiopian Studies with a special emphasis on the humanities and cultural studies.

(ii) To aid in the preservation of the Ethiopian Cultural Heritage by collecting, cataloguing, and displaying in a museum Ethiopian artifacts and items of historical value.

(iii) To aid in editing, translating, and publishing important works and documents on Ethiopia.

(iv) To aid and support the conduct of research on Ethiopian studies by acquiring and making available to interested scholars published and unpublished materials relating to all aspects of Ethiopia.

(v) To seek and aid in seeking financial support both from national and external sources for research and publications on Ethiopia on the basis of priorities and general guidelines set up by the Board (art. III, 1 below).

2. Management.

The Institute shall be governed by a Board and managed by a Director.

3. The Board.

Membership: The Board shall have seven members. The Director of the Institute shall be an ex-officio member and shall serve as secretary of the Board. The other member shall be elected by the Faculties of Arts and Theology on the basis of the following distribution:
(a) Three members from the relevant Departments of the Faculty of Arts.
(b) One member from the Faculty of Theology.

(c) Not more than two members from the community at large to be chosen by the above members from individuals who have gained stature in Ethiopian Studies.

(d) Up to three persons to be coopted, one of whom will be the Associate Academic Vice President for Research and Publication who will not have the voting right.

The members shall elect their own chairman and vice-chairman within the university community. Members of the Board shall be elected for a term of three years; no member will be eligible for a third consecutive term. For any departing member, a replacement shall be elected for the balance of the term.

III. Institute of Development Research

The Institute of Development Research is established for the purpose of promoting research in the social and behavioral sciences specifically aimed to help solve the development problems of Ethiopia. The Institute shall have the following specific objectives:

1. To initiate, coordinate, and direct interdisciplinary research on development problems of Ethiopia;

2. to develop teaching materials in the social sciences by utilizing research findings;

3. to cooperate with and provide consultative services to government agencies and other organizations on questions falling within the functional sphere and capability of the Institute;

4. to provide a forum for the exchange of views and information among those concerned with Ethiopia's development issues and problems in relation with other developing countries;

5. to initiate, plan, organize, and seek various foreign and local research grants and donations.

Administrative Structure:

The Institute shall be managed by a Director and governed by Board of Advisors, hereafter referred to as the Board.

A. The Board shall be nominated by the appropriate faculties and agencies associated with the Institute and appointed by the President of the University. Members of the Board shall serve for a two-year period unless otherwise specified and shall be eligible for re-appointment. The composition of the Board shall be as follows:

1. The Director of the Institute, whose term of Office shall be for three years and who shall serve as secretary to the Board; no Director of the Institute shall be eligible for a third consecutive term of office;

2. four members from the Faculty of Arts drawn from the relevant departments (two of the members for a three-year period);

3. one member from the College of Business Administration (for a three-year period);

4. one member from the School of Social Work (for a three-year period);

5. three members from outside the university, one of whom shall be from the Planning Commission. The term of office of the member from the Planning Commission shall be for three years;

6. up to three members from the other relevant units of the University. The composition and length of term of office to be determine by the above members of the Board; and

7. the Associate Academic Vice President for Research and Publications who shall serve as ex-officio, non voting member of the Board.

IV. Institute of Pathobiology

The Institute of Pathobiology is a research unit with some teaching responsibilities.

Purposes.

(a) To serve the university as a Research center and ensure long-term planning of research with due coherence between the Empire's needs and the university's overall development plans.

(b) To encourage, promote, and engage in research activities and advance the cause of Pathological Sciences.

(c) To contribute to and participate in such undergraduate and graduate teaching as is appropriate to the qualifications of the Institute staff and the needs of the university.

Objectives. In cooperation with appropriate Faculties:

(a) Engage in applied biological and/or paramedical research that is applicable to the framework of overall national development planning for Ethiopia.

(b) Utilize the professional staff for teaching specialized subjects to senior university students, graduate students, and students of medicine.

(c) Provide training in the fields of applied biology to science and paramedical students, and to research assistants.

(d) Offer supervision and advance laboratory and field training to Doctoral and Master's degree students who are engaged in dissertation research on subject matter related to indigenous Ethiopian problems.

(e) Initiate, plan, organize, and seek various foreign and local research grants and donations to materialise the objectives of the Institute.

Administrative Structure.

1. The Board

A Board shall be established for the Pathobiological Institute. This Board shall be nominated by the respective faculties and appointed by the President; members shall serve for two-year periods and shall be eligible for reappointment; it should consist of two members from the Science Faculty, two members from the Medical Faculty, two members from Pathobiology Institute, one member from the Alemaya Agricultural College, two members from the community at large, and three other coopted members from the community at large who will be designated by the Board. (No member may represent two bodies.) The Board shall elect its own Chairman from among its members. The Director of the Institute shall not be eligible to serve as Chairman.
The duties of the Board shall be

(a) to establish and formulate the administrative, academic, and research responsibilities of the Institute;

(b) to assist the Institute in its effort to develop sources of funds for research from extra-university sources, Ethiopian and international, to support the research activities of the staff;

(c) to review the budget of the Institute.

V. Institute for Scientific and Technological Research and Development

There is a proposal in the university, accepted in principle by the Faculty Senate, to incorporate the various scientific research units into a single center to be called the Institute for Scientific and Technological Research and Development (ISTRAD).

Purposes and responsibilities

The purposes for which the Institute is formed shall be:

1. To promote the educational purposes of the Haile Sellassie I University by encouraging, fostering, and conducting investigations and research in the physical, biological, geological, engineering, technological, and other related fields.

2. To carry out tests and calibration wherever applicable and to devote its resources to the advancement and extension of these investigations and research to the economic development of the country and to assist the University in the promotion and extension of learning and knowledge.

3. To promote and foster the application of science and technology in the development of commerce and industry, the discovery and development of methods for the utilization of natural resources, the industrialization of the country, and the improvement of the general standard of living and prosperity of the people.

Powers.

1. To provide, equip, and maintain laboratories, workshops, experimental, and other facilities for scientific and industrial research testing and calibration;

2. To utilize on loan basis the laboratories and equipment of the Faculty of Science, the Faculty of Technology, and other Institutions of the University, for the aforementioned purposes;

3. To engage, maintain, and develop a staff of qualified educators, scientists, and research experts to provide consultative services and to carry on investigations and research objectives of the Institute.

4. To establish a center for accumulation of information useful to scientific and industrial research and to utilize the existing libraries of the university to carry out the tasks set for the Institute; to foster an exchange of scientific and technical information with other research and educational institutions; and to publish and disseminate such of its findings as may be deemed of public interest;

5. To apply for, obtain, purchase, lease, own any inventions, patent rights, copyrights, trademarks, trade names, brands, labels, devices, formulae, processes, and all improvements and modifications thereof; to use, develop, introduce, sell, and grant licenses of rights for use;

6. To develop, plan, design, construct, and operate pilot and production plants for purposes of rent or sale to interested parties, enterprises, companies, private or governmental;

7. To make and receive gifts upon such terms and conditions as the Board of Directors may determine;

8. To make and enter into contracts permitted by law, with individuals, firms, associations, and organizations, municipal, governmental, or semigovernmental, and private, or any agency or department thereof;

9. To receive property by device or bequest, subject to the laws regulating the transfer of property by will; to convey, exchange, lease, transfer, or otherwise dispose of all property; to receive, hold, administer, and spend funds;

10. To do all other acts necessary or expedient for the administration of the affairs and attainment of the purposes of the Institute.

VI. The Debre Zeit Agricultural Experiment Station of the College of Agriculture

This pioneer experiment station together with the other experiment stations of the College of Agriculture at Alemaya undertakes the research and publication responsibility in the field of agriculture and the allied subjects.

VII. The Center for African Legal Development of the Faculty of Law

The Center has as one of its major premises the belief that Comparative Study of Legal Developments in Africa is not only interesting to the scholar but also potentially useful. It is also based upon the conviction that persons interested in comparative legal developments in Africa should not be required to go outside of Africa in order to study them.

In accordance with this conviction, the Faculty became engaged in the possibility of taking over the African Law Digest from Colombia University, with some assistance from the Ford Foundation.

VIII. The Creative Arts Center

This Center has as its purposes:

(i) To preserve the various indigenous arts of Ethiopia.

(ii) To analyze and evaluate the Status of Contemporary creative arts in Ethiopia.

(iii) To encourage the development of indigenous arts within the expanding Ethiopian society.

THE UNIVERSITY AND COMMUNITY
DEVELOPMENT
Gabriel Velázquez P.

This section is divided into three parts. The first is a summary of my experience at the Universidad del Valle in Cali from
1950 to 1972. I will emphasize the changes in concepts and programs
and give a few examples of how different schools, now divisions, went
from the early days, when the main goal was to develop in Colombia
a strong university and improve the quality of teaching and research,
to the last four or five years when several academic units have been
seriously involved in multidisciplinary research and experimentation on how to contribute to the well-being and development of the
community and the region. The second part will reflect present
innovative thinking and future plans of leaders at the Universidade
Federal da Bahia, Salvador, Brazil, where, during the last year, I
have had the opportunity to participate in several meetings and round
tables to discuss and analyze the role of this university and to the
university system in the development of Brazil's Northeast. In the
third part, I will attempt to present, in some rational order, my
personal concepts and ideas about the responsibility and the role of
universities in community development. Needless to say, in this
last effort, I will consciously or unconsciously reflect the thoughts
of many colleagues from Cali and Bahia, and readings on the subject.

Experiences at Universidad del
Valle, 1950-72

The needed innovative changes to fulfill the role of universities
in community development are difficult to get understood, accepted,
and fully implemented. Universities and educators are by nature
traditional and difficult to change. From my experience in different
countries in Latin America the best way to introduce innovative
change is by showing successful examples. But to be able to accomplish this, universities need to develop a critical mass of indigenous
scholars grouped under some strategic department or academic units
with facilities for "real-life" experimentation.

The Division of Health Sciences. This leading academic unit
has gone through five evolutionary changes. 1950-55: emphasis on
academic and scientific development. 1955-60: initiation of research
and education in family and preventive medicine. 1960-65: research
on community health problems and resources. 1966-69: recognition
of the need for an interdisciplinary health team, and creation of a

241

Division of Health Sciences. 1968 on: together with other divisions, multidisciplinary research and training in community development.

The Division of Education. If universities were logical in their structures and utilization of resources, the School of Education would be the leader in innovation and change of both formal and nonformal systems of education. Unfortunately at del Valle, as in almost all other countries in Latin America, this division has lacked leadership. Fortunately there are now some hopeful examples, such as the Educational Planning Institute and the Pilot School Program.

The Division of Economic and Social Sciences. In the work of this division we can see some practical examples of efforts to promote development, from studies on land use and tenure to the preparation of better managers for the private sector of the region.

The Divisions of Architecture and Engineering. These divisions, between 1960 and 1970, collaborated closely with the Divisions of Health and Economics in efforts to improve socioeconomic conditions of people living in urban and rural areas.

Better-integrated multidisciplinary efforts for rural and urban development. In the four years 1968-72, the Universidad del Valle has developed good models of practical efforts to involve staff and students from different academic units in practical experimental studies to promote development and to improve several of our social systems, such as the following: (1) the Center for Multidisciplinary Research in Social Systems; (2) the Center for University Research in Population; (3) the Norte del Cauca Program—in a rural area of the state of El Cauca, the Divisions of Health, Engineering, Education, and Economics and IDELAC (Instituto de la Construcción) in close cooperation with three governmental agencies, Instituto Colombiano Agropecuario, Caja Agraria, and the Corporación Autónoma Regional del Valle del Cauca, are working to test and experiment with practical models to improve well-being (agricultural productivity, nutrition, education, health, electrification, housing, and income) for farmers owning small plots; (4) the Union de Vivienda Popular Program (an effort to improve health and environmental conditions in a slum of Cali); and (5) the Center for Resources in Education and Teaching.

Present and Future Plans of Universidade Federal da Bahia

In 1968 the Federal University of Bahia (UFBa) joined other Brazilian universities in an intensive effort to modernize and strengthen its academic structure and improve its research and teaching programs both at graduate and undergraduate levels. Many isolated chairs were grouped under departmental structures, and the departments were organized under a better-defined university structure of schools and institutes. The number of full-time teachers was greatly increased, and opportunities for graduate studies were offered to the staff, so that the number of professors with Master's and Ph.D. degrees is continuously growing. The president's office and the general administration were carefully analyzed and restructured. The number of different diploma courses offered to young Brazilians increased as well as the total number of new students admitted every year. Research projects were encouraged.

Early in 1971 UFBa administrators invited the Rockefeller Foundation to study the possibility of undertaking a cooperative program to enable UFBa to participate in several projects that would contribute to the development of Brazil's Northeast. After several visits of New York officers, a preliminary agreement was reached, and during 1972 I was sent for several months to Brazil to study, in more detail, with government and university officers, the basis for such a program. An agreement was signed by both parties and was submitted for the approval of the Government of Brazil. The general purposes of the agreement are the general development of UFBa as a means to enable the university better to achieve its goals of accelerating the social and economic development in the Northeast of Brazil. This will be implemented through the strengthening of existing programs and the creation of new programs in research, teaching, and extension and advisory services related to an integrated development of urban and rural communities in the region aiming at the solution of social, economic, administrative, educational, housing, health, and labor market problems.

For the year 1973, plans include (1) the creation and development of a Graduate Center for Research and Training in Economic, Social, and Administrative Sciences; (2) the creation and development of a Center for Integrated Development of Rural Areas; representatives of several city, state, federal, and international institutions and agencies have been invited to participate in the planning and organization of these two centers and in their research, experimental, and teaching programs; a well-defined rural area, around the town of Cruz das Almas, will be selected to conduct projects to study how to improve well-being and quality of life of all the families of farmers with small plots living in the selected area; and (3) experimental studies, research, and training for urban development: A slum area of the City of Salvador (Bahia), Nordeste de Amaralina, has been chosen to develop models to improve health, environmental conditions, housing, education, and employment.

The projects mentioned above have the following similar characteristics: (1) they are long-range efforts, no less than 10 years, to develop models, strategies, and techniques for social and economic development of all the families living in the area; (2) they are well-integrated multidisciplinary, multiinstitutional efforts: Professionals and students from different disciplines, from different private, government, and international institutions will participate in a well-coordinated plan; (3) all kinds of efforts will be made to involve the families living in the area in the planning and implementation stages of these programs; (4) it is hoped that practical, efficient models of socio-economic development will be designed and later propagated and adapted in other stages of Brazil's Northeast; (5) a close working relationship will be established with the groups working at del Valle, in the hope that both UFBa and del Valle will profit by exchange of experience. Later the two programs will be very useful to propagate these ideas and experiences to other countries and to train leaders and experts in rural and urban development.

Personal Concepts about the Role of Universities in Community Development

In the following pages I will summarize some of our concepts about the role of universities in community development. In order to facilitate criticism and suggestions I have organized the presentation in two parts: First, some conceptual thoughts about the meaning of development and the role of universities, and second, some practical aspects regarding the work of universities that arise from actual experience and innumerable discussions in Cali and Bahia and also reflect readings on the subject.

Community development may be defined as a continuous process in which action programs and available resources are coordinated, adequately managed, and aimed at the improvement of the well-being of all people living in a given area.

To accomplish these goals, it is necessary to improve the use of existing resources and to increase the availability and accessibility of goods and services.

Obviously all people cannot be treated with the same emphasis; some will need more, others less. But, in order to decrease inequality, the distribution of the following factors, basic to an adequate standard of living, must be greatly improved: employment, family income, productivity of labor; education; food production, nutrition; health; sanitation and quality of the environment; housing; and human rights and opportunities for cultural development and recreation.

The fundamental long-range, or "terminal," goal of universities should be to contribute toward the well-being of the people—community development. "To contribute" indicates that universities cannot be expected to assume direct responsibility for all of the programs needed to promote community development. Rather, universities should participate as "agents or instruments for change" in furthering this development.

I would like now to present some ideas on how the universities can contribute to development.

Redefinition of university objectives and curricular changes. Intensive efforts are needed before staff and students truly understand and accept what the long-range goal of universities is. In my experience, too much lip service is paid to the topic of university participation in community development. Organization of seminars and conferences, lectures on the subject, distribution of papers and bibliographic material, and direct involvement of staff and students in research and experimentation are essential to bring about changes in the right direction. Promotion of salutary changes must include continuing curriculum revision to allow the introduction of courses to inculcate faculty and students with both the theory of community development and practical experiences with actual programs having this objective. Greater support and more academic status should be given to these types of programs and to staff and students participating in them.

Redefinition of development and "quality of life." Universities can and should make more efforts to define better the nature of development and to establish adequate indicators of "quality of life." Dr. Mahbub ul Haq, in his excellent paper presented in this volume, mentions the danger of using GNP growth, per capita income, and economic growth policies as indicators for development. He emphasizes the need for new perspectives for development and points out that this problem "must be defined as a selective attack on the worst forms of poverty" and "in terms of progressive reduction and eventual elimination of malnutrition, disease, illiteracy, squalor, unemployment, and inequalities." If attempts to promote development are to be successful, better definition and quantification of levels of living are needed. This is a difficult technical problem. What are the indicators of health? Of human rights? Of quality of the environment? How are the measurements made? On what scales? How can one define degrees of human and cultural values to compare with health and education on the same scale? Or with housing? Or with the quality of the environment? There is a great opportunity for university participation in attempting to find answers to some of these questions.

University participation in planning for development. To act as efficient "agents or instruments for change," universities should be involved in regional or national planning (regional if Brazil, national if Costa Rica). They should participate in studies of problems and resources of different social systems; in research on constructing, experimenting with, and evaluating different models for operation of social systems; in search for innovative strategies and techniques to improve the delivery and distribution of social services; in efforts to understand and contribute to the formulation of national policies. In this regard I am impressed by the radical changes in thinking and attitudes of leaders of medical education in Colombia, as the result of the active participation of the medical schools throughout the country in the national survey of health problems, health resources and manpower, conducted between 1964 and 1967.

Adequate selection of partners. For practical and conceptual reasons universities should not act in isolation in their efforts to promote or contribute to development. On the contrary, these efforts should from the onset be coordinated with government and private agencies. If the universities are going to seek new strategies, techniques, and models for development, they must have full cooperation from existing agencies and access to all kinds of data. The routine adaptation and propagation of the models and strategies are the responsibility of the other agencies, not the university. Our experience has convinced us that the agencies are more willing to accept these tasks if they have had the opportunity to participate from the very beginning in joint efforts. If a close working relationship is established, the other agencies will share the cost of the research, experimentation, and operation of the models, and many opportunities will be created for staff and students to participate either as research assistants or as temporary employees. Most significant is the fact that by working with and through government agencies, universities will have a greater opportunity to influence the power structure.

Participation of the people. Efforts must also be made by universities to involve members of the community where the studies are being conducted. If the final goal is to improve "quality of life" the consumer has not only the right but a mandate to become involved from start to finish. He should participate in the definition of objectives, work directly in the development of programs, share in continuing evaluation, and help to redefine objectives. The advantages of this participation are that the community's views and priorities are given due consideration, unit costs are reduced, efficiency of the programs is greater, and the chances of success are greatly enhanced.

Utilization of modern sciences and tools. Our preliminary experimentation at the Universidad del Valle in Cali has shown us the close interrelationship of the different social problems—for example, the association between poor sanitation and malnutrition—or between sickness, illiteracy, unemployment, and poverty. If one expects an efficient delivery system of social services and maximum benefits from limited resources, it is necessary to use a more systematic approach, where modern techniques and tools such as operations research, systems analysis, and information and computer sciences may help provide a more comprehensive solution to the multifactorial problems of underdevelopment.

The need of a strong university. In our eagerness to analyze the role of the university, one should not forget the first and most important prerequisite: the need for a strong university. University development is an evolutionary process. In the first part of this paper I mentioned the five different stages of development of our Division of Health Sciences; a similar process is happening in the other academic units at the Universidad del Valle. A university, to play its role in community development, needs an efficient organization, well-selected and well-trained staff, and a majority of the faculty on a full-time basis. It needs to have gone through the evolutionary process from directing its efforts initially toward improvement of the faculty and building departmental excellence to the final phase of immersing itself in community problems, a phase that should enjoy greater status than classical academic activities.

The need for university reorganization. I have already emphasized the interdependence of problems afflicting a society. The solutions to these problems are also interdependent. But our governmental agencies are not usually structured to take into account this interdependence when decisions are required and when action is taken. Those of the power structure who make these decisions are products of universities. This perhaps explains their shortcomings. Doctors, engineers, architects, economists, or nurses, when forced to participate in community problem-solving, are well aware that they need information and knowledge about health, financing budgets, politics, and how "things get done." But the rigid departmental structure of our universities does not train an engineer or a doctor to understand the interdependence of all segments of society or how to solve problems except in the limited area of their specialized knowledge. The success of our modest initial efforts with the Centers for Multidisciplinary Research in Social Systems and for University Research in Population, mentioned earlier, has convinced us of the need for more aggressive experimentation and restructuring and reorganization of universities, so that the graduates are better able to cope with the larger problems of the community and of society as a whole.

The scientific approach to community experiments. One of the weaknesses of many university experiments in community development is the lack of an adequate scientific approach. Efforts are organized to improve rural health services, to solve malnutrition, and to improve houses or environmental problems, but it is difficult to find well-documented models, hypotheses, theories, or even

247

conjectures that relate sanitation to good nutrition, and this to employment, better income, and increased productivity. If universities are going to be effective as "agents for change" for development, they need to utilize a more scientific approach. There is a great difference between the casual observation of the effects of change in the community and the ability to predict and evaluate these effects with some precision. The degree to which universities understand community processes is measurable by the difference between the predicted effects (before the changes) and the observed effects after the changes. If this degree of understanding is measurable, so is the potential contribution of the universities to the development of the community. This potential can only be realized by the utilization of scientific approaches that make it possible to bring predictions closer to reality.

Participation of students. Underdeveloped countries badly need leaders with a better understanding of underdevelopment, as well as trained and skilled manpower to attack the problems on a broad front. In addition to informed decision-makers, there must be groups of people who know how to apply technology for development. If the graduates of the university are expected to contribute to the solution of community problems, they will need prior training and supervised experience in attacking such problems. Unfortunately, in most university experiments or programs relating to community development, participation is limited to staff members and to a few lucky graduate students or research assistants. The number of students who take part in these experiments is appallingly small. More student involvement is essential if developing countries are to have the trained manpower that they will need for community development in the future. In order to facilitate students' participation, the curriculum must be flexible.

The need for long-range programs. This new role of the university, that of participating as an effective "agent for change" in community development, is a slow, difficult process that requires interdisciplinary efforts over a time span that is long enough to identify all of the needs and resources, to plan and implement action programs, and to discover and correct mistakes. In our opinion, no less than 10 years of continuous efforts are needed before a clear, well-defined program with quantitative objectives and indicators can be launched.

Need for internal stability. Reaching the final, regional, or national development goal takes time. Enough internal stability of university leaders, administrators, and directors of these experiments is essential.

Rural plus urban studies. Although special attention should be given to rural areas, where the majority of the world's population lives and where we may find the etiology of urban slum and ghetto

248

formation, we cannot forget the urban problem. Most countries in the world are plagued by varying degrees of rural-to-urban migration, and the resulting urban problems also merit university involvement.

The need for innovation in formal and nonformal systems of education. I would like to call attention to a very challenging and perhaps unique opportunity for universities, their role in reorienting and redesigning the formal systems of education and in strengthening and promoting a more vigorous and widely utilized nonformal system of education.

Notions of some difficulties. Undoubtedly the potential problems are innumerable. But from our limited experience one can single out the following:

1. Very few people in a university have the same concept of development. Each faculty member seems to have his own image of what it is all about, the image being colored by his discipline and by his own experience. Thus it is often difficult to achieve a meeting of minds so that when the word "development" is mentioned, everyone is receiving on the same wavelength. For example, an economist may incline quite naturally to a view of development couched in an economic framework; an agronomist, while implicitly recognizing that increased agricultural production should mean more money in the farmer's pocket, might tend to focus on production per se, almost as an end in itself, rather than how it relates to an individual's quality of life. The humanist has his own focus, as does the physician or the educator. One of the difficulties, therefore, is to draw people out of their natural barriers and to get them to think more broadly of inter-relationships and interactions.

2. The creation of a multidisciplinary team, and particularly one that may involve participants from more than one institution may not always be easy but presents no insurmountable problems. The difficulties start once a development team is formed. Will the team members listen to each other and really hear? Are they willing to learn from each other? Can they subjugate their interest in a particular field or specialty if this field, initially at least, is given low priority in action programs? Will each participant be able to understand the idiom of the others? Will he or she be willing to spend the amount of meeting time required to develop a common understanding of terms? Are some members of the interdisciplinary team, because of their personality or articulateness, likely to dominate the group and thus pressure consensus in what may later prove an ill-advised move or policy decision? Will everybody in the group, experts all and prestigious as well, be able to stand up under the stress of constant give and take, or will they get fed up and just go their own way? Essentially many of these are problems of group dynamics, very real problems and not easy to resolve.

3. There is a tendency for university staff to be satisfied with research "studies" the results of which are set forth in published papers that may bring kudos and promotion for the author or authors but rarely lead to application in the form of changes in existing systems or action programs that have an impact on an entire community. Academicians may feel that their job is finished with the publication of the fruits of their research; putting new knowledge to use is viewed as the sole province of action agencies. This attitude, passive in most respects, is essentially, "OK, boys, we've done our research. Here are the results, and you can do what you want with them."

The difficulty here is the lack of follow-through, or the abrogation of responsibility at least to try to promote utilization of the new data in a practical way by the appropriate action agencies. A more positive approach by the academic researcher in this regard will be obtained if personnel from action agencies are included in the research team, so that the subsequent translation of results into action comes more naturally because the agency was a participant in the research from the beginning and therefore has a vested interest in seeing that something constructive emerges.

4. Universities, and the community at large, have little <u>quantitative</u> knowledge about the way in which community processes—"social systems"—function. The community is unlikely to gain this knowledge unless the university is willing to experiment until it can predict in advance the amount and rate of change to be expected if the process were altered in a certain way. So far, universities tend to study rather isolated parts of community processes, but seldom is the process as a whole investigated. Even more rarely do universities, either by suggestion or through their own efforts, predict the results and then evaluate the introduction of change into a community process, and thus evaluate their own abilities to be "agents of change."

<u>A "pool" of supporting agencies and a "consortium" of university experiments.</u> In closing, I would like to make a strong plea. The role of education in promoting development, although broadly accepted, has not been defined clearly and operationally. More research and orientation is needed. There are probably many ways of tackling this existing challenge. I am one of those who strongly believe that universities may be very effective in searching for answers. I would like to suggest the idea that the assistance agencies undertake a joint effort to create a permanent task force that, under a permanent secretariat, will attempt to identify a group of universities that would accept leadership in this new role. They would be strategically located in different regions and countries. Senior staff of these universities should agree to devote part of their time, and a good amount of their institutional resources, to the important task of research and experimentation in education for community development. If properly

supported, and for a long enough period of time, and if an adequate system of communication to share information and experiences between them is created, I have no doubt that such a group of universities will constitute a very powerful mechanism to learn, from real ongoing experimentation, how education can contribute to quality of life—to community development.

5

IMPLICATIONS FOR
EXTERNAL ASSISTANCE
TO EDUCATION

THE REDEPLOYMENT OF EDUCATIONAL AID
H. M. Phillips

This is written from the "donor" standpoint, which may appear
an artificial point of view in the sense that "recipients" are sovereign
states and decide themselves what aid they want. But it is also true
that aid for development is, or should be, a form of partnership.*
So long as this is made clear, there is no artificiality in discussing
separately the functions of each of the partners. Thus the posture
assumed in the paper is that the "recipients" are masters of their
own educational policies, and that "donors" are free to decide what
types of program, within these policies, they are prepared to aid.
On this basis educational aid operations result from dialogues, followed by negotiations, between the cooperating partners in development.

The reason this essay has been written is that both partners
are saying a great deal about the need for regeneration and innovation
in education, but that neither partner appears to be matching its words
with deeds. From a donor standpoint it would be easy to say that
this is a policy matter, and therefore the blame rests with the other
partner. But this would omit the basic dialogue and reduce the creative element in international cooperation. We have therefore to face
the problem that while it is true a change of policy in recipient countries would be necessary to totally regalvanize aid, what can nevertheless be done on the donor side to contribute to this process?

This involves some examination of donor intentions and performances. The state of educational aid was reviewed in 1968 by
the Development Assistance Committee of the OECD, which concluded
it should be "reassessed and redefined on the basis of a more comprehensive understanding of country developmental objectives."[1]
The 1969 Review of Development Assistance referred to the contribution of donors of educational aid as "often at present reinforcing
irrelevancy."[2]

The Pearson Report, prepared in 1969, went further and stated,

On the whole, however, it must be said that aid from
abroad has served mainly to buttress classical methods,

---

*For brevity, the expressions "aid" and "donors" and "recipi-
ents" are used in this section. The correct expression for "educational aid" is "international cooperation for education purpose between the more developed and the developing countries." The expression "education" in the paper means both formal and nonformal
education.

applied by unquestioning teachers, both local and foreign, trained in a mold cast over a hundred years ago. Attempts to establish the kind of dialogue that could lead to a new education conceived by and for developing countries have been made, especially in the field of teacher training, but are still too rare.

Three years later the 1972 review prepared by Edwin Martin, chairman of the Development Assistance Committee, commented on the situation as follows:[3]

There is as yet no sign of a general improvement in the unsatisfactory state of education in the developing countries, nor have aid agencies been able to do much to redeploy their resources in favour of educational regeneration and renovation.

The purpose of this section, therefore, is to discuss (1) Why are there not apparent very significant new trends in educational aid for development, although there has been consensus for the last three or four years that changes are necessary? (2) What specific obstacles can be identified affecting the redeployment of educational aid? (3) What are the possibilities of hastening redeployment?

The answer to these questions may be basically political. Much of the present literature on aid is heavily charged with criticism of the insufficiency of the political will of the wealthier countries to give greater and more disinterested help to the poorer. It could be that, although the need for redeployment is recognized, the forces in each country that prefer tradition to change may retard the redeployment of aid at the stage that specific changes have to be made.

Alternatively there could be forces of delay and inertia in the actual mechanism of aid supply, which are neutral policy-wise but impede any type of operational change. These may operate even when the political will to change is strong, though they are more powerful when it is weak. It might, therefore, be possible that this is an activity where much change cannot be expected to appear in three years, either because it is still in the pipeline, or because a longer time schedule is in the nature of things, and cannot be avoided.* Political factors in any event are unlikely to be solely

---

*Some parallels can be taken from industry: New processes, whether technical or organizational, usually take far more than three years to materialize. Or from political economy: It was five years after the appearance of the General Theory before Keynsian thought

responsible and may themselves turn out to be malleable if alternative policies are better defined.

Finally it has to be borne in mind that the chief criticism of educational aid is that it supports educational systems that are dysfunctional in terms of development. Notions as to what is functional and what is dysfunctional change as development objectives alter. The stresses now being placed on "democratization of education," "structural change," "life-long education," and "quality of life" make the evaluation of educational aid, like that of education itself, increasingly more difficult and involve longer time schedules for assessment purposes. It may be a long time before these notions become a practical reality in the developing countries, and they must not meantime be allowed to obscure present urgent and practical needs. Nevertheless, education is by nature a long-term investment, and it is by action now that the future contribution of education to development has to be improved. To reconcile this apparent contradiction aid agencies should clarify their strategy by grouping the projects they consider under time variables—for example, (a) short-term urgent or first aid work; (b) medium-term bridging operations; (c) longer-term improvements of structures, and so on. Resources would then be distributed between the three types of project with relation to the recipient's educational objectives and plans, and to the donor's capacity to assume commitments involving different time schedules.[4]

This kind of approach is rarely adopted at present, no doubt partly because most donors cannot assume long-term commitments. This is clearly a limitation to redeploying aid in favor of fundamental educational reform if each donor acts separately. If, however, donors could be persuaded to pass the baton to each other like a relay team, the time span would be longer. An alternative would be the proposal referred to later that some new type of aid agency such as an international fund free from the exigencies of short-term budgeting is required for the purpose of promoting fundamental educational reform.

There follows an analysis of what are the obstacles that inhibit the redeployment of aid in education, even when there is political will in favor of change. There is also a discussion of some of the

received governmental acceptance. Or from behavioral patterns: A little more than five years elapsed between the first success of the Beatles and the issue by the Prime Minister of new instructions to his barber. Similar delays occur between the appearance of new art forms and their use in advertisements. Caution in adopting new practices is due to experience as well as to prejudice. About a quarter of a million patents are registered yearly, of which only about 3 percent become revenue earning.

margins of maneuver within given policies. But first there is a brief, and for this reason it is hoped not too misleading, account of existing aid and aid policies.

Existing Educational Aid

Amount

The volume of educational aid for 1971 from all sources may be estimated* to be some $1.5-1.6 billion.

About half is official aid from DAC member countries, one-eighth from the centrally planned economies, between one-sixth and one-fifth from multilateral agencies, and just over a fifth from non-governmental agencies.

Sixty percent goes to Africa, the rest being divided between Asia and Latin America with the former preponderating. Relatively little goes to the Arab states, but there is some substantial mutual educational assistance among themselves. On a per capita basis, Africa has a very high proportion and Asia a very low one.

The DAC members that provide educational aid rank in the following order in terms of amount: France, United States, United Kingdom, German Federal Republic, Belgium, Canada, Switzerland, and Austria. The World Bank Group is by far the largest multilateral provider of educational assistance, followed by the Inter-American Development Bank.

Nature of Educational Aid: Where Does the Real Gain Lie?

About a fifth of the overall total is for capital aid, another fifth to a quarter for fellowships and training (of which about three-quarters is in the donor countries). The rest is for teacher supply and for experts and, to a small extent, equipment.

Around three-quarters of educational aid is in the form of grants, but the activities of the World Bank Group are increasing the element of loan and credit (at present running about half IBRD loans and half "soft" IDA credits). The centrally planned economies operate mostly by means of including educational aid in commercial credits.

_____

*Difficult items to estimate are the extent of aid from nongovernmental organizations, how to convert the effort of the centrally planned economies of Eastern Europe into dollar equivalents, whether to base the figures on disbursements or commitments, and so on.

Practically all educational aid consists of provision for specific projects and programs, agreed between donor and recipient. Financial aid to educational systems as a whole is limited to the relatively rare cases of overall budget support given by one country to another in which the education sector may share.

There are a number of gains and losses not reflected in the statistics of educational aid, such as the gain from the "hidden subsidy,"* which accrues to students abroad arising from their participation in the general social and educational services of the receiving country, and losses† that may accrue to recipient countries through a "brain drain" engendered by aid. One form of offset is the sending of remittances to their home country by expatriate teachers and experts; another is interest paid on loans, and there is some truth in the adage "experts mean exports" in the case of educational as well as commercial aid.‡

The real economic benefit of educational aid is the addition it brings to the human resources of the recipient less the cost of the reverse movements and the noncompetitive factor in tied aid and plus the cost of doing without it.

---

*The United Kingdom in 1969 for instance financed 6,250 students and trainees from overseas, but the total of foreign students for any year in the United Kingdom is 50,000.

†Illustrated in the case of the United States by a study made in 1966, it was estimated (see "Education, Manpower, and Welfare Policies," Journal of Human Resources 1, No. 2, Fall 1966) that the net cost to the United States of foreign students over the first part of the decade was $45 million annually; that when the value of the education absorbed by U.S. students abroad was added the balance was reduced to $18 million; and that when the nonreturning foreign students were taken into account there was a benefit to the United States of $16 million. Many of the students had of course been studying privately and not as a result of aid programs.

‡So long as mutual interest, in addition to humanitarian factors, is one of the declared principles of bilateral assistance (both in the free enterprise and the centrally planned economies) it is legitimate that bilateral aid for education should further commercial links as well as strictly educational purposes. The suggestion is made later in this section that this link be intensified in order to increase the outlets for school-leavers and the better planning for foreign investment. The idealistic view that aid should be governed only by moral imperatives is well expressed in Myrdal's "The Challenge of World Poverty," but his conclusion is that at present the only country proceeding on this basis is Sweden.

The sum of this equation varies according to the type of aid. Alterations in the pattern and direction of aid will bring considerable changes in real costs and benefits. These are difficult to identify without thorough study and should be a subject of research.

Educational aid is at present mostly concentrating on higher, secondary, and technical education and has neglected basic education and literacy, apart from previous French programs. This fitted the priorities of the emergent countries for the 1960s. But both rate-of-return analysis[5] as well as social considerations now point to greater priority for basic or minimum education.

Aid priorities are not necessarily the same as domestic ones of the recipient countries; some top priorities are best suited to internal rather than external instrumentalities. One of the reasons why little aid is given to basic education, other than primary teacher training, has been the difficulty of finding the right point of entry. If the point of entry now becomes experimentation with new types of basic education, using new methods and modern media, the contribution of aid can be much extended.

Thus educational aid emerges as an instrument of considerable delicacy used too much perhaps in rather a blunt way; though there have been many successes for both partners. It has not always had the results intended because of education's close link with intangible social and political factors in society, because the dialogue between donor and recipient has not been sufficiently sharp on either side, and because it does not have built-in mechanisms that make it respond rapidly to the needs for change.

Apart from "first aid" and bridging operations, the real gain from educational aid is its creative role in introducing new educational approaches and in sparking off explosions of domestic resources and talents.

This calls for more mobility and sharpness of application than it has at present, and more assistance to educational research and development.*

---

*There are some semantic traps that have to be avoided in discussing research and development (R and D) and innovation, and it is useful to follow the terminology in use in the economics of science. Research is study and analysis, which may lead to discovery and invention (though many inventions occur without research). Development (in the sense of R and D) is the process of trying out and adjusting inventions so that they can be put to actual use. An innovation is an invention that has survived the process of development, or did not need it, and is in actual use for the first time. Innovations are relative: What is a long-standing practice in one

Policies of Providers of Aid—Snapshots of the
Educational Policies of the Main Donors

France is the largest single donor, and the sheer size of their teacher supply program and its dependence on the progress of innovatory thought in the teaching profession in France itself are factors affecting the introduction of new educational methods. The main recipients are the French-speaking developing countries, but an important amount goes to Middle Eastern countries and a certain amount to Latin America. France has pulled out almost entirely from supplying teachers for primary education, though it still provides many teachers for secondary and higher, and experts and administration for primary. It is also engaged in some path-breaking new aid projects such as televised instruction in Niger and the Ivory Coast, a new type of rural primary education in Upper Volta, and animation rurale in a number of African countries. It is also extending its geographical range.

French aid on the average makes up about a quarter of the educational expenditure of francophone African countries. It contains active forces alive to the necessity for new approaches to educational assistance, and a government commission (the Gorse Commission) has made a report in connection with the preparation of the Sixth Plan, which has not yet been made public. The main policy considerations affecting larger-scale redeployment of French educational aid would appear to be the necessity of maintaining the political, cultural, and commercial links with francophone countries, which on their side wish to do so, as a matter of mutual interest, and the dependence of its action upon the rate of economic and social progress in the recipient countries themselves.

The United Kingdom is in a somewhat similar position as France in relation to the Commonwealth and its ex-colonial territories, but there are larger interventions of other donors in these countries because of the wider use of the English language. The White Paper on Educational Aid Policy presented to Parliament in 1970 calls for a substantial reorientation of policy. Policy features stressed are that there should be a more intensive dialogue with the recipients rather than simply responding to requests to provide the same types of aid as before. It also calls for a widening of the geographical

---

society will be an innovation when it enters into use in another society for the first time. The meaning of development in the sense of R and D is different from its more usual meaning, which appears elsewhere in the paper—that is, the economic, social, and cultural process by which whole societies mature.

distribution of educational aid from the United Kingdom. CEDO (the Centre for Educational Development Overseas) has initiated experiments in new learning patterns and the Commonwealth Education Fellowships Scheme has been revitalized.

Possible immobilities in respect to British educational aid are obligations assumed to ex-colonial countries, and the political, cultural, and economic interests of the Commonwealth in educational matters. As in the case of French aid, a limitation to change is in some cases the vested interest of the local elite, who were themselves educated along traditional lines. Further, British like French educational aid, is an organizational structure of long standing and some complexity, a factor that may also place limitations on the speed of change. Operations, and to some extent the formulation of policy itself, are undertaken in collaboration with the educational profession by means of committees and independent standing organizations representing the different educational sectors. This gives the program its technical strength, but confers a heavy task of communication and coordination upon the aid administration in order to keep the sectors informed of developing country plans and needs, and of agreed policies of the donor governments.

The educational aid from the United States, the second largest donor, is more widely distributed than most, and tends to be open to change. This positive element is to some extent counteracted by high exposure to public criticism through legislative procedures that are not always helpful to continuity and have at times unduly bureaucratized its administration. The new U.S. aid policy aims at separating development aid from strategic factors and at greater use of multilateral agencies.

U.S. educational aid has been operated by the instrumentality of technical assistance and capital grants and loans through USAID, volunteers through the Peace Corps, and fellowships through the Educational Exchange Program. The USAID has used the "project" approach of supplying teachers to meet the requirements of different educational levels. It has created a considerable number of new institutions, as well as aiding the range of standard educational aid needs, and has been responsible for some innovatory action with the new media (for example, in El Salvador). A notable feature of U.S. aid has been the financing of training of students from developing countries in other countries of the region (third-country training).

The USAID has recently put out important proposals for redirecting its educational aid toward promoting new approaches in both formal and nonformal education in the developing countries. Like the case of the United Kingdom, much depends on the channels of aid and the extent to which the administration can communicate new policies and coordinate them, and when new approaches are required using new skills to extend or change, if necessary, the channels themselves.

The educational and training aid of the German Federal Republic, the third largest donor after France and the United States, is relatively free from historical or political ties and reflects a combination of welfare approaches (for example, the use of the churches as a channel of public funds) and commercial links (for example, the emphasis on technical and vocational training). Germany is by far the largest supplier of training facilities and grants in recipient countries, but study by foreign students and trainees in Germany is also a form of aid to which much official importance is attached. The trend is toward increased assistance to training and higher education in the developing countries themselves, utilizing the methods of pilot or model projects and university to university cooperation.

Belgian policy is similar to French except that through heavy reliance on its nongovernmental organizations it avoided in the past some of the export of European standards unsuited to the African environment and thereby stimulated high primary enrollment ratios in its ex-colonies.

Canada's educational aid effort is notable for its rapid rate of growth over recent years. It has Commonwealth ties but also has a unique position as a bilingual donor and a geographical range covering francophone and non-Commonwealth countries. It favors the "integrated approach" and has been experimenting with aid through the new media and also used traditional methods such as teacher supply and teacher training. Limitations that might arise affecting redeployment of its aid for educational innovation purposes would probably be the time involved in building up or reorganizing the necessary expertise to match the challenge of educational regeneration and the growth and widening range of its geographical distribution. It would no doubt also have problems similar to those of the other donors in respect of conservatism of the educational profession expressing itself through the channels of aid.

Australia has for many years been helping Asian countries, with a high proportion of its aid going to grants for students to come and be educated or trained in its own universities.

Swedish educational aid has traditionally covered all the standard forms of assistance, with emphasis on vocational training and the education of women. Its amount is growing appreciably and a number of changes of emphasis have recently been introduced. Individual fellowships for study in Sweden have been discontinued in favor of training in third countries, and the proportion of aid devoted to adult education is increasing. The amount devoted to university and higher education has been negligible. The effort is being concentrated upon seven countries, some of it being channeled through UNESCO and the ILO as funds in trust.

Originally, Dutch educational aid was limited to study and training in the Netherlands. In recent years aid has increased considerably to include the setting up and support of higher-level education institutes and technical and vocational training centers. As a method it makes substantial use of joint financing with nongovernmental bodies, which also act as aid agencies.

The main Japanese contribution is scholarships and training programs in Japan. However, certain training centers have been established overseas, and a small number of experts have been sent to assist in the teaching of scientific and technical subjects in Asian and African countries. Japan also makes a special contribution to educational research through the Japanese National Institute.

Assistance in education and training from the centrally planned socialist countries has been primarily in Africa and Asia, although some assistance of this kind has also gone recently to Latin America. It has been heavily concentrated on technical education either in the donor country or on the building up of technical skills in the recipient countries, frequently as part of trade agreements or industrial development projects. The Soviet Union sponsors over half of all students from developing countries in the socialist countries of Eastern Europe. Science and agricultural education are given high priority. A considerable amount of equipment has also been supplied, notably to the Near East and South Asia.

UNESCO aims at giving aid across the whole area of education, influenced only by the normative standards set out in its constitution and conference resolutions. It is deeply conscious of the need for educational regeneration and renovation and has taken the lead in stirring educational opinion in this field. It utilizes for its assessment of needs the UNDP country programing procedures to which it contributes. In this effort it has received considerable support from the Report of the International Commission for the Development of Education (the Faure Report). It is, however, exposed like all educational aid agencies to difficulties of redeployment. The same is true of the UNDP, ILO, and FAO, except that they do not have a responsibility for the whole field of education.

UNICEF has a long record of aid to education carried out in collaboration with UNESCO. The two agencies have recently agreed to phase out UNICEF's aid to secondary education and to concentrate it on primary schools and youth who did not receive basic education, and as far as possible to promote innovatory projects, including nonformal education.

The World Bank Group is the largest single multilateral source of educational finance. While its material aid is in the form of buildings and their equipment with a small proportion of technical assistance, it employs under its cooperative agreement with UNESCO sophisticated methods of sector analysis and project identification and preparation, and its investments are directed at efficiency improvement combined with better relevance to development.

The Inter-American Development Bank (IDB) has used large investments for educational purposes mostly for higher-level education and in the forms of loans for buildings and equipment. It is at present reviewing its educational aid strategy. The other regional banks for Africa and Asia have made little if any investment in education. The OECD gives educational aid to its member countries, and services the Development Assistance Committee (DAC). The latter has contributed considerably over recent years to promoting new approaches to educational aid but has no operational program of its own other than of its individual members. The Commission of the European Communities has concentrated on scholarships and training grants and capital aid for the associated African and Malagasy states. The South East Asian Ministers of Education Organization (SEAMEO) has set up six regional centers of advanced training in different fields and operates a revolving fund to finance them.

Nongovernmental organizations, notably religious and welfare groups, are a major source of educational assistance, usually to local projects rather than at the national level. The Ford, Rockefeller, and Carnegie Foundations are the largest sources of foundation assistance, and there are numerous smaller organizations in Europe and the United States. Virtually all of the nonofficial assistance is grant funds, and most is applied as technical assistance.

The Ford Foundation provides about three-fifths as much as the UNDP, for a wide range of educational assistance. It is at present reviewing the coverage and levels at which its assistance can best be applied, including the emphasis it previously placed on higher education and education in science. The Rockefeller Foundation is especially active in Latin America and in agriculture and science and the Carnegie Corporation in general education in the Commonwealth countries.

Nonofficial sources of assistance are, at least potentially, more flexible than official, since they are less exposed to political hazards, though some of the nongovernmental bodies have restrictions of their own. In most cases there is a considerable delegation of authority to the field, which means that redeployment possibilities depend heavily on the background and quality of their field staff, and the speed of communication of new ideas among them.

When one considers the impressive amount of educational aid, it has to be borne in mind that (1) most of the educational aid total of the DAC member countries is made up of the supply of teachers and by grants to study in the donor country; (2) most of the multilateral aid is in the forms of loans and credit for buildings and equipment, though associated with educational improvement and reform; (3) the nongovernmental aid, though large, is dispersed over local projects and tends to lack impact on educational systems as a whole; and (4) the educational aid from the centrally planned socialist countries usually forms part of commercial agreements or development grants or credits.

The amount of aid resources devoted to the direct improvement of educational systems as such is thus only a small part of the total.

Switches of Resources Required

While educational requirements flow from given situations, some of the most important redeployment needs may be listed as follows. This list is based on the recommendations of the main governmental and expert meetings of the last few years. The "less" and "more" in the list do not necessarily relate to any individual country and are of course no substitute for diagnosis on the spot. They refer to the needs of the Second Development Decade seen in bulk. The utility of trying to see the needs in bulk is the guidance this should provide to the overall planning of aid programs and their administration, especially as regards changes in the channels and methods of aid, and the type of "backstopping" and "expertise" to be accumulated.

less emphasis on	more emphasis on
grants for study and training in the donor country	grants for study and training in the recipient or in "third" developing countries
supply of teachers	teacher training
supply of experts in administration and operation of traditional systems	supply of experts in methods of educational change, innovation, and nonformal education; use of institutions both in developed and developing countries to increase capacity to design and carry out reforms
overall literacy campaigns	functional literacy related to work environment

less emphasis on	more emphasis on
vocational training inside the formal educational systems	arrangements for participation of employers in mixed formal and nonformal projects
expansion of enrollment without sufficient regard to the internal efficiency of the system	reduction of dropout and repetition, nonformal education to meet local needs
limited manpower view of external efficiency of system	unified economic and social criteria of external efficiency
support of existing structure of educational system (cycles and pupil streams)	restructuring to adapt better to economic and social needs of environment
standard types of curriculum development and reform	integrated curriculum development (that is, combining reforms in teacher training with changes in streaming of pupils, creation of new learning situations, use of new media, combined with review of syllabus)
aid to educational systems as wholes regardless of the social distribution of access to education, and of "democratization" needs	special attention to educational deprivation—for example, for reasons of difference of language, and in shanty towns and rural areas: education of females; scholarship grants to aid social mobility
support of ongoing foreign or standard national types of education without careful evaluation	intensive dialogue with government and national experts, and through them with parents and teachers and local authorities

less emphasis on	more emphasis on
unstudied acceptance of national education plans and prevailing priorities	selective aid, consistent with development plan, but favoring only progressive objectives
"hard" loans for educational development	"soft" loans and credits
independence of educational aid from total aid	greater links with physical employment-creating aid
"prefabricated" projects emerging from aid agencies	country programing and local initiatives
competition among aid agencies	coordination (informal or formal) and use of UNDP country programing facilities
documentation and expertise mainly from developed country sources	creation of intellectual "backstopping" facilities in recipient countries or subregions
experts from donor countries	experts from recipient countries
use of individual experts	use of institutions in developing as well as developed countries
traditional media and methods, and academic approaches, sporadic and unscientific evaluation	new media, more scientific methods, and built-in evaluation, practical orientation
	home economics and family planning
assessment of aid effort in money value as part of total aid flow	use of cost-effectiveness studies

less emphasis on	more emphasis on
separate collection of country data by each agency	exchange of country analysis and information evaluating innovatory projects

Associated Problems

The Small Demand for Aid for Educational Reform and Its Implications for the Supply of Aid; Can Supply Create Demand?

Few of the developing countries are embarking on fundamental educational reforms, and there are accordingly few requests for aid for this purpose. Against this has to be weighed the role that aid could play in stimulating reform, if donors were to reduce the types of aid that "buttress" traditional methods and were to increase the availability of aid dedicated specifically to educational regeneration and innovation. Alternatives would be to specify that a certain proportion of a donor's existing aid, or that all increments of aid, should be devoted to these purposes.

If a donor were to act in this way, would it be politically acceptable to the recipient countries and how effective might its action be? Developing countries cannot with conviction challenge (though they sometimes do) the right of the providers of aid to determine what general categories of aid they can make available for individual countries to accept or reject if they wish. This is done regularly by the United Nations as well as by the bilateral agencies (for example, the UNDP for a number of years excluded aid to primary education but provided it for secondary, and UNICEF has just excluded aid for secondary in order to concentrate its efforts on primary). Thus in the case of an individual donor, the problem is not likely to be one of principle, and in practice difficulties that arose would likely be due to the particular relations the donor had with individual countries.

On the side of the recipients, however, there may exist a difficulty of principle. Few developing countries would be prepared to accept overtly such a policy, since educational reform is in principle a sensitive domestic political issue. This difficulty can be reduced if it is clearly recognized that educational reform is determined, not by political decisions alone but by the combination of political factors with technical feasibility. External aid may be as much needed for the latter as it is redundant for the former, provided the aid agencies are adequately equipped for this role.

269

This proviso is important because the sources of educational aid do not at present have on hand a stock of experience of assistance to educational reform. Existing expertise is heavily linked to "buttressing" rather than to innovatory methods. Relatively little effort has as yet been made by the providers of aid to sponsor original research and to participate in the development work and risks involved in setting up new types and patterns of education, suited to the needs of recipient countries.

If there were an increased effort to develop prototypes of new educational solutions, would the supply create additional demand? This proposition could be tested out in a selected number of instances. It is part of the rationale for establishing a new international fund or program to stimulate educational innovation. Funds would be needed for the initial support of recurrent expenditure for innovatory projects, a practice at present frowned upon by most suppliers of educational aid.

Methods of Allotting Educational Aid

A further constraint on redeployment is the fact that the volume of educational aid, although increasing faster than total aid, is not producing sufficient new funds in a form that would open up new possibilities of this kind. It is usually much easier to finance new policies from new resources than to have to cut back and redeploy existing programs in order to create new ones.

If the annual increment of educational aid were available to utilize in new ways, a major source of stimulus to innovation would be created. This raises the possibility discussed below that there might be some common agreement among the providers of educational aid to allocate annual increments as far as possible to supporting types of projects that were definitely innovatory and not of the "buttressing" type, and research and development. This would avoid, or give more time to solve, a number of the problems inherent in redeployment.

Legal and Administrative Obstacles

A further constraint consists of administrative and legal factors. Different policies have different administrative implications. If a donor country has been following a policy based on a special set of national purposes, its educational aid projects will be likely subject to a larger number of detailed regulations before they can be operative. If such a donor wishes to move toward a more "open" policy of meeting a greater variety of types of urgent needs, where they may arise, it has not only to change its policy and possibly its legislation, but also its administrative process and perhaps also the governing regulations. One major donor was found recently to have a checklist of 68 statutory criteria, only a small part of which had a relation to the purpose of a particular project, but all of which had to be fulfilled. A staff of some 700 officials were required to see that the regulations were followed. Obviously a set of regulations and a battalion of officials of these dimensions constitute in themselves an impediment to rapidity of redeployment.

At the other extreme nothing is easier than for highly placed legislators or officials to make "off-the-cuff" decisions out of friendliness while on field missions, this being one of the sources of poor projects.

Then there is the problem of inspection or observation of progress. It does not follow that, because new equipment has been supplied, it will be used. The headmaster may keep it locked up to ensure its safety, and new methods of teaching are liable to be eroded by old methods unless regularly observed and polished up. Joint observation groups in which both recipients and donors participate can play an important part in steering major aid projects.

Finally, since the obstacles to redeployment are considerable, measures of control and persuasion to see that it actually takes place are in order. Permissive agencies that do not issue central policy circulars to guide their field officers in the general operation of their delegated powers should review their internal communication system.

Organizational Difficulties

Similarly, organizational problems may constitute a restraint. A donor country or agency may decide for instance on a policy of subcontracting to educational institutions rather than continuing to use individual experts to supply its technical assistance to developing countries. Such a decision will not be operationally effective until the agency has been equipped to recruit institutions instead of individuals. Different sets of data and administrative actions are required for the two different types of operations.

Similarly a switch in priorities (for example, a reduction of aid to primary education and increase of assistance to universities) requires that the intellectual "backstopping" and documentation should also undergo change. Up-to-date expertise has to be prepared and stocked and new data collected. There is also the task of reconstructing the new stock of expertise and data not only at headquarters but all down the line. To enable switches of this kind to be carried out, it is necessary to have a flexible system of backstopping, and of staff adjustment, to permit the new priorities to be serviced.

It may, of course, be only a matter of months before in the first case the recruiting methods can be changed and the redundant staff moved elsewhere (the recruitment of individuals being much more time-consuming); in the second case a longer period is necessary since it takes considerable time to alter an organization's background of expertise. But these organizational changes will, however, only take place as rapidly as possible if they are foreseen and planned immediately after the decision is taken, or were foreseen as part of the analysis of implications of the policy decision. Unfortunately, what too frequently happens is that the attempt is made to put new policies into operation with old forms of organization.

Strengths and Weaknesses of the Channels of Aid

Aid agencies work through the education profession, which means the representatives of the different levels and types of education, and this is the basis of their technical strength. However, this situation sometimes produces a tendency for the different levels to develop projects in isolation, the results depending on the vigor and resources of money and men that are available rather than upon any overall assessment of priorities. To some extent this is inevitable under systems of working direct with the profession rather than relying on civil service or intermediary public bodies to carry out aid programs. However, there are alternative organizational possibilities under which the educational profession can still be the main instrument of giving educational aid, but the effort and the decision-making process could be better coordinated.

A governmental committee in which, in addition to majority representation from the educational profession, economists, employers, efficiency experts, trade unions, and sociologists could be associated, would seem indicated as the planning and evaluation channel of educational aid.

A multidisciplinary group of this kind would have to be fed by an analysis unit that would place before it the necessary data including diagnostic surveys of country needs. This analysis unit should have an independent status and not be simply a branch of one of the other departments.

Periodic meetings should be arranged with governmental officials and experts from the recipient countries, both at the bilateral and multilateral levels, for the exchange of ideas and to share in the results of the work of evaluation. No important switches of policy should be set in motion without prior discussion with recipient governments that would be particularly affected.

Lags in Communication and in Acceptance of New Policies within Aid Agencies

Unless there is good communication and ready acceptance of new policy by the staff concerned, new types of organization will cling instinctively to old policies. For a new aid policy to be effective, it has to be understood throughout the headquarters of the aid agency, and also among the field staff, who may outnumber the staff at the center. One major assistance agency working in the field of education has no system of centralized instruction for the purpose of indicating and explaining new policy changes to its staff. Each individual division or section sends out its own interpretation of the decision made by the legislative bodies. This leads to considerable leakage of effort.

Decisions changing priorities involve shifts of the weighting and the level of responsibility to different sections that are not always palatable to those who lose on the decisions. Thus while no staff member will overtly oppose a new policy, the "steam" will go out of operations unless there is a single power circuit. The same type of intervention is required for the intellectual backstopping section. The new effort required to recast analysis made previously and to adopt new lines of thought may also cause loss of "steam." Old styles of thinking assert themselves unconsciously in the minds of both communicators and the audience.

Time Spans between Planning, Decision-Making, and Operations

A further constraint of a different kind is the time lag that occurs between the identification of the need for change and the decision-making, and then between the decision-making and program implementation. This applies to all types of programs, but there are some special difficulties in the case of educational aid. One of these is the long-term nature of educational plans and the absence in most of them of mechanisms of rolling adjustment. Aid allocations are for shorter periods. The situation is one of two different-sized cog wheels that interlock imperfectly from time to time.

This type of difficulty points to the need for planning boards, discussed below, to act as a "clutch" to permit the cogs to interlock better. Planning boards also have the advantage of permitting the sections whose work is being reduced to participate in the adjustments in the agency as a whole. This may strengthen their participation in the difficult task of making reductions in their staffs and the transfer or reshaping of their skills for the new purposes. Lags that occur through vested interests clinging to their existing type of work are important real obstacles to change and should not be passed over unnoticed. Management methods have to be found by which the human as well as the material resources can be re-channeled between the decision-making and the new operations.

Diagnosis of Needs

At present the diagnosis of needs starts normally with a study of the overall demographic data, and the contents of the macroeconomic and social plan, of which the educational plan is a part. Out of the educational plan a number of projects are selected as needing external help and fulfilling the donor's criteria.

While this type of diagnosis will always remain necessary, there are additions that need to be made. First, the analysis needs breaking down into regional or district data. Countrywide figures obscure geographical disparities fraught with serious implications. The regional and local analysis not only should cover enrollment and school facilities. It should also discuss the type of educational attainments that are required for preparation in these localities as well as for citizenship in the country as a whole. This involves ascertaining the views of provincial and local administrators, and those of the other interests involved such as parents, teachers, and employers.

Secondly, the educational needs of the population should be looked at on a face-to-face basis rather than through the glass walls of the educational system, some of which are mirrors. The familiar statement appearing in every country analysis that "x" percent of the primary-school-age children are in school is in practice meaningless unless accompanied by some solid reasons for believing that in fact all children in the particular country should be, or could be, in school between the ages of 7 and 14 on the model of the developed countries. A better index, hardly ever used, is the proportion of children who have or have not acquired (1) minimum or basic education, defined in terms of literacy and the most elementary aptitudes required by their environment, and (2) suitability for entry to the second level.

The standard answer to the question why data are not obtained on a geographical and qualitative basis is that the statistics are not available in this form. But the cost involved in assembling this information would be a tiny fraction of the $1.5 billion effort represented by educational aid. Usually the information could be obtained by small contracts with local research institutes or industrial officials either by reorganizing existing statistical materials on a new basis (for example, in the case of primary schools, giving the proportion of children over 11 with under four years; four years; six years), or by conducting sample surveys.

274

A third addition is that at one point of the diagnosis the analysts should forget for a while the specifics of the educational system and examine the extent to which the children are actually acquiring, or not, the basic knowledge and learning skills relevant to their environment from all available sources. The findings should be discussed with local educators, parents, community leaders, and responsible officials as part of the consultations already mentioned.

A fourth addition is that if aid is to support social as well as purely educational and economic objectives, data must be shown on education as an instrument of social mobility (scholarship ladders available, class origins of students, and so on).

A fifth addition of particular importance is to show the relation of educational plans to plans for physical investment so that the educational component of them can be assessed (the relationship of educational output to the employment situation is usually examined as a matter of standard practice, but there is seldom an attempt to relate educational aid to physical investment). The dialogue should not limit itself to the technical aspects but, to be fruitful, should take account of the political viability in the recipient country of securing adoption of the proposals.

Criteria of Good Aid Projects

Needs have to be appraised also in terms of their suitability for being met with external aid, rather than by domestic resources alone. Criteria of a good educational aid project are that it should be clearly requested by the recipient country and meet a defined area that cannot be met domestically, quantitatively or qualitatively; that it is consistent with the national development plan; that it should be carefully related to the recipient country's resources as well as to its needs; that new institutions or methods introduced should be of a kind that is within the power of the recipient country to keep up when the aid terminates; that it should have a catalytic effect, which means that it must have the necessary critical mass and duration (either alone or through complementarity with other aid projects) to have a sizable impact and not peter out; also that it should take care not only of the direct needs but of those created by the repercussions of the direct aid (package projects).

Conversely, aid that generates recurrent expenditure that the national budget cannot afford should be avoided; pilot projects should not be at a level of sophistication and expensiveness that prevent them from being propagated more widely; loans and credits should not place an undue debt burden on the recipient country; aid programs should not overload the recipient with administrative work that it is not in a position to undertake because the projects are too complicated or too innovatory. Also from the standpoint of the donor, aid normally has to be identifiable in terms of its sources (a tax-payer or private contributor likes to see his effort ascribed to him). Further, in the interest of all concerned, it should have a mechanism of evaluation incorporated into it. It is also desirable that the project be coordinated with the efforts of other aid suppliers in the recipient country.

Political Factors; The Nature of the Dialogue;
The Relation of Aid to the National Plan

H. G. Wells records that, in his famous interview in Moscow in 1922 with the Soviet leaders, Stalin remarked that education was the most powerful weapon in the hands of the state and that everything depended on who held it and who was hit with it. Certainly education is a multipurpose tool of national policies, but it also has a surprising element of political independence, owing to the complexity of its interlock with economic and social factors.

An example might be a Country A, which gave the major portion of its study and training grants for students from developing countries to come and study at its national institutions rather than in their country of origin. The political motives might be a complex mixture of generosity and mutual interest, with an economic reasoning that "aid helps trade." However, Country A's economists might also argue that more would be gained from a policy of raising the general level of skill within Country B by helping it to build its own institutions. This would have a greater impact on the income of the country and the demand for Country A's products. Similar examples could be constructed for countries that had policies of maintaining the closest possible connections with their ex-colonies as a matter of mutual interest.

In the realm of the international agencies where similar problems arise, there is also much scope for alternative policies, but the problems of priority are frequently less easily resolved. Whereas in national governments decisions are taken in a relatively small cabinet, in international agencies today, as many as 130 representatives of sovereign states participate. Sheer numbers have tended to undermine conference techniques that had previously permitted the international agencies to arrive at clear consensuses on priorities. There are too many resolutions urging the horseman to go fast and slow at the same time. While this has the advantage of leaving a large area of maneuver for the secretariats, the secretariats themselves as a result may become overcharged and dispersive. What are required are conference techniques that permit consensuses to be established more clearly, and planning boards that will interpret them into programs with clearly assigned priorities and periodic adjustments of them.

Much of the aid process takes place, so far as educational aid is concerned, without the obtrusion of political undertones into the dialogue, partly because controversy is avoided (often at present by the dialogue being minimal) and partly because the subject does not attract controversy as much as some other aid fields. Nonetheless, when the dialogue is sharpened, differing views as to its appropriate nature emerge, a gradation of which might be as follows:

1. Aid should meet only the recipient's wishes, and the donor's role is limited to accountability.

2. The recipient has to be assisted to formulate his proposals, or at any rate they should be discussed, so that inconsistencies can be avoided and the demand be matched with the right form of supply.

3. The recipient's proposals have to be checked by the donor for conformity with certain fundamental principles (such as human rights).

4. The recipient's proposals (and the flows of assistance) have to be tested against the principles of internationally approved development strategy (for example, the UN and UNESCO resolutions on the Second Development Decade).

5. The recipient's proposals have to conform with particular aspects of donor legislation (for instance, to be tied to purchases of equipment from the donor country).

6. The donor may in addition restrict his type of aid in advance, placing the recipient in a take-it-or-leave-it situation except for operational aspects.

There are of course different variants and combinations of these points of view. In all of them policy may be said to remain the absolute prerogative of the recipient country since it has no obligation to accept the assistance offered. This argument is not wholly convincing morally, and in any event the availability of some types of aid rather than others, in addition to creating a temptation for its use, may affect the strategies of countries that accept it.

It may do so by diverting domestic resources to support and eventually take over the new ventures initiated with the help of aid. There will be cases where resources are usefully rechanneled as a result of the dialogue, and other cases where they are not, due to shortsightedness. The answer seems to be to improve the dialogue and in particular to use educational aid to strengthen the recipient side.

Means of doing so are assistance to developing countries to increase their expertise in educational planning, and the granting of subventions or technical assistance to their national or local institutions, or units in government, specializing in educational analysis, research, and evaluation.

Positive attitudes are required, on both sides, to the concepts of partnership for global development contained in the UN and UNESCO Strategies for the Second Development Decade. It would be as sad to see a "neoimperialistic" country (if there is one) trying to "sell" a project not in the interests of a developing country as it would be to see a chauvinistic government of a developing country (if there is one), representing only the elite sector of the population, rejecting genuine attempts to apply the UN strategy. The strategy does imply more active and more cooperative concern with global problems, and an obligation on those who accepted it (unanimously) to be active in trying to get it carried out.

Some Major Sectors of Educational Aid and Redeployment Possibilities

The attempt is now made to show briefly for the main sectors of educational aid the shifts of emphasis required and the implications. The attempt covers nonformal as well as formal education and discusses the overall volume of aid without reference to particular donors, since the applicability will vary from donor to donor. Each agency will want to evaluate its own situation under different headings. The areas of aid activity selected are; study abroad; investment; teacher supply and training; technical assistance; institution-building; curriculum reform and new learning methods and patterns; research and development; and educational planning.

Study Abroad

Study abroad is a well-tried educational instrument that can be very useful. But it is a blunt instrument in the surgery of modern educational planning. It does not eliminate the problems of the cross-cultural transference of education, since problems of the foreign expert not being able to adapt himself are substituted by those of the foreign student. It may also mask the need for the development of domestic facilities and leads to "brain drain" unless the programs are concentrated upon postgraduate students and those with commitments to return to their country of origin. Selective and efficient study abroad can produce clear and positive results for development purposes, together with some less tangible effects on international cooperation in the transfer of knowledge and mutual understanding. But better planning is needed.[6] The bluntness of the instrument can be reduced by subjecting programs to the rigors of cost-benefit analysis, and better selection and evaluation of results.

The liking that the recipient countries have for this form of aid, which has amenities as well as educational advantages, is illustrated by the response to the recent questionnaire issued by UNESCO on the brain drain.[7] Few countries replied, but those who did emphasized the advantages rather than the disadvantages to the recipient countries of study abroad, even though it tended to produce people with qualifications that could not be absorbed on their return home. The liking of donors is shown in the large place it occupies in their aid allocation, and there is some tendency to regard it as a mercantilist opportunity.

Study abroad has possibly been exaggerated as an effective method of educational aid for development. The undoubted advantages of study abroad, for general purposes, especially for the training of an administrative elite, can best be pursued under programs under different budgetary headings, while mercantilist ends are best served by including study abroad in commercial treaties. About half of the people appearing under the heading of technical assistance are students and trainees receiving aid (numbering some 80,000 annually). This amount may be too high as a proportion of the present total of educational aid for development. And, within the total, the proportion studying or being trained in their own countries, which is only about 10 percent, is too low.

Investment

Whereas in 1960, under half of the would-be school entrants were provided with school buildings, the proportion is now a good deal higher. School buildings are usually poor, but so are the other public service facilities. To increase the output of persons possessing basic or elementary education, the reduction of drop-out and repetition, curriculum reform, and the better use of existing facilities are required. For this purpose and to bring into education the unenrolled, investment is required in new types of formal and nonformal educational buildings and equipment (functional work-oriented literacy centers, community schools, preemployment centers, and so on). It will be important for providers of capital aid to keep in close touch with, and themselves to stimulate, the development of new teaching and learning models.

Since 1960, general secondary, technical, and higher education have been expanding more rapidly than primary or basic education. This has raised the proportion of capital costs in education budgets, since they use more capital than basic education. Heavy but selective investment is still needed for manpower reasons in technical institutions, centers of excellence, and teacher education.

But there is a widespread overproduction of general secondary-level school-leavers in terms of employment opportunities, and the ratio of benefit to cost is likely to be shifting in favor of basic education, quite apart from the question of social equality.

Moreover, doubts are growing about the utility of some of the investment in secondary technical and vocational schools, as compared with the alternative of more investment in efficient pre-vocation basic education of a nonacademic type and incorporating training into investment projects. There are also reasons, in a number of developing countries, for transferring some of the cost burden of technical education to industry, on the parallel of activities of associations of employers (such as SENAI and SENATI) in a number of Latin American countries.

There are already indications[8] of some shift in growth rates in favor of basic education taking place in developing countries. But, with some exceptions, this is not yet matched by an equal redeployment of aid. In any event the redeployment is usually in the form of increased allocations to traditional types of primary education.

A switch of investments in favor of basic education, both formal and informal, on the part of aid agencies, would have to be supported by increased emphasis upon prior survey work and feasibility studies, since this is a neglected field in which new ideas and more scientific "backstopping" is required. At present educational projects seldom receive the same degree of detailed feasibility analysis as is applied to physical investment projects. Moreover, the investment requirements are more localized and often more elusive to the external eye than is the case with investment in the second and higher levels.

A restriction on external capital investment is the amount of recurring expenditure it generates domestically, which, being of a continuing nature, reduces the flexibility of the use of education funds. "Hard" loans, in addition to generating recurrent expenditure, also increase the indebtedness and volume of loan repayments of recipient countries. To a greater extent these aspects of a less positive nature are reduced or masked by the fact that both investments and repayments are spread over a considerable period of time. But while this is valuable for development purposes, it is also a serious temptation to governments and ministers who do not expect to remain in office long. The rate of turnover of ministers of education in the developing countries is particularly high.

Teacher Supply and Training

Teacher supply is an area in which considerable redeployment is already taking place. When 1962 and 1972 are compared, there is an important shift to be recorded away from the lower reaches toward the higher in the supply of expatriate personnel, as local staff have become available. There has also been a greater supply of aid for teacher training and teacher education institutions and for expert administrators and educational planners. This is especially notice-able in the figures related to the programs of the main bilateral agencies concerned with teacher supply. In one country, the United Kingdom foresees a 50 percent reduction of its teacher supply at all levels over the next five years. It is also becoming increasingly true in respect of the volunteer programs. The U.S. Peace Corps, for instance, is now predominantly made up of specialized personnel rather than general teachers.

Nonetheless the supply of teachers from donor countries to recipients is still a major part of the aid effort, and further redeploy-ment is bound to become necessary as local facilities for training teachers develop. One obstacle is the tendency on the part of many developing countries to use expatriate personnel in the teaching pro-fession rather than in business and administration in order to meet shortages of people with modern and high-level qualifications. This means that the reduction of expatriates is taking place more slowly in education than in other sectors or countries that obtained their independence recently. Another factor tending to maintain the status quo is the link, particularly through the examination procedures, with the educational process in the recipient country due to historical reasons.

So long as the developing countries wish to have this expatriate source of supply of teachers under aid programs there is every reason for meeting their requests provided they are associated with develop-ment objectives. Measures of improvement would be the increase in the quality and continuity of the services of the expatriate teachers by reducing the more haphazard elements in their recruitment. In this respect valuable experience exists in certain donor countries of the successful linking of institutions in the donor and the recipient country to enable continuity and quality to be maintained. The intro-duction of the link between institutions, rather than handling teacher supply on an individual basis, could assume continuing responsibility for the evaluation of this form of aid.

While there is a good recognition among donors of the virtues of domestic teacher training as an alternative to the sending in of expatriates, a most important improvement, of which there are few signs at present, would be to treat teacher supply as part of integrated curriculum development. Teacher supply and teacher training are well understood as one of the most potent of all instru-ments of foreign aid, since education takes place through teachers, and four-fifths of educational expenditure is on their salaries. The weakness of the present arrangement, however, on both the recipient and the donor sides, is the failure to exploit fully the linkages between teacher training and curriculum development as an instrument of the overall regeneration of the educational system, and the virtual omission of nonformal education. This matter is taken up further in the section below on learning content and integrated curriculum development.

Technical Assistance

Technical assistance is the sharpest of the instruments of foreign aid and has the largest success record, and perhaps also the greatest number of mistakes behind it through trial and error. The amount of technical assistance funds that has been devoted to education is very high, probably about half of all the technical assistance funds of the bilateral donors. The difficulty is that most of it has been taken up by teacher supply and study abroad based largely on support to the prevailing educational systems. There has therefore not been as much innovatory technical assistance in education as there has been in industry and agriculture.

A reason is that whereas there is an available set of models and a body of knowledge based on scientific research and on considerable expenditure on the development of new processes that can readily be transferred covering industry and agriculture, the same is not true for education. Moreover in the case of the transfer of industrial and agricultural techniques, it is not too difficult to devise technologies of an "intermediate" order that will fit the local labor market, even if unfortunately this is too rarely done. In the case of education, however, few "intermediate" teaching and learning models are available to fit local educational needs, and to devise them is difficult. Thus the tendency—supported by the developing countries themselves—has been to reject attempts to set up "intermediate" educational patterns (for example, structures that would gear the primary cycle more to the needs of basic education and less to entry into secondary). Donors appear in a large degree to be encouraging assistance on educational quality, which becomes interpreted in European or North American terms, such as long primary cycles, with the almost inevitable result of high rates of drop-out and repetition instead of short efficient forms of mass education.

The channels of aid for technical assistance also need reassessing in many cases. An increased but more selective use of institutions seems called for, as well as a decrease of the sending out of individual experts. The use of institutions, properly selected and judiciously controlled, rather than individuals, ensures the maintenance of quality and continuity, and the correction of errors by "built-in" evaluation, since institutes have better "memories" than individuals. The hit-and-run aspects of assistance through individual experts can be reduced in this way. A similar favorable effect can be gained by grouping counterpart staff around specific units of the ministry with career prospects in the aid field and giving them training and incentives. The use of institutions, however, has to be handled with caution, since they themselves may employ hit-and-run tactics and not become sufficiently involved. Selected institutions are required that are prepared to accept a closer and controlled relationship with aid administrations as the basis of long-term commitments on both sides.

To make technical assistance more effective, there is the need for wider forms of expertise involving other disciplines as well as education, based on research and development and greater experimentation, and relying less on a standard repetition of previous types of projects.

Institution-Building

There have been important and effective examples of institution-building as a result of foreign aid, mostly at the level of higher and technical education, the weaknesses being that some have been too expensive in terms of unit cost. Others have been the result of competition between donors and led to overproduction of graduates, while some technical and vocational training institutes have not been able to channel the output to meet employers' demands.

Aid needs for institution-building are shifting away from those of the middle and lower middle range of developing countries toward those of the least developed, and toward "centers of excellence" (especially in the natural sciences and technology) that can serve larger states or groups of friendly neighboring countries. There is also a heavy need over the whole range of the developing countries for new institutions (such as preemployment centers and community schools associated with work projects) to deal with that part of the labor force, especially youth, that has employment or community work possibilities but lacks basic education, including literacy. University-to-university aid has been an important component of this type of aid and needs further development, on perhaps a more judicious and selective basis than hitherto, as a long-term basic form of educational cooperation. There has also been a limited amount of assistance through nongovernmental organizations and foundations.

Curriculum Reforms and New Learning
Methods and Patterns

The technology of education consists at any given moment of the sum of useful knowledge, scientific or based on common sense, and human or mechanical, about teaching and learning and how to organize them. For the promotion of development this knowledge has to be circulated and adapted to new situations, and its sum has to be added to by research and experimentation, and the results have to be applied. Application takes effect through teacher education, curriculum development, and organizational and material changes.

It is best where practical to take action that affects all of these factors in an integrated way. Teacher education is likely to remain for a long time the biggest single claim on external aid, and if properly linked to curriculum development and facilities for experimentation is clearly one of the most effective points of entry for assistance in educational regeneration and innovation. Linkages are also required between teacher education and activities to redefine learning needs in terms of the demands of the pupil's environment.

Additional measures are also needed to circulate the results of changes of method and their evaluation, not only from the more to the less educationally developed countries, but among the less developed countries themselves.

Changes in the form of educational organization and material facilities provided by the state (for example, new types of school) raise problems of a different order. Parent opinion, traditional prejudices, and institutional factors enter the lists, as is also the case if curriculum reform is pressed to the extent of changing the length of educational cycles and the examination and diploma system.

Many examples exist of aid projects that have been well conceived in themselves but have failed because the ancillary circumstances were not provided for. The effects of training teachers in new methods of learning, for instance, may be nugatory if the examination system is based on old methods. On these matters the far-sighted educator will recommend a "package" approach that will cover all of the integrated elements of the problem.

Aid agencies have to proceed warily in such matters, but if they have workable and tested examples to offer and if they have behind them the prestige of international recommendations and high expertise and if the choice is made of countries ripe for institutional reform, valuable changes may result. Other countries and aid agencies may follow the example if the results, including the difficulties and how they were overcome, are diffused.

The basic difficulty is the shortage of new models. This in turn derives from the shortage of resources devoted to research and experimentation. Of all the handicaps to the use of aid for educational regeneration and innovation, this is the most serious. It is, however, a handicap that could be overcome progressively if donors were willing to redeploy a proportion of their resources, which would not have to be a large one, away from automatic support of ongoing systems to the search for acceptable innovatory projects.

Research and Development
<u>Research and Development</u>

The amount of aid resources devoted to educational research and development is extremely small. This reflects a limited use of research and "rationality" approaches to education throughout, both in donor and recipient countries. It does not mean that considerable effort has not been directed by a number of experts and aid agencies to problems of curriculum reform. A good number of successes can be recorded. But this work has usually consisted of tinkering with the existing system, and the effort has been patchy and sometimes unconsciously undermined by the bulk of aid continuing to move in a traditional direction.

Recipient countries do not often ask for aid for educational research and development except as part of grants for study abroad or as part of the establishment of education institutions designed primarily for other purposes, perhaps not unnaturally attaching more importance to present needs than to possible future benefits. Moreover, many donors also feel it their duty to meet first the urgent ongoing needs and rarely supply the necessary additional resources required for research.

The climate of opinion among both recipients and donors is, however, shifting in favor of innovation, and some switch of aid resources to educational research and development would now be likely to be well received.

Action might be of the following kind: First, mass exchange of information on innovations that have been made and on their evaluation; more communication from country to country in respect to research projects and results; more seminars and research training courses for educators and officials. Educational research and development should be an integral part of projects assisting teacher training institutions at the post-secondary level. "Idea groups" and other forms of intellectual backstopping should be promoted.

Second, subregional research and development projects covering several countries could usefully be promoted and aided, as well as national institutes in individual developing countries. Much of this work would involve the testing out of new education and teaching patterns in terms of their education efficiency, their acceptability by the local population and their impact on living levels.

Third, more modest and less institutionalized forms of innovation should be encouraged by direct action with schoolteachers, headmasters, and parents utilizing the existing curricula, or modifying them where they need adjustments. This kind of work has to be undertaken through local institutions and public officials but could well be financed as part of foreign subventions to institutions. Increased linkages with industry for the purposes of recurrent education should also be the subject of study.

The function of aid in these different cases would vary. In the first, it would play a role of stimulating communication by having at its disposal data and research results concerning many countries. In the second and third, it would become involved in measures for reconstructing the educational systems leading to demand for educational facilities for teacher training, new text books, and equipment. This would imply somewhat longer-term commitments than are normally assumed. Under this heading, aid also has the role of sharing the financial and technical risks of experimentation. This implies a greater spirit of entrepreneurship and invention on the part of donors as well as recipients. Aid might also stimulate the whole process of diffusing in agreement with the recipient governments, throughout the "grass roots" of the educational system, renovative influences that would modify the attitudes of teachers and parents and the local community, and of the pupils themselves, to the teaching and learning process.

Educational Planning

Educational planning is regarded as a high priority by both donors and recipients as an area for aid. Conceptually, educational planning still derives largely from the problems of the 1950s and 1960s rather than those of the 1970s, the emphasis being mostly upon the valuable but limited task of forecasting macro-educational expansion with the quality changes determined by occupational needs.

Attempts to reassess the learning needs of the population in more pluralistic terms, both as regards objectives and conditioning factors,[9] and the groups to be covered, are relatively new, and there is little presentation and costing options, which would lead to fundamental change in the educational system. Pressures are mounting to apply newer concepts of educational planning—for example, what the Faure Report (p. 175) calls the ecological approach[10]—but the planning techniques and data-collecting services and forms of analysis required have not yet become established.

A similar widening is taking place in the concept of development, which like education had been relying too much on the dynamic physics of growth, and some new marriages between education and redeveloped economic theory are on the horizon. At the turn of the last century Alfred Marshall, who did so much himself to aid economic dynamics, was writing, "I think that in the later stages of economics better analogies are to be got from biology than from physics, and consequently that economic reasoning should start on methods analogous to those of physical statics, and should gradually become more biological in tone." He went on, "Progress or evolution, industrial and social, is not mere increase and decrease. It is organic growth, chastened and confined and occasionally reversed by the decay of innumerable factors, each of which influences and is influenced by those around it." He concludes that, "The Mecca of the economist is economic biology rather than economic dynamics."

Rediscovery is an important form of innovation. Marshall's approach applied to educational planning would not involve the rejection of the current type of educational planning expertise that figures in aid programs but rather its chastening by adding to it a wider variety of the human and social factors that both condition and foster educational evolution. Since these factors vary so much in different localities, and are so much a matter of policies and politics, this addition has essentially to be made on the spot by the countries themselves. There remains, however, a role for external assistance (preferably by multilateral agencies) in helping in problems of methods of analysis, data collection, and the international comparison of experience.

This applies especially in the aid field to the joint recipient-donor task of diagnosis and project identification. While aid is now being influenced by the UN strategy of the Second Development Decade, and by the spirit of educational renovation, the methodology is still that of the 1960s for the most part. Points needing emphasis include the following:

1. The point of departure should be the actual learning and teaching needs of the total population.

2. The "access to education" emphasis currently in use should be replaced by "delivery of learning facilities to the population."

3. The discrepancies between performance and needs should be established and evaluated by locality as well as nationally.

4. Consultations should take place with teachers, parents, and employers, as well as with the central government, as may be arranged by the government.

5. The present type of data on enrollment ratios should be supplemented by performance information and evaluation studies made under contract with local institutions.

6. Diagnostic and identification studies should be put into a common pool and shared, and opportunities for complementarity of effort brought to the attention of other donors.

7. The employment factor and linkages with physical investment needs ought to be brought out in each case.

8. The projects identified should be categorized under the three types of strategy set out in this section and appraised under the set of criteria of pages 276-277.

9. Projects selected need not be the same as the priorities of the educational plan but must be consistent with them.

10. Country programing is admirable but should not be used as an excuse to abandon joint project identification efforts and approved aid policies.

Summary of Principal Conclusions

The Problem

There have been many recommendations recently that educational aid should be redeployed, and international meetings have put out a good deal of material indicating the desirable direction of change. But the OECD reports show that there is little evidence at present of very significant new trends. Is this due to the time that inevitably must elapse before concrete steps can be taken to implement recommendations, or is there in the aid process a set of obstacles that delay or hinder change? Alternatively, is there a good deal of change going on that is not visible to the naked eye?

The readily visible change, such as it is, can mostly be attributed to automatic influences, such as a decline of foreign teachers as the supply of domestic teachers increases. There also exists a small number of important innovatory projects initiated with the help of aid funds, though some of these aim at technical improvements of existing systems rather than at fundamental changes in what is taught.

What can be done to expedite the redeployment of aid? Educational policy is the prerogative of the recipients. But donors have the right to restrict their aid to some aspects of recipients' educational plans and to withhold it from others and to offer new types of assistance. Innovation is a field in which supply can create demand. While any major redirection of aid must await a redirection of aid requests from the developing countries, the better supply and management of aid for innovative purposes can be an important creative element. How can this element be fostered? This is approached by looking at obstacles, and asking how aid can become a more innovatory influence, and at what is involved for its better planning and management.

Findings

Certainly more change is taking place than meets the eye. However, it is mostly of a day-to-day pragmatic nature, reflecting an attitude change rather than a reprograming, and is not systematized. The new wine is mostly being poured into old bottles.

During the enquiry, a number of suggestions were evolved and tested out with aid agencies—not in depth but in terms of initial responsiveness. There was general agreement that if the impact of educational aid is to change, there are a number of indispensable alterations to be made in its programing and management. These changes will vary greatly from agency to agency. Each may want to select for consideration those that may be applicable from the list of suggestions made below.

List of Suggestions

Programing the Redeployment of Existing Activities. Educational aid agencies could take stock of existing activities and in agreement with the recipient countries sort them into two categories:

Category A: activities that appear to be "buttressing" dysfunctional education (in the Pearson Commission's sense); and

Category B: those that appear to be geared to development needs (as defined in the UN and UNESCO strategies for the Second Development Decade).

This could only be of a rough sort and should be done by an interdisciplinary group. Difficult cases should be left aside for further study. Redeployment can only take place step by step, but every step is valuable (a 5 percent redeployment on each donor's part, for instance, would yield an annual total of $75 million for innovatory projects).

Agencies would then subdivide both categories into (1) projects filling urgent gaps in the existing system (first aid); (2) medium-term projects (bridging operations); and (3) longer-term activities affecting structures and basic content (educational reform). Both Category A and B projects have to be so subdivided in order to give the initial time perspective of possible redeployment.

The next step would be to attack Category A by marking against each of the activities as so subdivided the time period for which existing commitments have been undertaken and showing (1) those where a sudden break would greatly reduce the value of the effort already applied and so give negative results and (2) those in which the commitment could come to an end without serious dislocation.

If the aid agency followed this procedure, it would then have before it a schedule that would give a first indication of the amount and the time requirements for the redeployment involved and an analysis of the feasibility both as regards time and the substance of the phasing out of the various activities under Category A. Obviously this would be a vulnerable piece of analysis to be used with care, since a number of individual judgments are involved. It would, however, give the first framework for a redeployment policy within which more sophisticated planning could take place. No aid agency was found to have a framework of this kind.

Forward Planning and Management. Detailed advance planning of educational aid is neither possible nor desirable. Too much depends upon the evolution of the policies of the recipient countries and the actual circumstances in the field. Nevertheless there are certain broad measures of foresight that are essential if redeployment is to be effective, of which some are listed as follows.

Sharpening the dialogue. The dialogue has to be sharpened to bring out the creative element in the aid process. This means better project-identification techniques on the part of donors, and more aid to recipient countries to sharpen their own dialetic tools. These tools are research and data collecting, the study of prevailing educational objectives and priorities as compared with actual learning needs and achievements, and the training of counterparts. The dialogue should give special attention to educational renovation and possible innovations.

Conditions of successful innovation. For an innovatory project to be successful and durable it should contain incentives for parents, pupils, and educators to adopt it; it should have local sponsorship and if possible leadership as well as the necessary central support; it should not be so complex that its results are not easily measurable and communicable; and it should have the necessary critical mass to have an impact that will make an impression on the community and result in its being followed up when its success has been demonstrated. At present educational aid negotiations take place centrally often without consultation with local interests. Every effort should be made working through the recipient government, to increase local involvement at the project identification and preparation stage.

For the least developed countries, servicing units might be initiated in national educational institutes, or on a subregional basis, which would conduct surveys, examine the options, and forecast aid needs. Steps should also be taken to promote educational assistance between developing countries themselves with common languages and cultures.

The dialogue should emerge from initiatives in the recipient country, with as much freedom of action as possible, subject to

accountability and within the framework of the UN and UNESCO development decade strategies. Automatic acceptance of projects simply
because they are in country programs is not to be recommended.

Channels of aid. Many educational aid programs are carried
out through semipublic or nongovernmental organizations, or through
committees representing the different levels of the educational profession. This gives programs technical strength, but in periods of
change it is necessary to review the channels of aid to see if they
adequately cover the new needs. In some cases it may be desirable
to use additional channels and adopt new funneling devices—for example, to set up intermediate committees or planning boards at which
policy is settled with the channels of aid so as to ensure their commitment to redeployment. This applies not only to outside channels
of aid but also to the channels within aid agencies and ministries of
education.

A career service for institutions. A good deal has been said
about a career service for experts and counterparts to increase
involvement and continuity, but little about a similar service for
institutions. It is desirable to set up long-term programs with
selected institutions in both donor and recipient countries that will
permit the programs to train staff and create the intellectual infrastructure required. There have been difficulties in this matter in
the past due to the institutions not assuming the necessary commitments and to aid administrations not exercising sufficient control.
But a new look is required at what should be basically one of the
most important instruments of improving the quality of educational
aid and a means of creating in the developing countries themselves
an increased capacity to design and carry out educational change.

Flexible backstopping. The expertise of a program depends
not only on the experts employed but also on their technical backstopping, which is especially important in times of change. The
task of a fullback is not only to defend his goal but also to make
strategic passes to the forwards. A number of the backstopping
services both in aid agencies and recipient countries are engaged
too much in defensive play. In times of redeployment it should be
the role of these services to be constantly on the lookout for means
of attack—usually in the form of tested examples and research results and new ideas.

However, it is not much use for the fullbacks to make good
forward passes if the men in the forward line are looking the wrong
way. A good forward spends a lot of time looking backward in order
to see where the passes are coming from. Successful redeployment requires a great deal of play in midfield. Documentary and
other supporting services should be reinforced in order to provide
more active backstopping. Examples of educational innovations should

be evalauted and their results circulated on the basis of a common methodology. Small resource centers and data banks should be created and used. Aid should be provided to the recipients for action on this at their end.

Communication and coordination. Both the recipient countries and the staff of donor agencies should be consulted and informed of the overall strategies and the reasons for them. This process must be planned in advance; otherwise there will be great waste of time with misunderstandings, as well as ineffectiveness in execution. Sudden switches of policy should not take place without prior discussion and diplomatic preparation undertaken with the recipient countries. Seminars should be arranged under the aegis of international agencies to promote the communication of ideas and points of view between donors and recipients. Donors should also exchange information among themselves for coordination purposes at the country level under the initiative of the recipients.

Evaluation and control. Evaluation may be (1) ante hoc; (2) ad hoc; and (3) post hoc. The first two are more important than the third, which tends to be overcomplex and to give results too late to be used operationally. A good model of the first exists in the UNESCO-IBRD Cooperative Programme, though some further improvements could be made. A valuable model for the second exists in the Federal German Republic, which has both an aid inspection unit available as a "trouble-shooting" service at all stages of the aid process and also a team of observers in the field.

It would be desirable to reexamine aid to educational planning and to broaden its basis and to reexamine prevailing systems of project identification. Joint constituted observing units would be a useful form of standing evaluation. Post hoc evaluation is important but can be left largely to the academic community.

Financial Allocations. Redeployment versus new money for new projects. The annual increase of educational aid is running at a rate a little ahead of the annual increase of the educational budgets of the developing countries (taken together). If increases of educational aid could be identified and isolated as a sum available for innovation, problems of redeployment would be reduced. Obviously it is easier to use new money for new types of projects than to have to undertake switches of resources. However, the additional money coming into the educational aid process every year is not a disposable total, since it mostly represents increments along the various budget lines (with priorities applied as between them), and "free" new money does not in fact emerge.

An international fund for educational innovation. The lack of "free" new finance might conceivably be overcome by an international fund for educational innovation to which governments might be persuaded to contribute a proportion of their annual increase, if not the whole. This would simplify problems of redeployment, but the question of setting up such a fund is itself a controversial issue about which majority opinion is at present negative. It is agreed that innovation should pervade the existing resources and that no additionality would result from a new fund.

If educational aid continues to increase and to occupy a large proportion of official aid and if donors move toward the decade target of 0.7 percent of the GNP for aid purposes, considerable additional sums will become available—unless redeployment results, as it may, in reduced unit costs by substituting R and D for the transfer of more expensive resources.

Allocation of funds for educational R and D in developing countries. Another possibility therefore might be for each donor to place a certain amount of aid (preferably untied aid) at the disposal of the developing countries themselves for use each year only for R and D or for ongoing projects of an innovatory nature.

Redeployment Measures in the Main Categories of Aid. There follows a summary in schematic form of possible measures and new or additional approaches discussed in the study for the main categories of aid. They cover study abroad, investment, teacher supply and training, technical assistance, research and development, institution-building, curriculum reform and new learning methods and patterns, and educational planning.

Shift of Emphasis Required	Redeployment Measures	Obstacles to Redeployment	Additional Approaches or New Directions
1. Large shifts would seem indicated, on an overall basis, but position varies considerably between donors. The shifts would be partly from study-abroad programs to other activities, and partly within study abroad (for example, more use of the group fellowship system).	1. Distinguish between the more purely cultural and political and the more strictly development objectives, and finance them under different budget headings. 2. For development purposes, limit study abroad in the donor country to those categories of study for which facilities are not available in the recipient country. 3. Build up the necessary substitute facilities in recipient countries except where application of cost-benefit analysis gives a negative indication.	Recipient's side 1. Failure to define and plan study abroad in educational planning. 2. Lack of resources for creating facilities to substitute study abroad. 3. Antagonisms between neighboring countries, and national competition for locations of regional centers of excellence. 4. Amenities of study in the donor countries, and the prestige of study abroad. 5. Ruling groups with foreign diplomas	Recipient's side 1. Strengthen the links between the administration and planning of study abroad and overall educational planning. 2. Use international aid to examine domestic substitution as well as third-country and subregional possibilities. 3. Evaluate existing programs better and more regularly, and use results in overall requests for educational aid. 4. Divert unavoidable nepotism into the cultural studies.

Shift of Emphasis Required	Redeployment Measures	Obstacles to Redeployment	Additional Approaches or New Directions
	4. Assist study abroad in neighboring countries (third countries) and aid the setting up or growth of regional centers of excellence.	protect their own status; nepotism.	Donor's side
			1. Separate out quotas of expenditure on fellowships according to location in donor or recipient countires.
		6. Lack of coordination of requests for aid.	
	5. Apply more funds to internal scholarships in recipient countries to aid socially disadvantaged students.	7. Lack of familiarity with cost-benefit analysis, shortage of data.	2. Reduce allotments under first heading and increase them under the second. Give special attention to scholarships to the disadvantaged classes so as to aid social mobility.
		Donor's side	
	6. Denepotize the selection process and establish incentives or penalties to ensure the knowledge obtained is applied to the development of the recipient country	1. Confusion between more developmental and more purely cultural or political objectives.	
		2. This leads to insufficient attention given to cost, for example, of "hidden subsidies" involved in participation of foreign students in social insurance, general student facilities,	3. Give aid for the better planning of study abroad in recipient countries. and assist them in cost-benefit and substitution studies.
			4. Evaluate impact of

Shift of Emphasis Required	Redeployment Measures	Obstacles to Redeployment	Additional Approaches or New Directions
		and so on, and of student places forgone that could be used by nationals (for instance, half of the Graduate School of the London School of Economics consists of foreign students).	study-abroad programs as effective intruments of aid and publicize the results.
		3. Lack of data for and practice in cost-benefit studies.	5. Coordinate more effectively with the overall planning and execution of educational aid.
		4. Lack of regular process of evaluation and comparison with other alternatives.	
		5. Forces of habit in administrations and weaknesses of coordination and planning.	
		6. Exaggerated belief that returning students will	

Shift of Emphasis Required	Redeployment Measures	Obstacles to Redeployment	Additional Approaches or New Directions
		substantially influence the direction of commerce. 7. Absence of standing administration machinery that studies alternatives.	

Investment

Shifts of Emphasis and Redeployment Measures Required	Obstacles Affecting Redeployment	Additional Approaches or New Directions
A lesser proportion of aid to straight building programs for general secondary and higher. More help to "centers of excellence," especially in applied science and technology, and less to ordinary technical education and vocational training institutes. Ensure industry is involved in aid given for technical and vocational training.	Attractiveness to transient ministers of loans. Conservatism within the profession. Administrative immobilities and conservatism in agencies. Difficulty of controlling what goes on in the buildings financed. Shortages of expertise and data for innovatory approaches.	Strengthen the expertise and data collection required for the shifts of emphasis. Issue new instructions to identification and preparation missions. Examine social equity as well as economic factors and nonformal as well as formal education possibilities involving industry and the communications services in the community. Link aid to integrated curriculum development (creation of local teaching and learning situations in which subject

Shifts of Emphasis and Redeployment Measures Required	Obstacles Affecting Redeployment	Additional Approaches or New Directions
Link capital investment in education more closely to physical investment.	Difficulties of obtaining the necessary interdisciplinary breadth in project diagnosis, and shortage of data for the purpose. This applies both to agencies and recipients.	matter, teacher training, equipment, are planned as a whole).
A greater proportion of investment in (1) basic education (formal and nonformal), and (2) education oriented to local development possibilities especially for the poorer part of the population, and (3) employment-generating projects for youth.		Give capital aid for research and development for new educational patterns and risk-taking.
		Create necessary administration and technical link with other capital investment.
Greater emphasis on pretechnical preparation, especially of youth who dropped out prematurely.		Establish special units for this purpose in donor and recipient agencies to foresee and influence educational component of future employment situation.
Readjust the time perspective—for example, stress the short term by giving more aid to adult education, functional literacy, family, planning, and nonformal education generally, including "first aid" projects.		Search out, through the country's development plan and by employment analysis the areas where the labor force is not ready for modernization but industry will grow. Create preemployment centers.
Aim to make an impact on the educational level of the		Encourage, and even subsidize, more takeover by employers of technical and vocational training.

Shifts of Emphasis and Redeployment Measures Required	Obstacles Affecting Redeployment	Additional Approaches or New Directions
mean of the population within 10 years.		

Invest in the new media, but in a manner less related to the formal system and more as a means of using all the community's educational influences, including parents, trade unions, cooperatives, and local government services.

Teacher Supply and Training

The proportion of aid going to the supply of expatriate teachers is, to some extent, declining and being redirected to aid to teacher training and educational planning and administration.	The momentum of the existing recruitment system, contract renewals, and so on perpetuates the present type of teacher supply.	Reduce progressively the supply of expatriate teachers.
This process needs accelerating since the expatriates, while playing an important role, occupy jobs that nationals ought to fill and tend to maintain artificial salary structures inherited from the colonial era.	On the other hand educational expansion in donor countries is reducing number available for overseas. Supply is also diminishing by disillusionment with aid program owing to current criticism.	Increase aid to domestic teacher training and to the training of trainers of teachers. No aid to teacher training without relation to curriculum development. Encourage movement of teachers between developing countries with same language, to help meet shortages. Diffuse throughout teacher training improved teaching methods

Shifts of Emphasis and Redeployment Measures Required	Obstacles Affecting Redeployment	Additional Approaches or New Directions
Teacher supply and training tends to be too exclusively concentrated on the pedagogic or academic aspects of education, on the one hand, or on technical training, on the other. In the formal systems, poor teaching methods (such as use of rote learning) should be replaced by more modern ones involving public participation and use of the new media. More effort should be devoted to increasing teacher supply and training in basic education for children and adults also, including functional literacy, "first aid," and recuperative types of education, and instructions in health, nutrition, and family planning. The gap between education and work life should be diminished through training teachers to impart knowledge	The pace of teacher training in recipient countries is limited by domestic financial problems, and bottlenecks in the number of teacher trainers, in the quality of curricula, and physical facilities, and lack of pilot schools for experimenting and opportunities for in-service training. The gap between new theories and instructions and their practical implementation is difficult to bridge owing to conservatism of the profession and the isolation of many of the individual teachers. Salary insufficies and poor general education of teachers on which further training has to be built.	based on participation and creation of teaching situations rather than on instructional techniques and rote. Increase inspection of training. Ensure that old methods are not used to train teachers in new methods and so destroy credibility. Sponsor seminars for headmasters and local educational officials. Aid the setting up of more pilot schools, in which teachers can try out new methods. Concentrate on in-service training in first place, since the returns are highest. Use both material and psychological incentives to encourage teacher productivity. Ensure teacher training includes link with nonformal education, and propagates an understanding of work needs and the need for recurrent education.

Shifts of Emphasis and Redeployment Measures Required	Obstacles Affecting Redeployment	Additional Approaches or New Directions
of the work environment, and to promote the idea of recurrent education.	Lack of facilities for nonformal education.	Assist training of teachers for functional literacy, and preemployment centers education, especially for youth who missed formal schooling.
Teacher training should be integrally linked with curriculum development.		Help to attract into nonformal education parents, community workers, social service officials, and others as teachers, and provide centers for discussion and experimentation.

Technical Assistance

An increase of technical assistance is needed, but it should consist mostly of expertise that will aid educational regeneration and innovation.	The amount of expertise available for educational innovation is not large. There are few tried and tested models that the technical assistance expert can carry with him to new environments.	Equipment and experts should be provided for resource centers and data banks necessary for evaluating and reshaping educational output.
The need to concentrate upon quality and relevance of education, and to improve cost efficiency, means that technical assistance could take an increasing proportion of aid funds at the expense, if necessary, of quantitative expansion.	The obstacles to innovation in education in the recipient countries have their counterpart in similar conservatism in the	Technical assistance should be regarded as the main point of entry of educational reform and should be oriented to integrated curriculum development.
		Less reliance should be placed upon individual experts, and more on educational institutions in both recipient and donor countries. This

Shifting of Emphasis and Redeployment Measures Required	Obstacles Affecting Redeployment	Additional Approaches or New Directions
	educational provision in the donor countries.	would give more prestige and continuity to the operations, and would safeguard quality, though high-level individual experts with specialized knowledge should continue to be used.
	Reliance upon the normal channels will not necessarily produce new solutions.	
	Technical assistance is too often a hit-and-run affair, and it is difficult to leave lasting results unless there are adequate commitments and counterpart staff provided by the recipient government.	This would mean some administrative shifts under which recruitment becomes less a function of general administrators and more a task falling upon those responsible for the "intellectual backstopping."
	High turnover both of ministers and of staff, which creates breaks in continuity and ambiguities as to commitments.	In order to improve continuity, career services should be provided, both in donor and recipient countries, for individuals of proven competence. Incentives should be created to enable them to stay with the job as long as possible.
	Local costs are found to be a burden by recipient countries.	The "intellectual backstopping" services should be of a flexible nature and kept constantly under review in order to foresee and later implement new priorities.
	The level of the technical assistance from abroad can fall below the available level	

Shifts of Emphasis and Redeployment Measures Required	Obstacles Affecting Redeployment	Additional Approaches or New Directions
	of domestic experts unless careful regard is paid to the quality of the expert and his "intellectual backstopping" and briefing.

Technical assistance has to be supported by linkages with other types of aid such as provision of equipment and sometimes capital in order for its full impact to be obtained. This link is not always made. | |

Institution-Building

Shifts of Emphasis and Redeployment Measures Required	Obstacles Affecting Redeployment	Additional Approaches or New Directions
Less aid to general secondary and higher-level studies. Help build new types of institutions to meet new needs.

More aid to centers of excellence (especially in technology and the natural sciences) and to basic education. | Pressures from politically powerful sections of the population to expand secondary and higher education.

Lack of information as to cost-benefits of different types of institutions. | Better project diagnosis and identification in relation to development needs.

More coordination among donors and greater selectivity in choice of projects.

Encourage university-to-university aid, but increase the communication of new policies down the line. |

Shifts of Emphasis and Redeployment Measures Required	Obstacles Affecting Redeployment	Additional Approaches or New Directions
More to nonformal institutions, such as functional literacy centers, community schools, and so on. More to educational institutes and research and development centers.	Prestige value of diplomas and grandiose projects. Competition among donors.	Consult with other departments as well as educational authorities. Sponsor cost-benefit studies; take care not to perpetuate inefficiencies by "tinkering," except for clearly urgent short-term needs.

Curriculum Reform and New Learning Methods and Patterns

Reduce tinkering and go for deeper reforms. Modernize curricula by relating them more to the actual local needs of the majority of school-leavers, but also provide adequate streams to meet national needs and the promotion of excellence. Curriculum changes to be accompanied by changes across the board (teacher training, textbooks, design of school buildings and equipment, scholarship ladders, structural	Stability of existing system of expectation of parents Examination system and expectation of employers and pupils. Insufficient incentives for the study and formulation of curriculum reform programs. Lack of enthusiasm for integration among the activities that should be linked with curriculum development.	Consultations at all levels to discuss expectations and realities and diminish prejudices. Take more integrated approach, including review of examination system. Better data collection and evaluation of results of old and new curricula and methods. Financing of experimental projects, including certain recurrent costs. Aid setting up of new economical types of school, particularly suited to local needs, with bridges and ladders to the national system.

Shifts of Emphasis and Redeployment Measures Required	Obstacles Affecting Redeployment	Additional Approaches or New Directions
changes in the cycles).	Differences of prestige between the various educational streams.	Exchange of information on innovations to be organized on international basis.
Try out new organizational patterns of education and improve learning capacity of pupils.	Shortage of good tested models for basic education and experience of applying them.	

Research and Development

More resources to go into educational research and development.	Preference of both donors recipients for visible shorter-term results.	Allocate funds for research and development on an independent basis, so that they do not compete with short-term.
Within existing research more emphasis to be placed on studying ways and means to promote educational renovation and innovation, and use of new media.	Shortages of research staff and data. Failures to define problems adequately in formulating research.	Consider establishing an international center for educational research and development for the developing countries financed from ex-budgetary sources.
Research to be integrally linked with curriculum development and teacher training.	Pressures of certain expenditure on budgets leading to research costs being squeezed out.	Aid universities to increase resources devoted to educational studies. Set up a five-year technical assistance project to recast basis of educational statistics including aid.
Situation of the community as a	Overelaborate nature and	

Shifts of Emphasis and Redeployment Measures Required	Obstacles Affecting Redeployment	Additional Approaches or New Directions
whole, including other means as well as the schools.	clumsiness of many research methods.	Publish unenrollment statistics, like the unemployment figures, and not only enrollment.
Recasting of present form of educational statistics.	Difficulties of comparison with the past statistics.	Train more research staff and work out simple research methods.
Improvement of the statistics of educational aid.	Soothing effort of present form of presentation of statistics.	Provide experimental schools and equipment. Contribute to local costs.

Educational Planning and Project Diagnosis

Extend planning to take in noneducational factors that have a vital impact on educational performance.	Shortages of data and appropriate methods of analysis	More methodological studies and case investigations.
Give greater depth to project diagnosis.	Lack of time and staff.	Strengthen analysis teams on both donor and recipient ends.

Notes

1. 1969 Review, Development Assistance, published by the OECD, p. 144.

2. Ibid., p. 221.

3. 1972 Review, Development Cooperation, published by the OECD, p. 125.

4. See H. Hawes, "Planning the Primary School Curriculum in Developing Countries," p. 36 (IIEP Publication, UNESCO): "There have been cases of governments demanding, and one case of an 'expert' advising, that the whole primary school curriculum should be changed in one year. In fact, since new work in any one year depends on that covered in the previous one, the process usually takes

six to eight years depending on the length on the basic course. It is sometimes feasible to introduce new curricula into the first two or three years of the primary school concurrently and so save a little time, but this puts an enormous strain on facilities for teacher retraining and the supervision that follows it."

5. See data in Professor Blaug's paper in this volume. Rate-of-return analysis has not found operational use in individual projects, but it has value for the allocation of resources between educational levels taken as wholes.

6. See final report of International Committee of Experts on Training Abroad Policies, October 1971 (UNESCO). See also statement by assistant director general of UNESCO: "Very often there is no overall planning of training activities at the national level."

7. UNESCO 17/C/58.

8. Average Rate of Increase of Enrollment

	1960-68	1968
Africa		
First level	5.6	5.1
Second level	10.5	4.6
Third level	9.0	7.8
Latin America		
First level	5.3	6.4
Second level	10.8	5.8
Third level	10.4	13.4
Asia		
First level	5.4	4.5
Second level	6.0	3.8
Third level	11.0	6.9

9. See "Social Background and Educational Career" (OECD, 1972) by Torsten Husén.

10. See also statement by Sylvain Lourié (UNESCO) on page 48 of the Faure Report for a new definition of educational resources.

THE ETIQUETTE OF MULTILATERAL AID AGENCIES
C. Arnold Anderson

Relatively large proportions of foundation funds have gone into the training of developing-country personnel at centers of excellence and into associated institution-building. (Item III.) No one is so naive as to think that all these scholarships were good investments; the chance of disappointment in that kind of investment is always high in the individual instance, as professors discover when students come up for their big exams or when we see how last year's scholarship winners made out. Effective assistance to developing countries by this sort of policy is handicapped also by uncertainty as to whether trained individuals will return to their countries and to the sort of work for which they were trained.

At the same time, we continue to be ignorant of how to foster regional or intercountry collaboration for R and D work designed both to stimulate developing country capability and to diminish their dependence upon technical assistance personnel from advanced countries or multilateral agencies. (Item IV.) This major area for research, while far from neglected, can absorb large quantities of research funds. Though the number of trained men for R and D work multiplies, the proportion of research produced by the developing countries will remain slight for decades, and investments in centers of excellence will have to continue for many years yet.[1] For the most part this paper will deal with the special problems of multilateral (public) agencies, mainly those in the UN family. The goal remains dual: low proportions of funds put into unproductive projects and augmentation of the capability of developing-country specialists to make reliable decisions about education.

National Sovereignty and the Preservation of Ignorance[2]

I am unable to trace the route by which multilateral agencies accepted the obligation to consider themselves beholden to "member nations," which has automatically raised their costs of operation and reduced the quality of the advice they render. (Item II.) Nor can I prescribe how it might be possible to substitute the rule that UN agencies are serving peoples, not states. But especially in the area

---

This essay has been excerpted from the original text of the paper by Professor Anderson, which appears in Chapter 3. "Items" refer to Appendix to the earlier essay, which begins on p. 183.

of education, efforts should be mounted to depoliticize agency operations so that the people of recipient countries may have greater confidence that the advice they receive reflects the professional judgment of competent specialists—with political judgments set carefully apart from technical judgments. As things now stand, doctrines of national sovereignty frequently operate to impede effective aid policies even from nationalistic perspectives of the developing countries.

My values call for a major expansion in resources devoted to "development assistance." Yet I am uneasy at the proportion of available funds spent in moving teams of specialists and secretariat members over the world, ostensibly assessing needs and setting priorities among projects (say, in education) without public availability of the data, the analyses, or the conclusions of these teams. If pronouncements about land redistribution or vocational education could be accepted as merely expressions of piety, designed to uplift the spirits of the world's publics, then what agencies decide, or do, or pronounce would be comparatively unimportant. But if policies are intended to augment "development," then the interchange of multilateral reports and decisions with national bureaucracies rather than with the world's top professionals or the more informed and concerned sets of local leaders threatens to subvert the resources and potentialities of multilateral programs.[3]

I leave aside obstacles such as rivalries among the agencies. I accept the enormous load of negotiation entailed in sharing out resources among all the world's nations on "pork barrel" principles. One must acknowledge also that on many topics informed opinion is divided. But the present policies of restricted discussions and documents unduly lengthens the time until our technical knowledge can become more nearly adequate. It is jealously sovereign nations who suffer most from their own acts in blocking the accumulation of tested knowledge, an indispensable condition of which is open criticism of work by "missions."

Dysfunctionality of Managerial Hypertrophy

Speaking as a U.S. citizen I cannot overlook the irony that a country so stubbornly resisting centrally planned controls over local affairs expends so much money through multilateral agencies for the encouragement of the contemporary vogue for centralized "planning." (Item X.) The paternalistic impulse disguised as "programs" for "planning" permeates the multilateral agencies, and the tendency is not retarded by the fact that most of the specialists who go on missions to developing countries become attached to governments, not to private agencies. Yet encouragement of capability for managing voluntary organizations and for active participation as citizens in the policies of educational (or other) programs remains an avowed aim of aid agencies.

This propensity for centralized management is encouraged also by the heavy reliance within at least some of the multilateral agencies upon a succession of slogans, each one more or less synchronized with the succession of agency general conferences. As yet we cannot with confidence encourage a belief that land redistribution will be economically effective in the absence of complementary institutional rearrangements that often go unrecognized or are quite beyond the economic or political resources of the developing country. There is little reason to conclude that acceptance of affirmations in support of "lifelong education" will help the people of either Ecuador or the Camerouns, or even of India or of Ghana, to improve their limping educational systems. Each new target tends to be put on top of previous ones, to be accompanied (when not tacitly ignored) by multiplication of new jobs for what we are always being told is a "shortage" of high-level manpower. Each new program tends to widen the distance between central officials delegated to maintain liaison with the multilateral agency and its new program and the concrete schools or extension programs or malaria-control efforts that presumably are the stuff of development.

The speed with which these (preponderantly) deleterious tendencies spread over the world results partly from the speeding-up of all news dissemination, partly from the expansion of overseas study and partly from the implanting of more multilateral suboffices and the steady undertow of more and more international conferences. Cumulatively added targets for education can confound the decision process with the piling up of aims, to the extent of diminishing the capability or interest of local citizenry to improve their own schools by participation in their support and management. (Item I.) Managerial hypertrophy is encouraged also to the degree that we reify "groups" (be they tribes, language clusters, or nation-states), for such reification encourages us to move away from consideration of actual educational problems of definite pupils and families and to move toward more and more thinking in the abstractions of agency "pronouncements."

The constant multiplication of national goals, supported by pronouncements on policy by assemblies and secretariats of big agencies, also encourages managerial hypertrophy. These pronouncements on goals are largely going to serve to uplift spirits rather than objectively to test achievement in education or health. The same outcome is encouraged by large projects or programs with large sums of money that presuppose skills officials and specialists in developing countries cannot be persuaded to believe that they possess.

310

Alternatively, given indoctrinated developing-country people who have studied or worked abroad and have fed on these high ideals, large funds will encourage ill-considered investments and resistance to advice from more ecumenical and disinterested technicians. Agencies are tempted to complement project assistance with technical advice, and the whole package of circumstances leads many developing countries to become unwittingly dependent in more subtle ways than their ideologies had conceived. Dependence is inevitable. The question is whether dependence will be upon a giant multilateral agency, upon a political patron country, or upon comparatively detached sources of judgment within national, neighboring, or advanced-country research agencies.

The foregoing paternalistic tendencies and accompanying varieties of dependence are fostered further by the device of voting by national units on agency programs. The very many embodiments of this goal in operating programs encourage readiness to accent a "plan" for one's educational system. In passing, I offer the opinion that it is less the poor implementation of plans than the inherent difficulties of conceiving a coherent and consistent program for a whole section of national life that gives rise to many of the difficulties. I have already cast doubt upon such "plans" in vogue as the search for a neatly "adapted" educational system or for widespread expansion of formalized vocational education. At the same time, multilateral agencies are in my judgment too hesitant in encouraging applications of benefit/cost analyses in evaluations for educational policy in various contexts in the developing countries. That kind of assessment criterion has the special advantage that it has an inherent logic for decision-making in that it entails direct or indirect comparisons among alternatives; it encourages scrutiny of disaggregated programs, thereby allowing developing country specialists to relate local data to multi-nation schemes.

The Need for Independent Judgments

Within the most active development sectors, and certainly especially within education, we have comparatively little hard evidence on which to base policies and relatively little experience in designing R and D work for educational systems of which we have not personally been a part. Accordingly, it is in these sectors particularly that multilateral agencies should seek ways to open their work to scrutiny by systematically organized panels of autonomous critics. Such a procedure would help to foreclose agency publications of histories of nonexistent programs. It will help to relate sensitive parts of an area (as education) to identifiable topics of strength and of weakness

among the specialists in that sector. Not least, by making clear the
interconnections of one education feature (as efforts to ruralize village
curricula) to fiscal or administrative complexities, the nonagency
and academic specialists will more rapidly be made capable of adjusting their analyses to the terms in which multilateral specialists often
have to discuss potential projects with developing country officials.
And by widening the sphere about which multilateral documents become available, specialists within developing countries will find their
confidence in looking at their actual society (rather than some fictional
"developing society") measurably enhanced. "Openness" in the
sources of technical discussion within multilateral agencies will
reduce the fears associated with "dependence" while at the same time
demonstrating that the sources of counsel about development are more
numerous and more diversified than had been believed.

Multilateral agencies (and of course bilateral agencies and parts
of some foundations) display a zest for multipronged attacks on the
problems of the third world. They participate in goal-setting conferences (in which the least developed countries vary greatly in the
degree to which they are passive participants.) They provide money
or technical personnel to assist in projects; and they offer various
sorts of training programs to inform developing countries as to which
kinds of projects are most suitable for them and even to help them
learn how to ask for the assistance. This combination of activities
borders upon conflict of interests, but more important is its tendency
to throttle the sources of independent advice about development,
especially if potential advisers can promise little tangible aid in
money or personnel.

It would seem that the day should be approaching when the
separation of these three kinds of assistance will be seriously considered. One approach to this goal would be to focus even more upon
the training of capable analysts by increasing the amount of foreign
study and by helping to thicken the network of scholarship and of
policy among sets of developing countries. Such policies would also
have the effect of shifting the balance, slowly and haltingly, from
creation of slogans toward technical assessment of projects and toward encouragement of the necessary underlying research. Put
statistically, we want to shift the country contributions of new ideas
from the present highly skewed distribution toward a more symmetrical
one, though we know that will take a century or more.[4]

Surely a large part of the R and D work relating to education,
even that which is especially suitable for application in the developing
countries, will come from centers in "advanced" countries. We need
more attention to deciding which questions especially belong in this
category, and we need also to identify more clearly the research
(apart from political pronouncements) that will be most useful for

the problems of the developing countries. For example, proposals that children should not enter school until around age 10 or 12 and that they will learn just as much need testing in societies not possessing all the elaborate extraschool educational stimuli with which we are so familiar. If this sort of policy is going to have any success, problems must be reduced in scale (as well as tailored to local conditions) so that researchers in developing countries will tackle them in confidence. And, as said already, of critical importance here is training people how to make the systematic analytical judgments required for cogent decisions on policy.

One contribution by the aid agencies would be to weed out of their position or sector papers the host of sophistries and half-truths, even if many confessions of ignorance must be substituted.[5] Such confessions can stimulate good research in those developing countries possessing a few capable investigators. By seeking to persuade developing countries into using evidence in discussions of education, multilateral agencies will not become less intrusive into local life, but they may become less offensively so. Until criteria of capability to absorb assistance (in at least certain sectors) are widely accepted by developing countries, dependence tied to the prospect of loans or technical personnel will subvert the needed training of competent educational researchers. It must become widely believed that research techniques are truly supracultural and that only by such techniques can a developing country attack its own problems with hope of success. But only if such techniques are used in the open and as part of a broad program to train competent analysts of social change will investigation of local problems yield knowledge of general value. Few organizations have any collective memory; the best approximation to such a socially useful resource is the set of bibliographies and abstracts on the shelves of a lively research center. Fortunately, the bibliographic apparatus for education has been expanding at great speed of late.

Not least among the benefits of open analysis of developing country problems is the supplying of individual developing countries with clues as to where they can find competent counsel on the kinds of questions they have put at the head of their lists of national problems.

Notes

1. One is reminded of the studies by Main of the settlement of Kansas; it took three families on a farm under the harsh and unfamiliar conditions before the fourth family moved onto the farm and succeeded in domesticating it.

2. There may be some value in reviewing the study by Richard Merit on Symbols of American Community: 1735-1755 (New Haven, Conn.: Yale University Press, 1966); his results suggest that it is just the kinds of educational efforts (and other space-transcending activities) we are talking about that create national unity; I infer that to defer to nationalist whims of officials is to defer the coming to maturity of those nations.

3. In my judgment the World Bank's Education: Sector Working Paper (1971) is a very uneven set of pronouncements, many of which will not stand up to scrutiny by specialists in comparative education of "development education."

4. Christopher Freeman, "Measurement of Output of Research and Experimental Development," UNESCO, Statistical Reports and Studies, no. 16, 1969.

5. I contend that UNESCO's Educational Planning: A World Survey of Problems and Prospects (1970) borders on being a chronicle of nonevents.

TECHNOLOGY, DEVELOPMENT, AND CULTURE:
A MEMORANDUM FOR DISCUSSION
Soedjatmoko

For all the care that has gone into the formulation of the strategy for the UN Second Development Decade, a number of disturbing questions have in the last two or three years injected themselves into the public consciousness in developed and developing countries alike, which make it almost impossible to take the assumptions and goals of that strategy for granted.

There is in the first place the new realization that contrary to expectations, industrialization—especially in the more populous developing countries—is not accompanied by decreasing unemployment. The statistics show that as a result of the population explosion, unemployment figures in many Asian and Latin American countries are rising despite increasing industrialization. This phenomenon has eroded the validity of the earlier assumption that economic development resulting from industrialization, increased international trade, and foreign investment—in other words through the gradual expansion of the modern sector in these former colonial economies—would automatically take care of unemployment. Parallel with the unemployment problem another phenomenon has come to cause considerable concern, namely in the educational field. It is now obvious that, again as a result of the population explosion, present educational systems in the developing countries are failing to expand rapidly enough to accommodate the additional numbers. The absolute number of illiterates in these countries has started growing again; so has the number of those who fail to gain access to the educational system, as well as the number of drop-outs. In some developing countries already, now more than one-third of the children reaching school-going age cannot be absorbed by the school system. And the problem is getting worse. Compounding this problem, there is the growing realization that the educational system itself may unwittingly have helped to reinforce the movement of young people from the villages to the big urban centers by educating people away from needed work in the villages to illusory employment opportunities in the cities and raising future expectations of an urban character.

In addition to this "internal brain drain" caused by the educational system itself, other aspects of existing development strategies are now being questioned. It is now for instance also becoming increasingly clear that unless deliberate compensatory policies of income distribution and social justice are effectively implemented, growth by itself is bound to lead increasingly to inequalities that continue to widen the gap between the rich and the poor in the country and thus strengthen the power position of its elite to the point that the

315

adoption of remedial policies becomes impossible. Many developing nations have also become sensitive to the danger that opening up the countryside through rural development may in the end only lead to increased dependence of the villages on big-city products, from the country's own metropolitan centers or from abroad, and therefore perpetuating rural stagnation at a new plateau instead of triggering self-sustaining nonagricultural activities in the villages.

Such concerns raise the question whether a more relevant development strategy could not be worked out that could avoid these pitfalls. It should aim at growth, employment and social justice, local initiative and creativity, and, most importantly, a sense of self-reliance.

Reinforcing the need that is increasingly being felt to work out development patterns that are not simply a repetition of the phases and directions that the industrial nations have gone through in the past, is the new awareness about the ecological cost of present socio-technological systems and the realization of the finiteness of the globe's life-supporting systems, forcing all of us to reconsider a civilization's relationship to nature. The raw materials crisis that is beginning to loom ahead as a result of the predatory economies of the industrialized societies and their pursuit of continued growth raises the very real question whether the globe's raw materials base will be sufficient to support a world economy in which the developing nations—even at present population density—could even hope to reach the level of affluence that, say, Europe now enjoys.

It would in any case appear likely that especially the more populous developing countries will have to work out a development pattern that will enable them to live with a population density probably twice as large within 30 years as the present level while consuming less natural resources than presently industrially advanced countries do. They will have to pursue employment-oriented growth policies in the industrial and agricultural fields and to develop "intermediate" technologies, fitting their resources base. It will have to be a development strategy that clearly and consistently aims at increasing self-reliance, increasing capacity for self-help at each step of the way, especially in the rural areas, and at the welding of the social structure, which would make this possible. Such a strategy would also require the reorientation and restructuring of the educational system in a way that would provide the skills to handle "intermediate technologies" for rural activity, local pride, self-employment, and innovation. It will also require a much more deliberate effort to provide access to education and relevant skills for those who fail to gain entrance into the school system through new out-of-school education policies in a way and on a scale that is commensurate with the magnitude of the problem. Furthermore, such a strategy should also be capable of nurturing a shared ethos of social justice and national solidarity, which, with the help of policies of equitable income distribution and access to opportunities and resources, will help keep within manageable proportions the social tensions that cannot be entirely avoided. Most likely such policies should in the first stage aim at a material sufficiency for all, rather than self-defeating affluence for a narrow elite.

The big question, however, is, Will the developing nations have the time and freedom to work out such an alternative development pattern? Will such a course require a period of isolation and protectionism? Is such a period of self-imposed isolation possible or even desirable? If for practical reasons, for instance because of the country's geography, or out of ideological preferences, such self-isolation is rejected, what problems will have to be faced? One of these is obviously the need to develop intermediate technologies appropriate to their situation. The developing nations will of course also have to develop capabilities in the field of high technology for production processes in certain fields, but the need for "intermediate technologies" is even more pressing.

There are two reasons for this: The first is that "intermediate technologies" should enable these countries to develop labor-intensive production techniques that will make possible the necessary rural emancipation through diversification into nonagricultural activities. Secondly, unless the developing countries develop such "intermediate technologies," they are doomed to remain captives of the very dynamics that will lead them to repeat the development patterns of the industrialized nations.

But the development of new technologies is quite expensive and the developing countries clearly have neither the resources nor the scientific and technological capabilities to do it on their own. The industrial countries should therefore help in its development. Lester Pearson's appeal that the industrial countries should spend at least 5 percent of their R and D funds for problems of international poverty must be taken seriously. Foreign business in the developing countries could and should play a much more active role in helping the economies of the host countries to move in this direction. Unfortunately until now the transfer of technology to developing countries through the operation of private businesses has not been very impressive. Also the operation of foreign business in developing countries itself, especially that of the highly efficient and powerful multinational corporations, may make it very difficult, if not impossible, for "intermediate technologies"—understandably less efficient at least in their early stages—to take root. Self-sufficiency may not always be compatible with optimal efficiency, yet unavoidable in certain fields for sociopolitical reasons, primarily in order to create employment opportunities.

Furthermore the presence of a large foreign business and professional community may give rise to consumption levels and patterns among the elite that are too costly for the country as a whole and therefore dysfunctional in terms of meeting overall development requirements. It certainly makes the maintenance of a regime of austerity and self-restraint, needed to maintain a broad basis for development, much more difficult. In this light it becomes obvious that the developing nations have considerably less latitude in working out their own patterns of development than one would have thought at first glance. The weaker and less developed its industrial base, the fewer the options open to a developing country.*

The problem is further aggravated by the involuntary impact of the outside world on a developing nation, once it is, through trade, aid, and investment, plugged into the international communications system. The almost random messages that reach the populations of the developing countries through radio, film, TV, books, and magazines tend to create not only unattainable expectations, attitudes, and life-styles that are totally unrelated to the developing nation's own situation, but worse, they threaten to overwhelm and stifle indigenous cultural creativity. In this way many developing countries run the risk of being gradually reduced to the status of mere consumers of manufactured as well as of cultural products from other civilizations. If that happened, the vicious circle of continued and possibly increasing dependence would be closed. Nevertheless it is most likely that precisely on the cultural level it may be possible to avoid this threat. On the cultural level the developing countries may be able to find the key to the drive, motivation, and self-assertion needed to work out new and different development patterns. Creativity and self-reliance are after all embedded in a sense of national and cultural identity, and in the pride and self-esteem that goes with it. The wellsprings for social action of most societies are to be found in their religiocultural matrix. It is here that we should find the stronger and more durable motivation for indigenous development patterns.

The conception of development as the mobilization of a hitherto stagnant social system in the pursuit of new goals further emphasizes the importance of motivation, purpose, and meaning in the process of national self-renewal. Unless the goals of development make sense not only in terms of improved material well-being but also in terms of the broader purposes of life as crystallized in the traditional cultures of many developing nations, it is unlikely that the impulse for change, creative adjustment, and innovation will be continuous and self-sustaining.

---

*It is also open to question whether present aid philosophies and policies could support such a new departure.

318

The search for a development strategy leading to an alternative social system and using a different kind of technology should therefore be tied up with the endeavor of our traditional cultures to redefine themselves so as to cope not only with the challenges of modern life, but also with the search for the purpose and the meaning of life, especially in the much more crowded and more confining world of tomorrow. The specter of existential emptiness that seems to stare those in the face who have lost themselves completely in what is called modern cosmopolitan culture may in this way be removed by a renewed process of cross-fertilization with the world's traditional cultures and religions. The narrow range of human faculties engaged by modern civilization may then be again broadened, the content of modern man's human experience enriched, and his creativity stimulated in new ways by the greater likelihood that it is within the context of a man's traditional cultures and religions that he can come to grips with the ultimate questions he is confronted with, such as life, death, purpose, and meaning.

The search then is for a new civilization, a new culture, one that aims not at continued exponential growth and affluence, but at dignifying employment and a widely spread material sufficiency; one that is less wasteful of the globe's resources, one that postulates a different relationship to technology and to nature. Most likely, the greater population density the world over will require a new balance between the notion of basic human rights and man's social obligations, in order to ensure the survival of the species and of its various cultures.

One would hope that it would still be possible to strike such a balance by a process of free choice on the basis of new ethics befitting such a crowded world. The industrial countries may have to search for such new directions, away from their affluence and dissatisfactions. Likewise the poor countries, out of their poverty and social stagnation and with the help of new and appropriate technologies, will have to move toward their answers to these goals.

It is obvious that it will be impossible for the developing countries to strike out in this new direction on their own. As mentioned above, even the development of the technologies appropriate to this course may require the support of the industrial countries and possibly a redirection of some of their technological thrusts. Even with such help it will require a clear vision and a sense of moral purpose strongly held for the developing countries to move against the stream, to forgo the relatively easy rewards in life-style and consumption levels in exchange for a greater possibility of increased self-reliance and freedom for a larger part of their society. It will require a clear idea of what kind of society with what dominant values is desired and what vision of man will enable one's nation to meet the new

319

challenges for survival. In facing this challenge the developing countries are of course not alone. The rich nations face essentially the same need for redirection and redefinition. We are all in the same boat, for there is not going to be a separate future for the rich and for the poor countries in this world. There is either going to be one future for all of us, or none at all. Concrete solutions will have to spring from the genuine cultural creativity of mankind and especially from the commitment of the mental and spiritual energies of the young generation all over the world, toward these ends.

ditions for successful, 55; dynamics of, 49; educational implications of, 88-89; human resource approach to, 84-85; need for more research on, 250; participation of students in, 203, 248; potential problems of, 249-250; redefinition of, 245; social and cultural, 225-227

development administration, 219

Development Assistance Committee, 255, 256, 258, 265

development planning, university participation in, 245-246

"development with social justice," 83-84

donors, lags in communication and in acceptance of new policies of, 273; policies of the main, 261-266

dropouts, 26, 135, 137, 144, 164, 167, 267, 279, 282, 315

earnings foregone, as a major private cost of education, 51

Economic Development Institute, 139, 143

economic growth, interactions with education, 50

economics of education, contribution to policy makers, 35

education, "allocative benefits" of, 51-53, 56; and economy: relations between, 35-36; as cause or consequence of economic development, 38; as a consumption good, 4, 16; as a developmental force, 135-136; as a factor of growth, 36, 40; as an instrument of social mobility, 275; as an investment, 41, 94, 257; as a social good, 3; as the "third factor" of growth, 39; benefits of, 6, 51; contribution of to growth rates of National

Income, 40; contribution of to rural life, 89-90; cultural, 226-227; demand for, 3-6, 7-8, 11, 12, 18, 19, 115, 117-118, 121, 217, 230; demand for: as related to four variables, 9-11; economic value of, 25, 28, 50; economics of, 23, 31, 33-34; external aid to, 34; "for National Development", 206; function of, 130; health and medical, 202, 207, 208-210, 236-237, 246-248; indirect costs of, 28; investment in, 3, 55; physical, 110; private benefits of, 5, 9, 14; private costs of, 4, 9, 10, 13, 19, 118; private rates of return to, 28; role of government in, 115-117; rural, 110; service function of, 92; social benefits of, 5, 51; social costs of, 14; social rates of return to, 28; structural analysis of, 64-65; supply of, 3, 8, 12; technical assistance in, 166

education, informal (see nonformal education)

education of women, 56, 175, 267; in reduction of fertility, 54 (see also mothers)

education, social demand for, 180; governments as instruments of, 118

Education Sector Review (Ethiopia), 130, 139, 216, 217-219

educational aid, annual increment of as applied to innovation, 270; criticism of, 257; evaluation, of 257; existing, 258-260; methods of allotting, 270; real economic benefit of, 259; relation of to national plan, 276-278; role of in stimulating reform, 269 (see also donors)

educational aid, redeployment of, 255-307; diagnosis of needs of,

274-275; legal and administrative obstacles to, 270-271; organizational difficulties of, 271-272

educational aid agencies, clarification of strategy of by project grouping, 257

educational aid project, criteria of a good, 275-276

educational aid supply, mechanisms of, 256

educational cycles, modification of, 108

educational efforts, local initiation of, 146

Educational Exchange Programme, 262

educational expansion, 3, 6, 7, 13, 129, 144; past policies of international donor agencies with respect to, 6, 21; rates of future, 7, 21

educational expenses, 38

educational investment, boundaries of, 52, 56; implication of, 56; planning, 117

educational opportunities, rationing of, 5, 19, 21, 99; supply of, 5, 16, 17, 137

educational opportunity, equality of, 29, 30, 163

educational planning, as management of innovation, 150; literature on, 61-62; redeployment of aid to, 286-288; "social demand approach" to, 30; youth as participants in, 159

educational reform, 129; acceptance of, 145; as a domestic political issue, 269; positive presentation of, 146-147; resistance to, 147; role of local social science research in, 148; small demand for aid for, 269

educational research, questions of, 137 (see also research)

educational research and development, redeployment of aid to, 285-286

educational services, distribution of, 120-121; supply of, 116, 117, 118, 119

educational supply, manipulation of, 16, 17 (see also educational opportunities)

educational system, as a rationing mechanism, 17; assessment of productivity of, 167; indicators for assessing qualitative outcomes of, 166; points of entry to, 155; rate of growth of, 38, 39; reform of, 143; relevancy of the objectives of, 163

educational technology, 91, 284

educational television, 139, 172, 230, 261

efficiency criteria, demise of, 114; "manpower needs for development" as, 114; "social rate of return" as, 114-115

elementary education, investment in, 52 (see also primary education)

employment, as primary objective of planning, 80-81; as requirement for entry to post-secondary education, 67; as secondary objective of planning, 76; in modern and traditional sectors, 4, 5, 8, 11, 17, 18, 20; local rural-centered, 218; rationing of, 17-18; universal, 86

Encarnación, Dr. José, 200

enrollment, average rate of increase of, 307n.; proportion of by level and area, 204

equity, 5, 114-123; criteria, 114; objective measure of, 120

Ethiopian University Service, 216

examinations system, 65, 66, 68;

reform of, 69, 155, 157

expansion of educational systems, 180; quantitative, 59

experimentation, as a priority activity, 7, 21-22, 92; lack of, 69; need for scientific approach in, 247-248

extension education, 90, 218, 226

FAC (Fonds d'Aide et de Coopération), 132, 136, 140

FAO (Food and Agriculture Organization), 264

Farrell, Joseph, 182

Faure Commission (see International Commission for the Development of Education)

Faure Report (see International Commission for the Development of Education, Report of)

feedback, 150, 157, 221

Ford Foundation, 136, 140, 143, 265

formal education, 24, 58, 63, 88, 166, 167; as factor in upward social mobility, 169

Foster, Philip, 26, 62, 89

Freire, Paulo, 130, 136

functional literacy, 132, 167, 170, 266; as a function of social progress, 102

GNP (Gross National Product), 30, 36, 38, 76-80; 84-86, 173, 245, 293; level of schooling and: correlations between, 36

Gondar, 216, 219 (see also Haile Sellassie I University)

Gorse Commission, 261

"Green revolution," 76, 84, 195

Haile Sellassie I University, 214-240

Haq, Mahbub ul, 127, 245

Harbison, Frederick, 84-85, 86-87

Harambee school movement, 12, 63, 65

Harrar, J. George, 197

Head Start, 51-52

higher education, costs of, 219, 221; in developing countries, 204; overinvestment in, 23, 29; priority tasks for, 218-19; relation of to rural sector, 215-216; shift of resources to, 118

"Higher Education for Development, Study of, xxi n

high-level manpower, requirements for, 215; "shortage" of, 23, 310

Huberman, M., 158

IBE (International Bureau of Education), 134-137

IBRD (International Bank for Reconstruction and Development), 28, 91, 117, 130, 132, 136, 139, 140, 143, 258, 264-265, 292

ICED (International Council for Educational Development), xxi n, 132

IDB (Interamerican Development Bank), 131, 143, 258, 265

IDRC (International Development Research Centre), 132, 143

IEA (International Association for the Evaluation of Educational Achievement), 140, 164, 166-168

Illich, Ivan, 135

Illiteracy, as factor of population growth, 96-97

ILO (International Labour Organization) 22 n, 64-65, 75, 131, 139, 263, 264

INACAP (Instituto Nacional de Capacitación Profesional), 136

Income differentials, 20; distribution, 78-79, 122-123

Innovation, 101-102, 116, 221, 226; diffusion of, 156, 182; micro,

155; need for, 249, 255
Institute of Development Research, 224, 225, 235-236 (see also Haile Sellassie I University)
Institute of Development Studies, 201
Institute of Ethiopian Studies, 226-227, 234-235 (see also Haile Sellassie I University)
Institute of Pathobiology, 236-237 (see also Haile Sellassie I University)
institution building, redeployment of aid for, 283
"Intermediate" educational patterns, 282
intermediate technology, 76, 76 n, 140, 282-283; need for development of, 317
International Commission for the Development of Education, 130, 150; Report of, 151, 264, 286
international cooperation, new strategies of, 231-233
International Maize and Wheat Improvement Center, 203
international professional standards, as factor in university emigration, 212
Iranian Primary Reading Project, 168

job market, relation of to educational system, 42
job opportunities, rationing of, 5; supply of, 6
job status, in traditional and technological societies, 86, 87

Kasetsart University, 202
Keynes' General Theory, 79
Ki-Zerbo, Joseph, 128

labor market, absorption capacity of, 42 (see also employment; job market)
language, 99, 136 (see also mother tongue languages)
Learning To Be, 130, 150 (see also International Commission for the Development of Education, Report of)
literacy, 3, 6, 18-19, 52, 103-104, 122, 163, 266; adult, 24; and per capital income: correlations between, 36; training, 14
local personnel, training of, 172-173
local research, 140-141, 145-149

Mahidol University, 202
Makerere College, 201
managerial hypertrophy, 310-311
manpower forecasting, 7, 24, 33, 43, 144, 219, 221; disillusionment with, 23, 24, 27, 114
Marshall, Alfred, 287
Martin, Edwin, 256
mass education, 112, 132-137
Mead, Margaret, 158
media technology, development of, 230
Mediterranean Regional Project, 43
Mexican Agricultural Program, 203
microeducational decisions, importance of, 181-182
Miller, Ralph, 128
mother tongue languages, 103-107; use of in adult literacy, 107
mothers, education of, 51-52; level of schooling of, 55
motivation, 28, 61-62, 64, 134, 138, 178; as factor in educational reform, 148; lack of, 165; relation of cultural factors to, 148; structural reform and, 63-64
multilingual societies, problems

of, 136

national development, as ultimate
goal of institution building, 203;
integrated approaches to, 209,
210
national development efforts, suggested focus of, 206-207
national sovereignty, as impediment to effective aid policies,
308-309
Nickel, John, 201
nonformal education, 58, 66, 85,
86-87, 121, 163, 218, 223, 266
Nyerere, Julius, 204

OAU (Organization of African
Universities), 107
ODA (Overseas Development Ad-
ministration), 132, 136, 140, 143
OECD (Organization for Economic
Cooperation and Development),
255, 265, 288

Peace Corps, 262, 281
Pearson, Lester, 317
Pearson Report, 88, 255-256, 289
per capita income, 4, 77-78, 80
planning, centralization of, 309;
micro, 223
policy decisions, social indicators
as a basis for, 182-183
primary education, 131-133, 164;
reallocation of funds to, 29;
underinvestment in, 23, 26
private benefits and costs, as related to social benefits and
costs, 5, 19

rate of return, 41, 114; analysis,
25-26, 260; private, 62, 116,
117-118; structure of private,
118
recruitment, patterns of in developing areas, 169

redeployment of educational aid,
summary of principal conclusions
about, 288-293
reform, key factors for, 142
research, and development, 128,
172-176, 260, 293, 308, 311-313,
317; as priority activity, 7, 21;
cross-national, 140; experimental, 69; external assistance
to, 130; local, 138; on economic
growth, 39; on education in rural
areas, 141; strengthening of
local, 143; suggested emphasis
for, 134, 138-140; university
and, 224-225
resources, misallocation of, 15-16;
mobilization of, 61, 89, 156, 223;
required switches of, 266-269;
scarcity of, 58, 150
Rockefeller Foundation, 131, 143,
195-203, 205-206, 265
Romulo, General Carlos P., 201,
203
rural development, 86-87; 218-
219, 222-224; high-level manpower implications of, 224;
role of university in, 212
rural education, 129, 132, 146
rural-urban migration, 15-16, 89-
90, 100, 248-249, 315
rural works program, 76

school, anti-democratic, 107; as
a factor in early school leaving,
134-136; as a factor of underdevelopment, 95; as an economic dead-end, 99; as an environment, 102-103; creative, 101;
insular, 97-98
school system, economic analysis
of, 35-36
schooling, benefits of, 54-55; interest of parents in, 108-109;
lack of integration between
working life and, 164

SEAMEO (South East Asian Ministers of Education Organization), 132, 139, 265
SENA (Servicio Nacional de Aprendizaje), 136
Second Development Decade, 266, 277, 278, 287, 289, 315
secondary education, redesign of, 218; role and impact of, 131
secondary level school leavers, over-production of, 280
selective assistance, as a priority activity, 7
SIDA (Swedish International Development Authority), 132
skills, new demands for, 49-50
small-scale projects, donor response to, 91; encouragement of, 90; experimental implications of, 91
"social demand," consequences of, 117-119
structural reform, proposals for, 66-69
student unrest, solutions to, 227-228
study abroad, 259, 278-279
syllabi, revision of, 69, 103

target planning, 150
"Taxonomical" method, 37
teacher education, 279, 284
teacher supply, as an area for redeployment, 280-282
technical assistance, as an area for redeployment, 282-283; as a factor in developing country dependence, 311-312; channels of aid for, 282-283; resources for, 167
technical education, 58, 65, 90, 108, 283
Thammasat University, 202
time, as a fundamental unit of cost, 53

trade unions, 11-12
training educators from the developing countries: Some things not worth doing, 176-178

undergraduate instruction, rate of return to, 52-53
UNDP (United Nations Development Programme), 117, 130, 264, 269
unemployed, level of education of, 3, 5, 12
unemployment, educated, 3, 8-9, 12, 15-18, 100, 119, 217; industrialization as a factor of increasing, 315; in urban areas, 3; measurement of, 75
UNESCO (United Nations Educational, Scientific and Cultural Organization), 37, 91, 102, 130, 132-133, 136, 139, 140, 143, 217, 264-265, 279, 289, 292
UNICEF (United Nations Children's Fund), 132, 136, 264, 269
unit costs, 133
United Nations, 107, 269
universal education, 19, 120, 165
universal primary education, 120-121, 163; irrelevancy of Western model for to developing nations, 167-168
universal secondary education, 120-121
Universidad del Valle, 200, 242, 246
Universidade Federal da Bahia, 200, 242-244
universities, developing: as modeled on Western, 205; structure and function of, 205
universities, monopolization of training of national intelligentsia by, 205; opposition from, 131
university, as an instrument of development, 231; contribution of

to primary and secondary education, 211-212

university centers, types of assistance to, 200-202

university development, 195-203; as means toward national development objectives, 206; efforts: coordination of with government and private agencies, 246

University Development Program, phases of, 197-200

university divisions, relation of to problems of development, 208-210

University of East Africa, 200, 201

University of the Philippines, 201, 203

University of Zaire, 200

university planning, as linked to national planning, 220

university reorganization, need for, 247

university staff, development of,

228-230, 232

UNRISD (United Nations Research Institute for Social Development), 37

USAID (United States Agency for International Development), 129, 130, 132, 136, 140, 143, 159 n, 262

vector planning, 150; illustrations of, 151-155; simulation and gaming in, 159-161

Velázquez, Gabriel, 200

vocational education, 27-28, 58, 91, 165; training, 218; within educational system, 28, 65-66, 179

wastage, 133, 134, 164, 175

Welch, Finis, 56

work, three distinct functions of 86

World Bank (see IBRD)

Wriston, Henry, 198

F. CHAMPION WARD is Program Advisor in Education to the International Division of the Ford Foundation. Before joining the Ford Foundation, he was Dean of the College at the University of Chicago. He is the editor of The Idea and Practice of General Education, and has contributed to numerous educational journals.

Dr. Ward received his B. A. and M. A. from Oberlin College, and a Ph. D. in philosophy from Yale University.

EDUCATION PLANNING AND EXPENDITURE
DECISIONS IN DEVELOPING COUNTRIES:
With a Malaysian Case Study

> Robert W. McMeekin, Jr.

EDUCATION, MANPOWER, AND DEVELOP-
MENT IN SOUTH AND SOUTHEAST ASIA

> M. Shamsul Huq

EDUCATIONAL PROBLEMS OF DEVELOPING
SOCIETIES: With Case Studies of Ghana and
Pakistan

> Adam Curle

ECONOMIC GROWTH IN DEVELOPING COUN-
TRIES—MATERIAL AND HUMAN RESOURCES:
Proceedings of the Seventh Rehovot Conference

> edited by Yohanan Ramati